The Artist's Mind

For the past century psychoanalysts have attempted to understand the psychology of art, artists and aesthetic experience. This book examines how contemporary psychoanalytic theory provides insight into understanding the psychological sources of creativity, modern art and modern artists.

The Artist's Mind revisits the lives of eight modern artists, including Henri Matisse, Marcel Duchamp, Jackson Pollock and Andy Warhol, from a psychoanalytical viewpoint. It looks at how opportunities for a new approach to art at the turn of the twentieth century offered artists a chance to explore different forms of creativity and artistic ambition. Key areas of discussion include:

- developmental sources of the aesthetic sense
- psychological functions of creativity and art
- psychology of beauty, ugliness and the Sublime
- co-evolution of the modern self, modernism and art
- cultural context of creativity, artistic identity and aesthetic experience.

Through the examination of great artists' lives and psychological dynamics, the author articulates a new psychoanalytic aesthetic model that has both clinical and historical significance. This book is essential reading for all those with an interest in the origins and fate of modern art.

George Hagman, LCSW, is a psychoanalyst and clinical social worker practicing in both New York City and Connecticut. He is also a member of the faculty of the National Psychological Association for Psychoanalysis.

"Hagman invites the reader to join him on a fascinating and audacious psychoanalytic tour of the minds of significant artists of the 19th and 20th Centuries. Tracing their personal histories he demonstrates how psychological factors contribute to the aesthetic resonance in works of art and architecture. An innovative contribution to the dual fields of art and psychoanalysis, *The Artist's Mind* is an engaging read."

Joy Schaverien, Jungian Analyst and Visiting Professor in Art Psychotherapy at Leeds Metropolitan University, UK. Author of *The Revealing Image*

"In his second book Hagman pursues the development of a novel theory about aesthetics and creativity from self psychology and relational perspectives. He sees aesthetic experience as rooted in idealization of early attachment of the infant to his mother. In the present work he expands his ingenious formulations to Modern art which encourages personal idiosyncrasies, subjective expression, and aggressive abandonment of tradition. In this thoughtful and well researched text, he illustrates his theory by a detailed examination of a number of well known painters including, Degas, Bonnard, Duchamp, Pollock and Warhol. The list is extensive enough to enrich our understanding and appreciation of varied and at times opposing attitudes towards the process of artistic creation."

Francis Baudry, faculty New York Psychoanalytic Institute

"The author's psychoanalytic readings of the eight artists are compelling like princesses in a fairy tale, each of whom is 'more beautiful than the last,' I found each treatment to seem more fascinating than the other."

Ellen Dissanayake, author, *Art and Intimacy: How the Arts Began* and *Homo Aestheticus: Where Art Comes From and Why*

"*The Artist's Mind* offers a vitalizing, new analytic perspective on the importance of aesthetics and art as a 'dialogue with the world', shedding light on the evolution of modern art through the lives and works of major 20th century artists, and expanding our understanding of art into the 21st century."

Carol M. Press, Ed.D., author, *The Dancing Self: Creativity, Modern Dance, Self Psychology, and Transformative Education*

The Artist's Mind

A Psychoanalytic Perspective on Creativity, Modern Art and Modern Artists

George Hagman

Routledge
Taylor & Francis Group
LONDON AND NEW YORK

First published 2010
by Routledge
27 Church Road, Hove, East Sussex BN3 2FA

Simultaneously published in the USA and Canada
by Routledge
270 Madison Avenue, New York, NY 10016

Routledge is an imprint of the Taylor & Francis Group, an Informa business

© 2010 George Hagman

Typeset in Times by Garfield Morgan, Swansea, West Glamorgan
Printed and bound in Great Britain by TJ International Ltd, Padstow, Cornwall
Paperback cover design by Lisa Dynan

All rights reserved. No part of this book may be reprinted or reproduced or utilized in any form or by any electronic, mechanical, or other means, now known or hereafter invented, including photocopying and recording, or in any information storage or retrieval system, without permission in writing from the publishers.

This publication has been produced with paper manufactured to strict environmental standards and with pulp derived from sustainable forests.

British Library Cataloguing in Publication Data
A catalogue record for this book is available from the British Library

Library of Congress Cataloging in Publication Data
Hagman, George.
 The artist's mind: a psychoanalytic perspective on creativity, modern art and modern artists / George Hagman.
   p. cm.
 Includes bibliographical references.
 ISBN 978-0-415-46705-6 (hardback) – ISBN 978-0-415-46706-3 (pbk.)
 1. Artists–Psychology. 2. Art–Psychology. 3. Creation (Literary, artistic, etc.) 4. Art, Modern–19th century. 5. Art, Modern–20th century. I. Title.
 N71.H228 2010
 701'.15–dc22
                                                                2010000076

ISBN: 978-0-415-46705-6 (hbk)
ISBN: 978-0-415-46706-3 (pbk)

To my wonderful children
Peter Davila Hagman and Elena Christine Hagman

Contents

	Acknowledgements	ix
1	Introduction	1
2	A new psychoanalytic model of aesthetic experience	6
3	Art and the artist's mind	18
4	Modern art and modern artists	33
5	Edgar Degas: The psychological edge of modernism	37
6	Pierre Bonnard: The seduction of beauty	47
7	The creative anxiety of Henri Matisse	58
8	The beauty of indifference: The art of Marcel Duchamp	72
9	Modern art in America	87
10	Joseph Cornell's quest for beauty	91
11	Form follows function: The selfobject function of Frank Lloyd Wright's art and architecture	107
12	Jackson Pollock: An American's triumph and the death of modernism	128
13	The birth of postmodernism: Andy Warhol's perverse aesthetics	142

14 Postscript: The world after Warhol   161

   References   167
   Index   171

Acknowledgements

As I wrote this book I was supported and encouraged by a number of people: Carol Press, the late Carl Rotenberg, David Shaddock, Leslie Hogan, Karen Schwartz, Julia Schwartz, and members of the Self Psychological and Psychoanalytic communities who read my papers, reviewed my earlier book, and attended workshops and paper presentations. Most importantly, Carol has supported my work and me over the years, and I owe much to her and our friendship. I also acknowledge my friend and collaborator the late Carl Rotenberg, M.D., with whom I discussed several of these papers and who supported my initial ambitions in this area of study. In addition, I want to thank Jon Mills, Ph.D. and Eric van Brooekthuizen at Rodopi Press for publishing my first book *Aesthetic Experience: Beauty, Creativity and the Search for the Ideal* as part of the series *Contemporary Psychoanalytic Studies*. That book is the foundation of the present one, so I am grateful for their interest and support. Some chapters in this book were written for and presented at a series of workshops that Carol, Carl and I have conducted over the past ten years at the Annual Meetings on the Psychology of the Self. I also want to thank the members of the Connecticut Self Psychology Study Group for their friendships and stimulating discussions: Allison Brownlow, Nancy Boksenbaum, Larry Ludwig, Lois Fox, Alexis Johnson, Nancy Bronson, Mikey Silverman, Grete Lane and Susanne Weil; and the membership of the Connecticut Society for Psychoanalytic Psychology, an organization I have been proud to serve as the Scientific Program Chair for the past five years. I would like to thank my children, Elena and Peter, to whom this book is dedicated – they are the joy and pride of my life. Finally, thank you to my wife Moira, whom I will love forever.

Chapter 1

Introduction

Ever since Sigmund Freud published his monograph on Leonardo da Vinci in 1910, psychoanalysts have attempted to understand the psychology of art, artists, creativity and aesthetic experience. Over several generations new psychoanalytic models have been promoted which reflect the evolving nature of theory and practice – each explaining art and artists in its own light. The perspective I will use is a contemporary psychoanalytic one, with an emphasis on mind as embedded in cultural, developmental and relational contexts, as well as the importance of self-experience and idealization. In an earlier book (Hagman, 2005) I elaborated the theory behind this new psychoanalytic model, pointing out the developmental origins of aesthetic experience; the role of idealization in early attachment and its bearing on the creation and appreciation of art; the dynamics of the creative process; the nature of beauty, ugliness and sublime experience; and the multiple dimensions of human subjectivity in culture, what George Gadamer calls "festival" (Gadamer, 1986, p. 39). In this volume I will apply these ideas to our understanding of modern art and modern artists. My hope is to illustrate a new psychoanalytic approach as well as increasing our appreciation of the role of individual psychological dynamics in larger cultural developments.

I acknowledge that there is no clear-cut boundary or single definition for modern art or, for that matter, modernism. That being said, I view modern art as beginning with Manet and the impressionists and ending with the abstract expressionist work of Jackson Pollock. It is a broad category that contains many philosophies, various groups and myriad individual practitioners. However, I will work with the following assumptions: modern art and modernism challenged "classical conventions" and continually pursued approaches that disrupted old assumptions and promoted innovation. Aesthetic quality in modern art was diverse and perspectival, it expanded notions and forms of beauty and encouraged subjectivity, expressionism and idiosyncrasy. It was also self-critical; as artists sought to innovate they also inquired into the nature of art itself. Freedom of expression required the aggressive abandonment of tradition and even the deconstruction of the notion of what art is. Modern artists were a new bunch. Unlike the middle-class craftsmen serving the aesthetic tastes of the church, the upper classes and the royals, modern artists were often rogue loners and aesthetic revolutionaries. They hungered to be freed of restrictions so as to execute the most original and personal artworks. They were only satisfied when their creations reflected their most personal, inner vision, and they viewed creativity and art as opportunities for a transcendent, state of self-fulfillment. For them art was a chance at self-healing and, perhaps, a fantasy of immortality.

In other words, this book is about the psychology of art and artists during the late nineteenth and the twentieth centuries. The importance of this period for art, artists and modern culture is well known, and I will not try to review the myriad perspectives from which the modern period has been viewed and analyzed. The perspective that I will take is that modern art placed the individual subjectivity of the artist at the center of aesthetic experience and the creative process. Many different factors contributed to this change, such as the availability of cheaper high-quality mediums, the expansion of the middle-class art market, the waning influence of large art institutions and academies, and, importantly, the elaboration of aesthetic experience as an internal private process arising from the individual person's relation to art. However, my argument will be that the new types of people entering the art world also fueled the cultural and institutional changes in aesthetics and the nature of art, as well as the psychology of art and artists. These new artists, coming from outside the traditional art communities, brought a different type of motivation to the artistic career, a motivation to succeed in the modern marketplace, within which the individual genius, the aesthetic revolutionary and the innovator became increasingly important to western culture's idea of the arts and of artists.

I have chosen a number of artists whose work and lives most clearly represent the technical and psychological aspects of modern art and modernism. They are Edgar Degas, Pierre Bonnard, Henri Matisse, Marcel Duchamp, Frank Lloyd Wright, Jackson Pollock and Andy Warhol (in Chapter 4 I explain my choice of artists and their relation to my project). It is the psychodynamics, professional ambitions, creative methods and aesthetic values of these artists that will be my focus. I will attempt to explain why each chose to become an artist; and I hope to explain the developmental source of the unique contribution which each made to the development of modern art. Most importantly, the entire book argues for how the drive for innovation and the creation of a unique individual art form was powered by each artist's psychological, developmental and relational background. In other words, this book is not a work of art history or of art criticism, or a treatise on aesthetics (although it is partially all of these things), it is a psychoanalytic investigation into the psychological lives of some important modern artists, which I hope sheds light on how the personal, the relational and the cultural play a part in bringing about major artistic changes at a particular time in history.

As a group these moderns were new types of artists. Reacting against tradition, developing new artistic mediums, attacking old assumptions about subject manner, style and even basic ideas about the nature of art, each artist created out of his individual intrasubjective experience new creative approaches and aesthetic forms. The result was an explosion of artistic innovation. At no time in history was art subjected to such intense competition, analysis, attack and revolution. No longer constrained by the traditional art institutions or the financial limits of the art marketplace, these men and women were not just free to do what they wanted, they forever changed the nature of art, the art world, the social role of the artist, and the nature of the artistic self.

In order to understand the motivations of these modern artists we have to better understand the psychological dynamics of aesthetic experience, the creative process and the relation between art and the mind. It is in these areas that this book attempts to offer something new. Building on this, the following is a brief overview of a new psychoanalytic model of aesthetics, art and creativity.

Aesthetic experience is a fundamental dimension of human experience. It is as important as love, sex and aggression, and is part of all human experiences. Ellen Dissanayake (1992) refers to man as "homoaestheticus", declaring art and aesthetics to be basic to human identity and daily life. Her belief (which this book will support) is that art arises out of the most important aspects of relationships. It is the form of our bodies interacting, the rhythms of breathing together, the soothing or exciting touch of skin against skin, the music of voices in conversation. Out of these human communications is elaborated the dances, music, dramas and visual images that make up art. And it is art that becomes the glue of society; it gives shape to our towns and villages, it entertains communities, it decorates our appearance and our cities. Art is the means by which we celebrate and mourn. It makes real and concrete the subjectivity of people in communities that live day to day and exist over ancestral time.

The source of the power and ubiquity of art is of central importance to human attachment, interaction and interpersonal regulation. The mother holding and caring for her child is the first medium of aesthetic experience and creative life. The beauty of her child's smile, the shape and color of the child's body, the clothing with which she keeps him or her warm, all are aesthetically based and are chosen out of the mother's engrossment and love. And likewise the baby experiences the mother aesthetically: her expressions, the movement of her body, the ebb and flow of soothing comforts or mutually invigorating playing. The shared love and idealization between mother and baby invests the forms of feeling with beauty and special value. The aesthetic experience of this dyad is intense, exciting, and endlessly variable and expressive.

I believe that these basic aesthetics of relatedness are extended and elaborated into the endless forms of aesthetic experience and artistic creations that fill our cultures to overflowing. Art becomes the way mankind affirms its most basic nature, the forms of feeling and relating that characterize our self-experience and our relationships. But art also perfects the human, idealizes the forms and meanings that hold and contain our lives. It is the idealized nature of the formal aesthetic organization of our cultural world which creates an environment that is meaningful, special and at times beautiful – in this way we are protected from the often empty and grim experience of the physical world.

Hence human cultures have encouraged and valued the creation of art. It is why large groups of people adopt familiar ways to dress, to memorialize, to decorate and entertain. A culture is the sum of its many and varied aesthetic forms and artworks. It is art that makes cultures human and it is by means of the arts that culture makes available resources for people to grow and prosper.

In all societies certain people are designated and trained to be artists. This special group is charged with elaborating and perfecting the aesthetic rituals and costumes of the larger group. In most cases they get together around their shared role and work. They share ideas and practices, tools and mediums. They come up with new ideas and new ways to improve on old practices. When they organize they can support and advocate for the artist's craft and status in society. It is these artists' special talents, training, learned skills, and shared values that maintain the culture's aesthetic infrastructure. This is the way that societies marshal and direct aesthetic resources, maintaining and developing new meanings and adapting to changes in the social makeup of society.

Unlike practical disciplines such as engineering, farming and hunting, which adapt to the changing demands of the physical world to increase the survivability of society, art adapts to the changing human environment, giving value and meaning to events that impact on and change society, such as death, marriage, birth, the harvest etc. All cultures tend to conserve aesthetic standards and art forms. Art becomes a means to preserve and maintain the life of the people and the way in which they live together. So cultures tend to resist major changes in art, gradually integrating change into existing paradigms. Change, and indeed revolutionary change, begins and is fueled by dialogue and individual effort. It is the day-to-day struggle of individual artists to survive in society and respond to the changes and demands of the environment (both natural and social) that leads to the rapid and diverse innovations that characterized the modern period of art. During the late nineteenth and early twentieth centuries the old cultural institutions changed, losing their control over the production of artists and the art marketplace. The rapidly changing culture made new demands on artists and offered new opportunities. As artists began to respond with innovations and increased production of artwork and ideas, the culture, grudgingly and sometimes violently, responded and changed around them.

As I said earlier, I intend to look at the individual developmental and psychological factors that contributed to the development of modern art. However, unlike prior analytic approaches, I do not intend to focus on artistic imagery or content, the symbols and unconscious meanings that may lie hidden in an artwork like the latent meaning of a dream. Rather, I will be interested in innovations in the creative process, and the artist's changed relationship to aesthetic experience and aesthetic form. I believe that the sources of artists' motivation to grapple with these areas lie in the earliest relational experiences and how they have been elaborated into the mature artist's self-experience, sensibility and creative efforts. Hence I will take each artist in turn and look for the sources of each person's particular aesthetic innovation and contribution to the development of modernism. As you will see, I believe the sources are in early developmental experiences (some of which were traumatic, but not necessarily) which posed particular challenges for each artist. These conflicts, deficits, preoccupations, etc. contributed to the selection of the artistic career and specific aesthetic projects. I will tie this directly to attempted solutions for early developmental dilemmas and, most importantly, to efforts towards self-healing through art.

A note to the reader: I have chose not to include images of artworks in this book. There are few instances where we will be discussing particular artworks in detail and images of these works are easily available in standard art history textbooks or on the internet. In fact, rather than analyzing specific works, the discussions that follow emphasize the broad sweep of the artist's career and the evolution of his aesthetic style. Given this, for the reader to get the most from the discussion of the various artists, I recommend familiarizing oneself with a selection of the artists' works so that engagement in the discussion of the development of style and aesthetic approach can be informed by knowledge of the paintings, buildings or sculpture which that artist produced.

Chapter 2

A new psychoanalytic model of aesthetic experience

> When the artist passes from pure sensations to emotions aroused by means of sensations, he uses natural forms, which are calculated to move our emotions, and he presents these in such a manner that the forms themselves generate in us emotional states, based upon the fundamental necessities of our physical and physiological natures.
> (Roger Fry, 1909, in Frascina & Harrison, 1987)

This chapter presents a new psychoanalytic approach to aesthetics and creativity from the perspective of contemporary psychoanalytic theory, and clinical practice and research. It includes recent advances in psychoanalytic thinking and self psychology, especially an appreciation of the relational context of aesthetic experience and the role of relatedness and intersubjectivity in aesthetic experience. Several of the most important points of this new perspective are highlighted, specifically: 1) that the source and enduring core of aesthetic experience is found in early childhood; 2) that the special, idealized quality of aesthetic experience has its source in early experiences of mother–infant interaction; 3) that the sense of beauty is an aesthetically organized selfobject experience, tied to specifically maternal aspects of this initial relationship; 4) that the intense aesthetic experience known as the Sublime is tied to the relationship with and experience of the father; 5) that the violation of aesthetic organizations of experience is experienced as a sense of ugliness; and 6) that all aesthetic experiences and artistic efforts possess three dimensions of subjectivity: the intrasubjective, the intersubjective and the metasubjective.

I will start with a brief review of the issues of intersubjectivity and self-experience in the psychoanalytic literature on aesthetic experience. I will then discuss the work of Gilbert Rose, Daniel Stern and Ellen Dissanayake, which links aesthetic experience to the intimacy of parent and child. This idea will be extended to recent psychoanalytic ideas about idealization, beauty, the Sublime and ugliness. I will close with a brief overview of the multi-subjective model of aesthetic experience.

The intersubjective source of aesthetic experience

Psychoanalysts have studied art, aesthetic experience and the dynamics of the creative process for generations. Initially creativity and art were viewed as sublimations, defending against forbidden sexual wishes (Freud, 1908, 1910, 1925a, 1925b). Hence Freud's approach to the study of art was interpretive in that the symbolic forms of artistic expression were unmasked, revealing hidden fantasies and wishes. This view of the psychology of art and creativity as a type of dream work or defensive operation has been the center of classical psychoanalytic aesthetics. Later analysts viewed art more progressively, with the ego harnessing the resources of the unconscious for the purpose of self-expression (Kris, 1952). This ego-psychological perspective continued to emphasize symbolism, but now saw regression as being at the "service of the ego" rather than the other way around. Eventually analysts such as Gilbert Rose (1980) and Jerome Oremland (1997) would elevate creativity to the status of a complex developmental accomplishment resulting in a higher level of human experience. In keeping with the classical analytic perspective on the mind as a self-regulating system, most analysts have approached the psychology of art and the artist from a primarily intrapsychic viewpoint, only tangentially related to other people (for example the potential audience). This is consistent with contemporary culture's myth of the artist as a solitary rebel who defies convention and critical judgment. However, some recent thinkers have argued that the artist is a far more social being than has generally been admitted to (Rotenberg, 1988; Dissanayake, 2000; Press, 2002; Hagman, 2005). I believe that the major limitation of the analytic approach has been its focus on the intrapsychic dynamic of the individual artist's mind. This shortsightedness has become increasingly obvious given the recent revolution in psychoanalytic thinking which views human psychology as more relational and intersubjective than previously thought.

Given that Freud saw art as a compromise formation between conflicting parts of the mental apparatus, the issue of the relational and developmental sources of art was not relevant to him. Freud viewed art as one of the many manifestations of the defense mechanism of sublimation, which, despite cultural trappings, was at heart an intrapsychic phenomenon. The ego psychologist Ernst Kris viewed art as resulting from regression in the service of the ego whereby earlier forms of mentation and instinctual life are temporarily allowed access to consciousness, permitting aesthetic expression for the purpose of mastery (Kris, 1952). However, once again the source of art lay in the functions of the ego, which made use of infantile modes of thinking, but these early forms of mentation did not constitute aesthetic experience itself. Ultimately the notion of the elaboration of the products of regression during the later phase of the creative process placed the heart of successful creativity in the mature emotional and mental capacities of the artist.

Gilbert Rose, in his monograph *The Power of Form* (1980), argued that artists seek through their art to recover lost ego states, specifically early experiences of fusion with the ego ideal as well as the archaic mother. Rose believed that artists as part of their normal capacities have a greater ability to merge with reality and then to disengage. They immerse themselves in an unconscious psychological process in which there are rhythmical disintegrative and integrative states. Unlike Kris, Rose viewed these regressive processes as capacities which, rather than just being at the service of the ego, have progressive, creative potential in and of themselves. He wrote regarding the artist's creative process:

> Later in life, a person's ego may scan back over unconscious memory traces of early fusion states. Unconsciously reliving these memories of dissolving and reforming early ego boundaries is an attempt at mastering the potential traumas of the original situation. It is often accompanied by unconscious birth fantasies. They signify the re-establishment (rebirth) of ego boundaries from the fusion of primary narcissism. The re-emergence from narcissistic fusion and the re-establishment of ego boundaries carry the possibility of altered, perhaps even innovative, arrangements of the building blocks of reality.
>
> (Rose, 1980, p. 70)

Rose described this scanning back as an *autonomous capacity of the ego* to which some aspects of reality are readily available as "malleable or plastic material to be adaptively reintegrated in the light of more customary aspects of reality" (Rose, 1980, p. 77). Creative imagination restructures reality and deepens and expands our understanding of the world. The production of art is according to Rose essentially an enhancement of normal capacities and processes by which all people test and master reality, "relating inner and outer in repeated fusion and separations" (Rose, 1980, p. 78). Ultimately the goal is an externalization of the early ego ideal that the artist has endowed with all the perfection of the parents. "By creating it, and loving it and being loved by the world for making it the artist is rematriated" (Rose, 1980, p. 64).

Through this notion of rematriation Rose moved towards a more relational view of creativity in which the core of aesthetic experience could be said to contain an intensely interactive component, the mutual engagement of artist with artwork and audience, resulting in the emergence of an archaic state of self-experience associated with the early bond with the mother.

The psychoanalyst and infant researcher Daniel Stern (1984) supported the notion that mature creativity involves the activation of archaic affective states and cross-modal perception. In the following quote Stern emphasized the emergent organization of the infant's subjective world as a template for aesthetic creation:

> Infants are not lost at sea in a wash of abstractable qualities of experience. They are gradually and systematically ordering these elements of experience to identify self-invariant and other-invariant constellations. . . . This global . . . domain of human subjectivity . . . is the ultimate reservoir that can be dipped into for all creative experience. . . . That domain alone is concerned with the coming-into-being of organization that is at the heart of creating and learning.
> (Stern, 1984, p. 67)

Stern supported Rose's argument that early regressive ego states and experiences play a part in creativity but additionally he stresses that it is the progressive organizational capacities of the infant, not just regression, that underlie the creative processes in later life. Surprisingly, Stern did not emphasise the relational context of these archaic processes. However, one would assume that these organizational capacities emerge and are elaborated within an interpersonal context. Mature forms of creativity involve the type of rematriation discussed by Rose, but additionally the self-experience-in-relation-to-other which Stern's research highlighted.

From a self-psychological perspective Charles Kligerman (1980) explored this area in his discussion of the motivation of the artist to recapture the experience of an archaic selfobject tie. In his formulation Kligerman speculated that the prototypical artist is someone who experienced consistent mirroring of his or her grandiosity in childhood. Eventually this selfobject experience fails and the artist-to-be is cast out from this state of perfection. Kligerman wrote how the artist confronted with selfobject failure possesses:

> the need to regain a lost paradise – the original bliss of perfection – to overcome the empty feeling of self-depletion and to recover self-esteem. In the metapsychology of the self this would amount to healing the threatened fragmentation and restoring firm self-cohesion through a merger with the selfobject – the work of art – and a bid for mirroring approval of the world. We can also add a fourth current to the creative drive – the need to regain perfection by merging with the ideals of the powerful selfobjects, first the parents, then later revered models who represent the highest standards of some great artistic tradition.
> (Kligerman, 1980, pp. 387–388)

For Kligerman art is linked to the recreation of early experiences of relationship with important caregivers and involves the expression and embodiment of psychological processes of idealization and merger associated with selfobject experience. This self-psychological perspective while clarifying the psychological function of art and creativity in self-experience does not capture what we now know to be the intensely relational nature of infantile experience. In light of recent insights in infant research and the intersubjective nature of human psychological experience, some authors have started to consider how the fundamental drive for and experience of mutuality and intimacy plays a part in aesthetic experience and the creative process.

In her book *Art and Intimacy*, the anthropologist Ellen Dissanayake (2000) argued that the source of the arts lies in the intimate mutuality of mother and child, specifically in the affective and behavioral attunement between the members of the dyad. Referring to the burgeoning field of infant research, which has elucidated the complex interpersonal relatedness of the human infant, Dissanayake highlighted the affective interplay that characterizes the infant–parent dyad. She argued that the infant is born expecting rhythmic-modal behavior from its caretakers and its exercise becomes the bedrock of the aesthetic forms, values and experiences that eventually develop among people in a culture. In fact, Dissanayake believed that one could find the intimate aesthetics of mother and child in the rituals and art forms of the larger culture, which seeks to increase connection and coordination among members through the evocation of developmentally early experiences of attunement. Dissanayake wrote:

> It is in the inborn capacity and need for (1) mutuality between mother and infant (the prototype for intimacy and love) that four other essential capacities and psychological imperatives are enfolded and embedded and gradually, in their time, emerge. Mother–infant mutuality contains and influences the capacities for (2) belonging to (and acceptance by) a social group, (3) *finding and making meaning*, (4) acquiring a sense of *competence through handling and making*, and (5) *elaborating* these meanings and competencies as a way of expressing or acknowledging their vital importance.
>
> (Dissanayake, 2000, p. 8)

Dissanayake believed that the creation and valuing of art derives from one of the most important human imperatives – the need for relatedness and self-experience. She felt that communities create artistic culture as a means of coordinating individuals and thereby contributing to individual and group survival, and that individuals work within the given artistic culture to achieve experiences of meaning and personal competence. But her idea of *elaborating* emphasized how meaning is not just in terms of everyday realities; rather, individuals as artists seek to create works that possess special power, authority and beauty so that the importance of the work in the experience of the community is made manifest. Dissanayake argued that underlying even the most idiosyncratic creative efforts is the evolved impulse to elaborate biologically important concerns, using the "rhythms and modes" of these archaic experiences of self with other.

Beauty, ugliness and the sublime

In an earlier book I defined beauty as the formal aspect of the experience of idealization (Hagman, 2005, p. 87). The self psychologist Charles Kligerman claimed that the artist idealizes beauty and that "by and large the artist is concerned with exhibiting a beauty that was originally his own (or that of the idealized maternal selfobject)" (Kligerman, 1980, p. 386). It is the experience of perfection that is at the heart of the sense of beauty. Beauty is an invariant characteristic of anything that is experienced as ideal. We all value and seek beauty as an opportunity for selfobject experience. When we are in the presence of something beautiful we are enlivened, we feel whole and happy. Beauty is a special element in the aesthetic experience in which the investment of reality with subjectivity creates an experience of that reality as both ideal and harmonious with our inner life (see also Lee, 1947, 1948, 1950; and Hagman, 2002). George Santayana described a similar experience:

> The sense of beauty is the harmony between our nature and our experience. When our senses and imagination find what they crave, when the world so shapes itself or so moulds the mind that the correspondence between them is perfect, then perception is pleasure, and existence needs no apology.
>
> (Santayana, 1896, p. 269)

Santayana described what he believed characterized the general human experience of beauty that could occur spontaneously and without obvious effort. For the artist this experience is something that he or she seeks to bring about through his or her own creative efforts. While in general artists do not make the creation of beauty a conscious goal, nonetheless a characteristic of all successful artistic efforts is that the result evokes the experience of beauty, which often transcends the artist's intention. With this in mind it makes sense to say that beauty can never be produced (except by imitation) but only evoked as a result of the pursuit of perfection and the memory of a lost ideal. Jacques Maritain in his monograph *Creative Intuition in Art and Poetry* stated: "Art engenders beauty, it does not produce beauty as an object or a thing contained in a genus" (Maritain, 1953, p. 173). In the same work Maritain quotes the artist Robert Henri: "Things are not done beautifully. The beauty is an integral part of their being done" (1953, p. 174). In a similar sense the artist does not make or produce a selfobject experience, he or she through the creative process brings about an opportunity for selfobject experience, and thus the experience of beauty, whether in the experience of the external attributes of the object or in the interrelationship among the ideas that are concretized in the work.

Art cannot be limited to what is considered beautiful. In fact I would argue that art is not primarily about aesthetic experience; rather, the artist as he or she works to perfect the forms of expression in the artwork evokes aesthetic experiences such as beauty. In fact The opposite of beauty, ugliness, may actually be the outcome of many works of art, especially in the work of modern artists who systematically deconstructed and transformed accepted cultural standards of aesthetic value, artistic practice and art products. In ugliness many modern artists found a world of alternatives which permitted the expression of highly personal and at times forbidden aspects of self-experience and relatedness. Ugliness was a means to directly challenge many of the restrictions that artists felt were blocking the development of new forms of art and new ways of being an artist (Higgins, 2002).

In the experience of ugliness, the expectation of beauty is radically disrupted. Instead of resonance, there is dissonance. The ideal is replaced by corruption and degradation. Harmony and wholeness are replaced by conflict and disintegration. For example, from a classical analytic perspective, it is not just the observation of the primal scene or the female genitals that evokes a sense of ugliness; rather, it is the expectation of one thing (loving affection between the parents and the presence of a penis, respectively) and the shock of encountering a form of violation of that expectation that results in anxiety, revulsion, and the sense of ugliness. In object relational terms, it is the expectation of unity and wholeness that is violated by the encounter with chaos and disintegration. In other words, the experience of ugliness is that aspect of an experience that leads to the disruption or shattering of the formal/aesthetic structure of experience. Hence, ugliness offered an alternative means of aesthetic organization that disrupted established aesthetic standards and therefore liberated the artist's mind and skills to permit the expressions of formerly hidden and denied psychological states and experiences.

While beauty is the aesthetic of maternal preoccupation, the organization of the ideal elements that composed the formal sense of the interaction between mother and infant, and ugliness is the disruption of maternal order, meaning and balance, the Sublime is the paternal dimension of aesthetic experience, characterized by power, formlessness, obscurity and immensity.

Psychoanalysts have rarely discussed the problem of the Sublime. However, we may be able to approach the subject through its accompanying affect – awe. Several decades ago, the psychoanalyst Phyllis Greenacre (1953, 1956) argued that awe before the Sublime was derivative of the child's first encounters with the father's phallus. Its strangeness, size and power (all inseparable from fantasy) became the prototype of all experiences in which we perceive the Sublime and extraordinary. Building on Greenacres's view, awareness of the Sublime develops as the infant moves outward from the enclosed and managed aesthetic space of the mother, into an open, dynamic and uncontrolled engagement with the world as introduced by the father. The father's relative size; the child's fantasies of the father's power, aggressiveness, and perhaps even omnipotence; the perception of immense and obscure reality beyond and outside dyadic experience, all these combine in the first aesthetics of awe and astonishment. Many of us are drawn to seek out and cultivate such experiences. The Sublime functions to bring a number of different terrors within a containable, ordered universe (normally the father is experienced as protective and containing, as well as exciting). Through its powerful discharge of desire and aggression without catastrophe, the sublime experience can allow the result of discharge without the destruction of self or loved one. Death, sexuality, aggression, loss of self, vulnerability and isolation are embraced and overcome, although not by being negated or denied. Paradoxically, the experience of these terrors in the sublime experience is vitalizing and self-confirming, not disorganizing. There is an emotional state of arousal/tranquility. What is internally threatening is safely put outside the self. There is an externalization of fantasy, desire, and fear.

In other words, the Sublime is the experience of vulnerability from a position of safety. It begins with the father as observed from the arms of the mother, and continues with the world surveyed from within his firm grasp. It is the rawness of affect, the passion of fantasy, and the shock of the new, contained and expressed within a formal structure that is experienced as astonishing and ultimately transcendent.

Mature forms of aesthetic experience often involve the simultaneous apprehension of the beautiful and the Sublime. It is that aspect of our experience in which the sense of quality, formal value and beauty combine with the recognition of failure and mortality. Aesthetic experience is pleasurable, vitalizing, and accompanied by a feeling of "fittedness" and positive self-experience, but in addition the person encounters the reality of disjunction, transience and even death. It helps us to live with the recognition of our vulnerability, our tragedies and our mortality. Aesthetic experience can range from the transcendent (as in a visit to the Sistine Chapel) to the commonplace (as in the gleam of rain on a city street, or the sound of rain on the roof at night). In the experience there is recognition that these transcendent things are temporary, limited and will ultimately fade and be lost. For mature adults it can be said to be an ever present aspect of all experience; however, in instances such as art appreciation, aesthetic experience achieves a heightened, even ideal level. In other words, aesthetic experience is an aspect of a mature level of self-organization. The sense of reality is organized according to processes of idealization amalgamated with the recognition of the other in the world. Otherness includes acceptance of the inevitability of the failure of reality to meet the needs of the self in fundamental ways – failure, loss and death. Great works of art possess great beauty and contain terrible truths. Oedipus Rex is the best example of the Sublime and the tragic.

There is a mature level of awareness of the tragic nature of life and of one's own humanity, but this awareness is articulated in a form (visual, verbal, linguistic, musical) that is of such a refined quality that tragedy is given expression beautifully. Thus tragic man transcends his or her vulnerability and mortality through aesthetic experience. In this way great art offers an opportunity for extended dialogue – it evokes a response, enhances self-experience and recognition. The great work never intimidates but elevates the self-experience of the viewer.

The aesthetic experience of the artist

> Because it combines the sense of fusion with the sense of object-otherness, we might say that art is an emblem of the state of being in love: this seems true if we emphasize the infantile projections and reparative attitudes that are strengthened by the state. These attitudes are the font of Form. When the artist joins them in the creative process, infantile psychic tensions concerning sense-data renew in him some freshness of vision, some ability to meet, as for the first time, the phenomenal world and the emotion it carries.
> (Adrian Stokes, 1957, p. 407)

The viewer of art often comes upon it unawares and the aesthetic experience is thus surprising and spontaneous. The artist on the other hand must work to achieve aesthetic experience through the incremental perfection of his or her craft as well as the often arduous struggle to perfect a specific piece of artwork. In fact, the artist's aesthetic experience is attenuated and exceedingly elusive. If creativity is like love it also shares many of the characteristics of a love affair in which vulnerability, anxiety and doubt accompany, or perhaps shadow, the joy of discovery. True love often involves an unsettling recognition of the other as a real person with flaws and limitations (especially to one's own fantasies). Thus the reparation of art and love is not easy or safe; rather, it is often tragic and incomplete. When the Kleinians talk about the reparation of art it may be at times the rush of idealization, but for the artist especially the reparation comes at the cost of hard work, personal vulnerability and even fear.

There is a dialectic within the artist's mind between the imminence of aesthetic experience and of anxiety. While aesthetic experience involves feelings of harmony and balance, anxiety results from the experience of malattunement. The artwork and the individual's systems of meaning are in disjunction. For the artist there are two options: 1) accommodation to the new aesthetic experience through change and expansion of personal meaning systems; or 2) rejection and/or withdrawal whereby the artwork is expelled from one's life world through denigration or exclusion. Even as she marks the canvas with the first tentative brush strokes, the artist appraises the forms, their textures, relations, relative intensities, resonance. She feels within her a stirring of aesthetic experience coupled with anxiety (or the potential for anxiety). As the artist works the tension between anxiety and aesthetic experience acts as a form of signal affect, guiding her towards increased refinement, balance and perfection. She might even seek to increase her anxiety towards some unknown or uncertain expressiveness or new formal order. Anxiety may even suddenly convert to joy and expansiveness, as a new aesthetic form is discovered and elaborated.

Art appreciation is enhanced when one engages the artwork, attending to one's critical attitudes as well as one's sense of resonance and conjunction. The art appreciator "meets" the artwork. There ensues a process of implicit, preconscious procedural knowing in which the formal, visceral and representative aspects of the work, which are the concretized subjectivity of the creator, impact on the viewer eliciting a response on multiple levels. Archaic, self and other experiences are activated during the encounter with the art object. In the best of cases this experience of meeting is intensely affective and profoundly moving – a perfect experience. In the language of first relationships, the good feed becomes the ideal feed in which all is idealized and made well again.

Festival

> If we ask ourselves what the true nature of art is, then obviously we must reply that it consists in an experience of community that is difficult to define in precise terms. We celebrate inasmuch as we are gathered for something, and this is particularly clear in the case of the experience of art. It is not simply the fact that we are all in the same place, but rather the intention that unites us and prevents us as individuals from falling into private conversations and private, subjective experiences.
>
> (Gadamer, 1986, p. 40)

The festival that Gadamer is referring to above is not any specific group of activities but the continual human engagement in the unfolding dialogue of art and aesthetic experience. The festival is the dynamic hubbub that has characterized creativity and the discussion of creativity throughout history and across societies. The individual creative act occurs within the present confluence of meaning and dialogue, but also arises out of the historical context of the society's vital art history. But in the end Gadamer is uncertain about the ultimate purpose of the art festival. However, in this chapter I have argued that aesthetic experience is fundamentally tied to the archaic infant–parent relationship; therefore I would argue that the communal institution known as Art would also be linked to the way in which a society as a whole attempts to elaborate the aesthetic experience (and thus the archaic selfobject tie) across the social landscape, structuring and giving value to the most intimate as well as the most public of human relationships and institutions.

In her book *Art and Intimacy*, Ellen Dissanayake (2000) argued that there is a fundamental connection between the archaic sources of art and the larger cultural activities of a community. She wrote:

> The arts evolved not as stratagems for male competition . . . but as physical correlates of psychological concern. The inborn rhythmic-modal sensitivities of mutuality, through cultural elaborations, became adaptive means for arousing interest, riveting joint attention, synchronizing bodily rhythms and activities, conveying messages with conviction and memorability, and ultimately indoctrinating and reinforcing right attitudes and behaviors. . . . As rhythmic-modal sensitivities and capacities evolved to enable the emotional dispositions by which mothers and infants engaged in mutuality, so could elaborations of these sensitivities and capacities become vehicles for social coordination and concord, instilling belonging, meaning, and competence, which are feelings that comprise psychological well-being.
> (Dissanayake, 2000, pp. 139–140)

Art is one of the means by which human communities extend and infiltrate these archaic interpersonal processes of shared experiences of self, relationship, community and world. The arts are the activities that reflect and embody these archaic aesthetic experiences – creating and enjoying art are the occasions for the shared experience of attunement, vital engagement and mutual regulation. In this sense art is conservative and transformative. It holds and preserves communal subjectivity in the face of mortality and change, and provides opportunities for new experience and the facilitation of social development.

Aesthetic standards are the formal configurations that the group establishes as the optimal and expectable embodiment of metasubjective attunement and mutual regulation. They are social ideals in which communal subjectivity is concretized and given form and value. However, art is also responsive and evolving. The artwork allows for the sense of mutual creation and recognition. Art is intersubjective; there is always a sense of interaction, of dialogue between subject and object.

Some analysts have claimed that art is biologically based and has an adaptive function. However, if art is adaptive, then there must be a way for art to change in response to new developments in society and the environment. This is where the three dimensions of subjectivity come into play, the cultural standards of society are reworked through dialogue and new artists and new forms of art emerge and innovate. The creative churning of the festival, the ongoing tension between iconoclasm and conservatism in art, between social institutions, creative dialogue and individual artistic struggle, is the beating heart of culture. But the deciding process is the way in which society finds its group subjectivity reflected in the multifaceted, perfected mirrors of experience whereby they are both confirmed, confronted and changed.

Conclusion

By means of aesthetic experience we are held psychologically by the formal perfection of the work, object or experience. The real is conjured and confronted in an ideal form. It is at once beautiful and also terrible. Our fearful imaginings are reconciled with the dreadful truth – they are merged within the perfect image. The fragments of our inner lives, of our self-experience, are brought together, coordinated and held together in and by the aesthetic experience. The terrors of unconscious fantasy and desire are made manifest to consciousness and enter into communal life. We are a crowd of vulnerable human beings as we enter the Sistine Chapel together, whereupon we become like gods. The most powerful and terrible fantasies of our culture are expressed through forms of such an ideal nature that we may believe that we have transcended our fragile humanity, at least for a moment – together.

Chapter 3

Art and the artist's mind

> Art creates nature, even human nature.
>
> (Field, 1957, p. 139)

When an artist puts brush to paper, hand to clay, or fingers to keyboard, the boundaries of his or her mind expand. No longer is the artist thinking solely within the confines of the individual mind; rather, consciousness, mind, subjectivity, even self-experience shift fundamentally within a transitional field within which there occurs a dialectic between the internal self and the emerging externalized self concretized in the artwork. But more precisely the artist's mind now exists in the dynamic psychological space in which both inner and outer are contained, interact and affect each other. I believe that a new definition of art may help to identify the nature and processes within this psychological field in which art and artist interact and create each other.

My goal in developing a psychoanalytic definition of art is to identify the psychological function of and motivation behind both art creation and art appreciation. In other words, why do people go to such trouble to make artworks, and why do we grant art such value and find it so enjoyable? I am not satisfied to say that art is just a means of sublimation and that the thrill of art is simply modified sexual excitement. In this chapter I will propose a definition that defines art and distinguishes it from everything else, and I will identify the specific dynamics, functions and motivations which make art an important part of psychological life.

Although psychoanalysts have been interested in art, there has never been an attempt to define it from a specifically psychoanalytic perspective. Freud accepted the existence of art as a human activity with artworks being the result of certain behaviors and psychological processes. But he did not distinguish art from other forms of psychological productions, such as dreams and cultural artifacts. In this sense, for Freud art was a given, another type of activity in which the human need to sublimate forbidden instincts and defensively symbolize unacceptable fantasies resulted in culturally acceptable and at times highly valued objects. But Freud used a common sense definition in which much of the question of art's specific nature was put to the side. The question of what art is did not seem to trouble Freud. After all he stated at several points that before the question of art psychoanalysis must remain silent, seeming to indicate that many questions about art would be left outside the explanatory range of his theory.

Over the past several decades a number of analytic writers have offered new perspectives on art – from object relations, self psychology and developmental perspectives – in an effort to expand on the classical model. What these writers have in common is their understanding of the relationship between artist and artwork. Most importantly they all grant the artwork a dynamic role, not as the passive canvas for the artist's elaborately disguised fantasy life, but rather as part of an active realm of psychological experience, in which there is the possibility of something new, both out in the world and within the artist. The creation of art according to these models serves a psychological function for the artist not secondarily, but primarily as part of the artist's mind, a concrete embodiment of his or her subjectivity. For example, in several papers the Kleinian analyst Hanna Segal (1991) emphasized an important new dimension of art – its restorative function. Segal wrote:

> The artistic impulse is specifically related to the depressive position. The artist's need to recreate what he feels in the depth of his internal world. It is his inner perception of the deepest feeling of the depressive position that his internal world is shattered which leads to the necessity for the artist to recreate something that is felt to be a whole new world. This is what every major artist does – creates a world. This creation of this inner world is unconsciously also a recreation of a lost world.
> (Segal, 1991, pp. 86–87)

The artist through the creation of art brings together parts of the lost object that have been split apart by aggression, and thus unifies and restores the whole object to the creator and audience. In this way the damage to the inner world that results from the dissociative mechanisms of the paranoid-schizoid position are brought forward into the depressive position. The desire to create is driven by this longing for reunion and healing, and the enjoyment of art appreciation is the joy of experiencing this restoration as embodied in the artwork – a return to a once lost harmonious inner world. However, although I feel that this approach identifies an important psychological function of art, it does not offer the definition that we need. For example, interpretations in therapy help to restore internal splits, but interpretations are not art, despite having some aesthetic qualities when done well.

Marion Milner, writing as Joanna Field (1957), suggested another view from Winnicottian object relations. She argued that art was not primarily about restoration of lost objects, but the creation of something new, in which the artist engages the world and brings into existence not something lost, but something that can be discovered, which is significant and new. Through the creative process the artist offers an opportunity to experience something special in the world – that special object being created out of the artist's engagement with reality. This she felt is an enlivening, self-affirming experience – it makes both artist and audience feel more vital and alive. She wrote:

> The importance of a work of art may be the lost object that the work re-creates; but for the artist as artist, rather than as patient, and for whoever responds to his work, I think the essential point is the new thing that he has created, the new bit of the external world that he has made significant and "real" through endowing it with form.
>
> (Field, 1957, p. 160)

Similarly to Milner's approach, D.W. Winnicott argued that creativity occurs naturally in the potential space between subjectivity (the subjective object) and the object objectively perceived, between what he called "me-extensions" and the "not-me" (Winnicott, 1971, p. 100). He believed that the capacity to engage the world in this way develops in the primary experience between the baby and the mother where she allows the baby to play with her, the elements of projection and reality intermingling and influencing each other freely and creatively. With good enough mothering the baby acquires the desire and ability to blend inner and outer, bringing "other-than-me" substances into the self and also investing the experience of the world with fantasy (and vice versa). In instances where the mother impinges on the child his willingness and desire to engage with the world in this way is blocked. Reality remains unrecognized and alien, and the inner world remains walled off and protected from intrusion – creative engagement is stifled.

Winnicott also differentiated between two means of dealing with objects in the world. The first is "relating", where unconscious fantasies determine our experience of the world and objects are just bundles of projections – the external object remaining unrecognized. The second is "using", what the person, after experiencing the survival of the object over time in the fact of repeated attempts to "destroy it" is recognized as independent from the self, having its own being and nature (Winnicott, 1971, p. 86).

In other words, Winnicott viewed the aim of art and other creative activities as a person (artist) engaged with the world so that his subjectivity transforms objective reality and vice versa. This is how the world is humanized (being both "out" there and "in" here, simultaneously). And for the individual person it is how he is able to feel "real" and fully engaged with the world.

The most valuable contribution made by both Milner and Winnicott to a theory of art is their description of the process by which something "new" is created. For them art is not just the projection of fantasy, the externalization of lost memories, or the sublimation of forbidden drives. They describe how the artist is in a dynamic encounter with the real world, inner and outer impacting and changing each other and bringing about in the potential space between (a space with both physical and psychological dimensions) a brand new object – the artwork. It is important to recognize that Winnicott did not view this new object as either subjective or objective; rather, it is the result of the dialectic tensions between these two worlds, an amalgam of psychological and physical realities.

Similarly, Susan Deri (1984), a student of another object relations theorist, Michael Balint, viewed art as a "reordering of the universe" in which the artist's perceptions of the external world are filtered through their apperceptive and symbolizing schemata, which imbues the artwork with "subjective symbolic significance". While the artwork's deeply subjective elements may derive from the artist's unconscious, the formal organizing principles stem from the preconscious–conscious system. Deri described how

> in the course of creation, a "dialogue" takes place between the artist and the work. There is a continual matching (probably on the preconscious level) between external and the internal that takes shape through the "dialogue" between the artist and the visible work. The outside feeds the inside, which again looks out – maybe changed due to the effect of what has been seen on the canvas. The final work possesses a self-consistent system of relations, which is the essential "subject matter" of all art forms.
>
> (Deri, 1984, pp. 170–171)

Like Milner and Winnicott, Deri believed that art was a dynamic, creative activity between the inner world of the artist and the external world, which the artist perceives and alters according to unconscious organizing principles. She argued that the artist must step in and out of the potential space, at one time immersing himself in the artwork and at other times "stepping back" and assessing and judging it. Later I will make the case that this dialogue is at the heart of creativity but is also one of the ways that we can distinguish art from other human activities. For as Deri said, the dialogue that the artist engages in is not with an other completely separate from the self, but the other as constructed and reordered according to inner principles. In other words, the artist's dialogue is with externalized aspects of his own subjective life, aspects of his self which have engaged with and reorganized the external world in the form of his symbolic schemata.

More recently some self psychologists have elaborated a theory of creativity and art, which is similar to the object relations approach. For example, Carl Rotenberg, in his 1988 paper *Selfobject Theory and the Artistic Process*, argued that once an action is taken and an aspect of subjectivity can be said to be expressed in the work, this externalized subjectivity becomes to a greater or lesser degree disjunctive with self-experience (due either to the effect of the object on the form of self-expression or the rapid unfolding of the self-experience of the artist). The artist then acts upon the subjective object as both internal and external to self-experience. There is a unique dialectic that is established between internal and external aspects of subjectivity. As a consequence of this dialectic further actions are taken and the artwork develops towards perfection. Carl Rotenberg described this process:

> The area of interaction between the artist and his own work, he puts his own puzzles and mental ambiguities outside himself and then reacts to them as if they were other than his. In a sense, once the artist begins a work, he surrenders to it as though the work were dominating him, demanding a solution of its own ambiguities, and requiring completion. The artist experiences selfobject functioning of the artwork as alive, active, and interpretive and eventually having transformative capabilities, to the extent that inner puzzles of the artist are worked through this externalization.
>
> (Rotenberg, 1988, p. 209)

Rotenberg described a unique form of intersubjectivity where the artist engages with an "other" which was in fact once part of self-experience but is now external, possessing through concretization in media or language a separate subjectivity. That which has been made external, in other words has been "expressed", is the artist's self experience. But Rotenberg believed that what the artist was driven to express were "puzzles" about the self, and the work of creation was not just the externalization (that is the first step) but the solving of the puzzle through engagement with the new object, which is gradually transformed by the artist into a perfect solution. The result is that the artwork functions as a selfobject experience, mirroring the artist's perfection, or offering an ideal opportunity for admiration of its beauty.

Gilbert Rose, in an approach very similar to Rotenberg's, felt that that which was being externalized through art was the mind itself. However, he is explicit about the special nature of the artwork and of the appreciation of it. Once again art is not just externalization or projection of subjectivity – the artistic creative process works out the psychological puzzles contained in the art object, and through a process of skillful perfecting and refinement, the form of the artwork becomes more articulated, special, even ideal. Rose wrote:

Thus, the art object not only stands for the working of the mind, but the mind idealized; so, a partial fusion with the art object is fusion with an idealized object standing for the self. The recurrent merging and separating from the art object (standing for the harmonious workings of the mind) enhances self-esteem.

(Rose, 1980, p. 13)

Of course this enhancement accompanies only successful artist effort; artistic failure leads to depression even despair and self-hatred. But what Rose suggests is that artists have a powerful motive for art creation – the affective thrill of what I will later refer to as *aesthetic resonance*, the vitalizing, self-confirming impact of a successful creative effort.

A new psychoanalytic perspective on art

Human beings act upon objects in the world and change them to embody human interests and experience. In many instances these changes make objects more useful and/or functional, but for many others the goal is simply to transform the non-human into something that can be included within and help to construct a human environment within which social life can take place. Universally human beings work to create a world that is of human scale and reflects back to them who and what they are. Through craft we change the environment and objects and give them human meanings and social roles. But in the end we are perfecting something external to ourselves, and though it reflects a human need or wish, it is in and of itself something other; a bowl, a knife, a clock, a hat, all may be creations of human intension but they are in the end, objects. On the other hand, art occurs when people act upon their own subjectivity and perfect it. They do this by externalizing subjectivity (paint marks on a blank canvas) and then working to perfect the subjective expression, the objectified subjective object. This is the only instance that I know of where human subjectivity becomes both external and real, but is also pliable, alterable and gradually transformed as a subjective object. Through the making of art the artist's subjectivity exists outside self-experience and becomes the focus of his or her creative intent. This is why art is so important to us – it is one of the only means through which we can experience what it means to be human in a form which intensifies and focuses human experience, so the viewer feels more alive, more aware and more valuable. Creating art and viewing art, we come into contact with the most perfect manifestation of human subjectivity and through it we both transcend normal human life and at the same time come into awareness of our deepest nature.

Psychoanalysis has traditionally linked artistic creativity to primary process thinking, the unconscious and, specifically, dreams; and while these do play a role in creativity (as they do in every human thought, feeling or activity) they are not sufficient for the understanding of art. A dream in and of itself is always internal and private. What we generally think of are reports of dreams, verbal accounts of private experience. In this sense dream reports can be art (for example, Coleridge's most famous example of dream into art in his poem *Kubla Khan*). However, an artwork cannot be just a symbolization of a fantasy or a feeling. Symptoms, doodles, angry arguments may put fantasy and affect into concrete forms, but these types of things are more simply expressive than otherwise. The form they take is clearly secondary to the function of expression and externalization. Although, as with dreams, these spontaneous actions and communications may be a source of artistic inspiration and/or sources of imagery, they are not art.

Art exists in the world – *thoughts* cannot be art, unless transformed into words, music, movement or imagery. It must be something external to the artist, even if that existence is as ephemeral as the sounds of music or as concrete and enduring as a block of basalt. However, as we have seen, the creative artist makes changes in objects or creates objects or experiences that involve the externalization of his or her subjectivity. Thus the object is the medium for an objectification of feeling, thought or fantasy. Subjectivity is literally *trans-substantiated*; it remains grounded in the self but has also become an other thing entirely. As a result of this process the artist's subjectivity is externalized – the artwork is a subjective object. The artist's subjectivity has a *real presence* in the artwork, but it is not simply a mirror of the inner experience of the artist. The artwork is a creation of the artist, based on his or her subjectivity, but not equivalent to it. The act of creation, as well as the movement of time, forces a disengagement between the inner experience of the artist and the artwork which now exists on its own terms. When the artist studies the artwork he both recognizes it as his own (of his own flesh, if you will) but it is also *other*, apart from the self, thus it can be known both for what it shares with the artist's mind and how it is different. It contains parts of her or him, altered by the very act of creation. Now the subjective object as artwork can be further transformed; thus the artist engages in a creative process with externalized aspects of his own subjective life which, as a consequence of externalization, becomes open to further elaboration. This is what makes art distinct as a human activity: the artist works to refine and perfect the expression of his or her subjectivity as it is concretized in the artwork. Hence *art is a unique, evolving dialectical relationship between internal and external aspects of the artist's own subjectivity*. The result of any successful creative act is a synthesis, or an aesthetic integration, concretized as a new object (or a new elaboration of the artwork). Of course, this synthesis continues to be the target of the artist's creative attention until the artwork is finished. Optimally, with a skilled and experienced artist, this dialectic leads to an increasingly refined and perfected articulation of subjective experience –

human life expressed at the most exquisite level. When this creative work is at its best and the artist's efforts are most successful the result is a thing of beauty.

The three dimensions of the artist's subjectivity

To fully understand art and artists we must expand what we normally think of as subjectivity. Most importantly individual subjectivity cannot exist out of context. Each artist brings to his work intrapsychic (individual), intersubjective (relational) and metasubjective (cultural) dimensions of his or her own subjective life. In other words, the artist is also embedded and inseparable from the social milieu within which he works, hence the importance of including in our model the role of the artist's relationships (past and present) and the cultural surround within which he developed as a person and artist, and in which he is creating his art. In fact, one of the theses of this book is that an understanding of the evolution of art requires that we consider the shifting prominence of these three dimensions of subjectivity in art history. Over historical time the balance between the three major dimensions of subjectivity has changed and this has affected the subjective nature of artists and their arts as well.

Throughout most of history the intrasubjective (individual mental life) has been in the background of creative work, with the metasubjective (cultural) taking the foreground of the creative process. In fact, individual subjectivity would largely play a role in the interpretation of cultural forms within a professional group with various standards and values. The intrasubjective in and of itself was in the background, while cultural images and art forms were in the foreground of creative effort. For artists prior to the modern age these meanings were predominantly social and cultural – the wars, battles and challenges faced by the heroes of Greek history and the role of the gods in human events and fate. For modern artists the predominant meanings and values have been about individual experience, the radical creative potential of private, inner fantasy and creativity.

Art and creativity serve different functions when you approach them from the vantage point of culture, relationships and individual subjective life. The social function of art in the preservation and enhancement of group relations within a particular society is quite different from the psychological function of art in the affirmation and enhancement of the self-experience of the individual working artist. Yet a complete analytic aesthetic theory must acknowledge the relationship between these different domains. Although in this book I will emphasize the creative process of the individual artist, the creative act is intelligible only from within the culture and social milieu out of which it arises.

Art and artists exist in cultures in which the forms and methods of art are established and the standards of quality are decided. This is true of even the most personal aspects of art. The artist in her studio relies on the tools, maps and measuring instruments of outside culture, and though she might challenge her culture, she cannot escape it. We take our artistic language from culture, which becomes the personal aesthetic idiom through which aesthetic experience and creativity is possible and intelligible.

Artists are also embedded in a network of relationships within which their aesthetic develops and is perfected. Many have noted the frequent occurrence of artistic dyads, where an artist or artists rely on dialogue with a valued other person who functions for them as a muse. It is out of this intersubjective matrix that many revolutionary aesthetic movements are spawned and sustained. These grouping of artists take from the metasubjective horizon of culture those themes, styles, values, and art forms that are best suited to express their special intersubjective vision. They then through dialogue create the unique aesthetic of their generation. It is the cultural and relational contexts that compose the working ground of individual artistic effort.

In the end, though, neither culture nor relationships have the adaptability and resourcefulness of the individual artist's creative process. This is why, although there are grand cultures and great movements in art, it is in the individual struggle of the single artist that these larger processes emerge. The artist working within, taking from and acting against the culture and relationships within which she lives creates something new. It is this domain of aesthetics that is the primary concern of this book. Therefore, I will emphasize the way in which self-experience (which includes the experience of self in relationship) is expressed in the formal structure of the artwork. However, it is crucial that I be clear that the individual intrapsychic experience of the artist crystallizes out of and is constituted by relational and cultural meanings which are also the artists motive, form and subject. In fact, artists may be more profoundly engaged with their environment and social milieu than others. In 1966 Heinz Kohut made this claim:

> The creative individual is less separated from his surroundings than non-creative one; the "I-You" barrier is not as clearly defined. The creative individual is keenly aware of these aspects of his surroundings that are of significance to his work and he invests them with narcissistically idealizing libido.
>
> (Kohut, 1966, p. 112)

Although Kohut utilized a classical model of intrapsychic mental life, the artist he described is intensely relational. The normal boundaries between self and other are fluid; the artist engages dynamically with the world. He or she is not introspectively ruminating in his or her own world; to the contrary the artist's self-experience is powerfully linked to the world of objects and others who are also, paradoxically, creations of the artist.

Extending Kohut's thinking I would argue that *aesthetics* is fundamentally intersubjective in this sense. It involves the externalization of self-experience intertwined with the discovery of the world. This is the process Dissanayake emphasized, where the rhythms and modes of archaic attunement become the templates for our aesthetic engagement with culture. It is similar to the concept of projective identification and Winnicott's transitional experience, but includes the notion of action, where the person does something to effect the object so as to express subjectivity. Once an action is taken, altering the object in some way, it can be said that subjectivity is externalized and the artist enters into a relationship with an object which is now invested with qualities of the artist's own subjective experience. I am not proposing a solipsistic model of aesthetics; rather, the qualities of the external object are essential (as in the mother–infant dialogue). In fact, the action taken upon the object *must* include the qualities of the object (its color, plasticity etc.) as well as the changing relationship between internal and external aspects of subjectivity.

Self-expression in aesthetic experience is not limited to emotion, affect or even specific ideas or impressions (although it may contain all of these). The form of self-expression contained in artistic creation is best captured in the idea of being, of conveying in the work aspects of how it feels to be the living person who one is. However, art is not simply a mirror, a representation of our selves, it is a new creation that evokes self-experience and embodies the self-in-relation through aesthetic perfection. This allows us to include within the idea of art the cosmic tapestry of the Sistine Chapel and the stark simplicity of a Rothko painting. As different as they may be, both can be said to contain within them some perfect expression of human experience.

Art: human subjectivity externalized and perfected

Self-experience is not unitary or unchanging. What we experience as our self (I or me) is protean, ambiguous and complex. For example, the psychoanalyst Phillip Bromberg (1996) explains how normal self-experience is composed of fluid, fluctuating self-state configurations, only some of which are conscious to us at any given time. The normal mechanism that Bromberg believes permits us to establish coherence in the midst of psychological chaos is *dissociation*, by means of which we separate out and focus on particular self-organizations that increase psychological safety. Therefore, when we say that the artist externalizes his or her subjectivity, we mean that the artist brings a whole range of conscious and unconscious options to the artistic task. During the heat of the creative process the artist's self can be viewed not as fixed and preformed but emergent and transitional, crystallizing in the potential space which defines the shared psychological reality of artist, medium and artwork. Internal potential and external emergent aspects of self-experience interact, co-create and define each other.

As noted earlier, once the artist uses a medium they are also changed in the process. The artist is no longer the person they were, and the object is no longer what it was. Technically the artwork has been placed there by the artist, but it is no longer a part of him. In fact, the art object was never part of him, it was always something else, a creation of his subjectivity but never equivalent to it. Throughout the creative process the developing artwork is in and out of sync with the artist's expectations – the artist struggles to reconcile inner and outer, accommodating his or her vision to the new reality, trying to see it for what it is and, hopefully, eventually celebrating it's existence. But for the artist the art object is experienced as part of the self; both of the artist and of the world, it exists in a transitional psychological realm within which subjectivity and objectivity are dynamically related and a new reality is co-created – the artwork is a *subjective object*.

Aesthetic resonance and selfobject experience

Artists engage in a special type of relationship with their medium and artwork. They are not satisfied with simply externalizing their subjectivity but must perfect the artwork.

Gradually, as a result of artistic effort and resourcefulness, there is an increasing sense of the inner and outer beginning to match, the intersubjective dialogue which has characterized creative work results in a sense of *aesthetic resonance*, with intrapsychic forms (those which arouse the emotional necessities of our physiological, psychological and relational natures) falling into sync with the artwork. Often fleetingly, sometimes only partially, and at times with a lingering sense of regret (even dread), the inner and outer are disengaged, and the process ends.

This unfolding dialectic between artist and artwork is accompanied by the fluctuation of states of emotional tension and self-experience. The sense of resonance between the external and internal aspects of subjectivity is self-confirming and pleasurable. Dissonance leads to varying levels of self-crisis. *Aesthetic resonance* is the degree in which internal aspects of subjectivity and the external aspects of subjectivity concretized in the artwork are conjunctive one to the other, the way in which the relationships between the colors and forms of a painting express the organization of the artist's internal world. Fundamental to this idea is that the artwork and the artist's subjectivity are a single intersubjective field in which inner and outer are from a certain point of view irrelevant. As a result of the experience of *aesthetic resonance* the artist feels vitalized, more cohesive, directed and alive. If the artist is successful in developing the work towards greater precision this inner state can be quite powerful and the artist's self-experience is idealized.

As we discussed in the last chapter, throughout life people seek out proximity to and engagement with idealized others. These relationships function psychologically to give form, vitality and meaning to subjective life. Self psychologists use the term *selfobject experience* for this psychological state and for the object, which provides the opportunity for the experience. The most important dimensions of these experiences are mirroring of one's value and specialness (the ideal self) and being with another who is felt to possess a high degree of value and specialness (an idealized other). The artist invests his or her relationship with the developing artwork with these fundamental qualities of selfobject experience. He or she seeks to create a relationship with an object that both reflects the artist's value and specialness and is also ideal in and of itself. This is a psychological experience in which a person enters into relationship to an object which is felt to have ideal qualities (an idealized selfobject) and/or experiences the object as reflecting back ideal qualities of themselves (the grandiose self). In most cases successful creativity involves both an idealized and a grandiose selfobject experience. The artist feels in the presence of an ideal object that reflects back an experience of the ideal self. As a result, if the artist is successful he or she, by means of the creative process, experiences the artwork as a selfobject. It is this ongoing search for the aesthetic selfobject experience that drives the creative process.

However, in reality selfobject experience tends to be precarious or fragile. The person inevitably experience *selfobject failure*, where the object, for whatever reason, is no longer experienced as ideal or reflective of one's grandiose self. An example of this disjunction is when an artist begins work in the morning and finds a confusing jumble where the night prior he had left a "masterpiece". In such a case externalized aspects of subjectivity are no longer in conjunction with self-experience and they are experienced as something other – at times as something far removed from what is imagined or desired. This leads to a state of self-crisis that can result in a permanent rupture of the relation to the artwork or, optimally, to further effort to restore the selfobject tie through creative work. It is important to remember that it is not solely the qualities of the object which determine resonance and dissonance but the relation between the internal subjective world and its externalization in the object. From the point of view of a third party the object may be beautiful, but the artist may nonetheless experience a sense of disappointment or even failure.

Successful art involves the artist's creation of an opportunity for self-object experience. He or she does this by externalizing some aspect of subjectivity by means of an action upon some aspect of the external world. She then enters into a dialectical relationship with these externalized aspects of her own subjectivity. The intent of this dialectic is to take further action to alter the artwork towards a goal of greater expressive perfection. On the other hand, the artist is affected by the artwork, his inner working model of the work and emotional state being responsive to the object, which is being created. Optimally the artwork not only resonates with inner experience, it also externalizes subjectivity in an increasingly ideal form. The relationship with the ideal artwork that reflects back the perfection of the artist is at the heart of the *aesthetic selfobject experience*. Heinz Kohut saw this as being at the heart of the creative drive. He wrote:

> Creative artists may be attached to their work with the intensity of an addiction and they try to control and shape it with forces and for purposes that belong to the narcissistically experienced world. They are attempting to re-create a perfection that formerly was directly an attribute of their own.
>
> (Kohut, 1985, p. 115)

In closing this chapter I would like to say several words about the connection between psychopathology and the creative arts. To this end I will briefly summarize the model which we have been discussing and see how it offers artists an opportunity for self-healing that is unique – however fleeting, illusory and fragile it may be in reality.

Artistic creativity is a manner of thinking, of feeling, of being within a medium and symbolic language of forms. It is a dialectical process, in which the artist alters the medium, infuses objects with subjectivity, and engages the new, subjective object (both actively and psychically). Thus artistic creativity is not just something the artist does, a pastime or occupation, it is a way of being in the world, and of experiencing their inner and outer life. Like breath or sight the creative act is inseparable from self and over time and effort it becomes the artist's primary medium of self-experience and self-in-relation to the world, and – as parts of the world – other people.

The fact that artistic creativity can provide an opportunity for autonomous, self-referential selfobject experiences explains why artistic creativity and an artistic career can be attractive to people with histories of insecure or traumatic attachment. A review of the lives of many great artists (especially in modern times) reveals that many of them had childhoods in which good enough parenting was absent. Some of these artists may in fact have disrupted or deficient aesthetic development which may contribute to depression and self-disregulation in adulthood. However, what if these people possess artistic talent? What if they discover the possibility of using that talent to bring about positive aesthetic experiences – within the limited scope of creative work – and that work provides the opportunity for selfobject experiences otherwise unavailable? For a self-disordered person the creation of an artwork may serve a powerful defensive or compensatory function – a longed for realization of archaic selfobject needs. In the most successful instances the artist may achieve an aesthetic experience of such perfection and emotional satisfaction that at least temporarily, he or she feels restored, whole and vital. This is the experience of having created something of aesthetic perfection, of beauty. I believe that this can explain the frequent phenomenon (especially within the community of modern artists) of the psychotic or character disordered artist, who in the midst of a tormented and disrupted life successfully organizes him or herself around a productive and aesthetically successful career as an artist. Oscar Wilde conveyed the protective function of creativity and art in the following quote:

> It is through Art and through Art only that we can realize our perfection; through Art and Art only that we can shield ourselves from the sordid perils of actual existence.
> (Wilde, 2007, p. 995)

Summary: art and the artist's mind

The unique qualities that characterize and define art as a psychological activity and which I believe are at the heart of any definition of art are the following: 1) Art involves the expression of the subjectivity of the artist and the process of perfection of that expression, as a function of the creative process; 2) The artist's subjectivity includes the cultural, relational and individual dimensions which make up all human subjective life; 3) Subjective expression in art involves externalization through the altering or creation of an object or external form of experience (I call this the creation of a *subjective object*); 4) It is in the formal aspects of the object that the subjectivity of the artist is concretized; 5) This process of externalization through the medium of art inevitably results in accidents and other unanticipated emergent phenomena; 6) Once the subjective object is "out there", existing separately from the artist's inner world, it can be acted upon, its form manipulated in order for the artist's internal and now external subjectivity to be perfected and refined – idealizing; 6) The perfecting of the artwork is experienced as pleasurable and self-affirming to the artist – a *selfobject experience*; 7) There is a feedback loop in which the new object influences the artist even as the artist further refines the object, an experience of *aesthetic resonance* results; 7) At least temporarily the artist feels more alive and more cohesive as a person when the creative process goes well; 8) This dialectic between the artist's subjectivity and his or her externalized subjectivity in the crystallizing work results in the emergence of new formal elements and unique organizations of experience, till then unknown or unseen even by the artist; 9) This entire process results in the perfection of an increasingly ideal object, the formal aspects of which embody the ideal manifestation of human subjectivity; 10) The artwork is not synonymous with or equivalent to the artist's self; rather, it is entirely new, independent and unique, an ideal product and, given this, a highly refined and perfected "making real" of human subjectivity itself; 11) The successful artwork, being the product of the artist, does essentially mirror the artist's creative self; even its externality becomes an important benefit to the artist, who can hold the fantasy that the fragile and ever changing uncertainty of his or her inner life and sense of self is now permanently contained and embodied in this special, ideal object; 12) An inevitable, hopefully non-traumatic, tragedy for the artist is that the artwork is ineluctably external and its function in confirming and vitalizing the artist's self fades, hence a new artwork and creative project must be pursued in a never ending search for artistic self-confirmation.

A note on chaos, complexity and creativity

I want to note before proceeding further that although I have not explicitly mentioned systems theory it nonetheless has played an important part in my thinking regarding creativity, artists and art. The lone artist in his studio, putting brush to canvas, is a special type of system engaged in a dynamic process in which aesthetic forms and internal psychological states interact.

In the following chapter I will show how this model of aesthetic experience, art and creativity can be useful in understanding the lives, works and times of a number of modern artists and their modern art.

Chapter 4

Modern art and modern artists

Introduction

As a psychoanalyst studying modern art and modern artists, I start with three fundamental questions: 1) What was the psychological context, the specific cultural milieu, which produced and then became influenced by the artist in question?; 2) Who was he or she and what types of relationships did they have and maintain which may have influenced the decisions and actions the artist engaged in as he or she created art?; and 3) What was the nature of the psychological life of the artist, his or her motivations, vulnerabilities, talents and conflicts, which impacted on the creative process and influenced their career, art productions and innovations as well as the art world of his or her time.

Since this book is a study of the psychological lives of individual artists I will not discuss the historical and cultural context in great depth. What I will do is introduce each section of the book with a short summary which will set the discussion of each artist in the context of his time and the particular state of modern art before and during his career. The intent is not to say anything new or definitive about the history of modern art; rather, I will try to help the reader by clarifying each section's relation to art history and, more importantly, linking it to the sections that precede and follow it. Since I will be discussing both European and American artists, I have organized the chapters accordingly and provided separate introductory sections. In addition, since the last chapter, on the life and work of Andy Warhol, deals with postmodern art, I have written a brief introduction to that chapter, setting it apart from the others and clarifying the special issues for art during the second half of the twentieth century. The rest of this chapter will introduce the reader to the historical and cultural context of modern art, while limiting its focus to European artists.

Prior to the nineteenth century artists were generally concerned with the expression of fantasy and imaginary depictions of historical events that reflected the values and meanings of the culture – specifically those of the institutions that supported and paid for the artwork that was being produced. Creativity did not emphasise private or even relational processes but the large communal themes of religious belief, heroism and nationalism. This does not mean that individual subjective elements were absent; rather, they were subordinated to the large subjective world of the cultural, institutional and political life.

However, in the nineteenth century this all began to change and the nature of art and artists would change as well. A new art economy emerged with a developing market for new art driven by the hunger of the new bourgeois business class for affordable, new types of art. The subject matter of art had to go beyond the historical themes that dominated earlier decades as artists attempted to appeal to the everyday lived experiences of the middle classes.

There are many characteristics that have been used to define modern art. For our purposes I will argue that the modern artist sought a new type of relationship to his or her artwork, and a new approach to the artistic creative process. The cultural and social influence in aesthetics dropped to the background and the artist's own subjectivity, his mind, became the subject and source of artistic inspiration and aesthetic form. From Edgar Degas to Andy Warhol modern artists struggled against the values, art forms and aesthetic standards which had defined western art for generations. Most importantly they thrust their own subjectivity into the creative process and made the subject of art their own minds. This led to a profound and enduring revolution within our culture and transformed how we think about art and, most importantly, it helped to change what art is. Once the domain of social expression and institutional production, art became defined by the self-experience of the artist himself. Its mooring to cultural traditions and standards became unfastened, and a compulsion to rebel and create new forms of art became the driving force behind modern creativity. The cultural definition of art and the professional skills and practices of the artist were swept away. This continual revolution was driven not just by the internal economics of the art marketplace, or the changing political and social world, but also by the new individualism that had taken over the west, and the elaborate new image of the artist as innovator, visionary and originator of aesthetic values and forms.

There were so many important and interesting artist's who participated in this aesthetic revolution that any list would be incomplete. I have not used the standard art historical line-up, namely Manet, Monet, Cezanne, Picasso, etc. Rather than being guided in my selection by art historical tradition I have selected artists whose psychological lives and artistic careers seem clearly intertwined. As you will see I am not claiming any internal connection between the lives of any of these artists that might explain modernism. However, I believe that each of the artists whom we will be discussing reflected a particular psychological relation to the modern movement, by responding to contemporary developments as well to actively producing cultural changes out of their personal creative efforts and struggles. To begin, in the next chapter I discuss the life and work of Edgar Degas who I see as one of the best examples of an artist who worked at the boundary between classical art and modernism. Struggling against the confines of classical traditions and the disciplines imposed by academic forms of learning, Degas challenged these conventions from within and eventually defined a personal aesthetics which (along with the other leaders of the avant-garde, impressionist group) redefined not only what was the subject of art or how that subject was painted, but the basic function of art as an activity, a social institution and a psychological experience. Our next subject, Pierre Bonnard, pioneered an aesthetics of imagination, in which color and light represented not the perceptual world of the impressionists but an inner imaginative world of beauty, the source of which was the artist's own self-experience. The next artist, Matisse, confronted the anxiety of change and broke through to a completely new and unencumbered aesthetic free of all ties to tradition and standards of taste – his was the first fully modern art form. Then we discuss Marcel Duchamp who abandoned the traditional mediums of art and the tyranny of perception for an aesthetics of ideas in which the artist's basic relationship to art and culture was altered.

Before starting I would like to make a short comment on the psychoanalytic study of dead artists. Clearly there is no way to verify any of the claims that I will make regarding the artist's inner life. The data that I will use – biographical facts, artistic imagery, symbolic communication, artist statements and writings – are unreliable at best and subject to interpretations that cannot be verified by the artist's associations. Claims such as the ones I will be making are hypotheses, and in the end they are only rhetorically true (I hope), having an internal consistency that resonates with the sympathetic reader's personal experience of the artist's work. In the end all that the analyst can offer is an interesting psychological perspective on the artist that may enhance the reader's experience of the artwork. The purpose is not to claim that a particular artist was "really" saying this or that, or that a particular experience (for example a mother's deafness) inevitably accounts for the artist's aesthetic stance. Traditionally psychoanalysts have subjected the artist's creations to an interpretive procedure similar to that used in dream analysis. In this traditional approach art is primarily viewed as symbolic – thus the goal of the analyst is to look behind the protective veil of style and image and reveal the unconscious truth that is really what the artist is saying. More contemporary analysts, using object relations and developmental models, try to explain art by conjuring up reconstructions of early childhood traumas that may be at the core of creativity. My view is that these approaches need not only to be kept in perspective (given that we can never really know the validity of our interpretations) but they also take the fun out of art. I would argue that the benefit of an analytic approach is to expand the possibilities of art, not limit its meanings. The analyst can be playful as he or she opens up the mind of the audience to unforeseen possibilities and rich new dramatic hypothesis, and challenges the viewer to confront and struggle with their "countertransferences" to the artwork. In this way psychoanalysis can free the viewer and stimulate an engagement with art that augments the inherent curative and vitalizing process. An analytic perspective not only analyzes artists and artworks, but also challenges and liberates the audience. If we see art appreciation as a dialectic, as a hermeneutic activity of interactive constructions of feeling and meaning, then the ability and willingness of the audience to be creative, to break through their own internal walls of tradition, greatly enhances the enjoyment of art. With this book I hope to explore ways which we have come to think about modern art, not to tell you "how it really was" but to expand the narrative, to engage in dialogue, to open up each other's eyes – the way that the analyst and patient open up each other's eyes and create new, less constricting narratives.

Chapter 5

Edgar Degas: The psychological edge of modernism

> Art is not the application of a canon of beauty but what the instinct and the brain can conceive beyond any canon.
> (Picasso, in Kuspit, 1993, p. 31)

In this short statement Pablo Picasso captures the psychological challenge of the modernist artist. From its beginnings in the late nineteenth century, modernism promoted a revolutionary aesthetic; no longer were artists just members of a guild, or an academic tradition defined by and judged by the conventions, values and institutions of traditional culture. Aesthetic life was "liberated" under modernism. The artist pursued a direct and often aggressively personal relationship to artistic forms, mediums, subjects and audiences; to do this he or she rejected the "canon of beauty" and encountered the world by means of instinct and pure brain power, pursuing art beyond the canon. Aesthetic experience became internal, psychological and idiosyncratic. The new bourgeois artist seeking to "make it" in a rapidly changing art world turned inward and away from society (even as he offered his artwork towards it), seeking ever different and provocative forms of self-expression. Of course what was once avant-garde soon became canon, and the drive for self-realization has required a non-stop push to construct more revolutionary interpretations of self-experience and to break through endless walls erected by society in it's hunger for tradition. Edgar Degas lived his life on the edge of this aesthetic revolution; his artistic career stretched from the age of classicism dominated by Ingre to the world-shaking, cubist revolt of Picasso and Braque. By examining Degas' individual aesthetic development we will glimpse the psychological underpinnings of this fateful cultural transformation.

The psychological function of modern art: The "breakthrough" of the self

The art historian and critic Donald Kuspit wrote the following regarding what draws the modern person to art either as creator or as audience:

People go to art to recover from unconscious breakdown of the sense of self and of the will to live brought about by their inability to tolerate the world's indifference to their inner life, and especially by their narcissistic need to be mirrored and to idealize. True art seems to care about inner life and respond to narcissistic need. It thus makes people feel alive, renewing their faith in themselves. More particularly, the playful unity of the true work of art – playful because it seems simultaneously disintegration of old form and an integration of new form – becomes a hopeful model to the self. True art gives the self leave to become playful. Leading it out of the wilderness of feeling like nothing into the promised land of feeling like something new. True art and true self seem in perpetual playful transition between old form, which embodies the feeling of being nothing, and new form, experienced as everything one would ever want to be.

(Kuspit, 1993, pp. 76–77)

I believe that Kuspit is correct in describing how art can revive, enliven and cure our self-experience and our sense of relatedness to the world – even mature and healthy people feel invigorated, challenged and entertained by art. In particular, modernist art has as its primary goal the enhancement, cure and restoration of the self. Through confronting old, tired customs and standards of aesthetic values, by breaking through and transforming mediums and art forms, the artist seeks to embody the experience of being alive in the modern world. And through the process of perfection, the creation of new forms of beauty, he or she transcends and moves beyond crisis into a renewed self-state (although this renewal is usually limited to the engagement with the artwork – art does not cure neurosis). Again, Kuspit:

A wall of tradition blocking the artist's path is destroyed by sheer force of artist will (and hard work); going through it, he finds himself in an unexpected artistic situation that remains to be explored. "Breakthrough" signals the ruins of the confining old wall as well as the passage to a new openness. The breakthrough – avant-garde, (modernism) – artist dissolves an old tradition perceived as a dogmatic trap, a stifling uniform . . . breakthrough is a change from the habitual to the mysterious.

(Kuspit, 1993, p. 30)

Edgar Degas: Living at the modernist edge

Edgar Degas' life defined the contours of the modernist edge as he moved towards a total transformation of the formal conventions of nineteenth-century art (biographical information on Degas is from *Degas: His Life,*

Times, and Work by R. McMullen, 1984). Struggling against the confines of classical traditions and the disciplines imposed by academic forms of learning, he challenged these conventions from within and eventually defined a personal aesthetics which (along with the other leaders of the avant-garde impressionist group) redefined not only what was the subject of art or how that subject was painted, but also the basic function of art as an activity, a social institution and a psychological experience. This chapter will suggest the psychological dynamics behind Degas' transition to modernism. In particular I will show how the artist sought to cure a split in the self in which his longings for his dead mother conflicted with his ambivalent identification with his traditional but living father. It was through the gradual transformation of the formal aesthetics of his art, from classical precisions and formal standards of representation, line and color, towards a freer more expressive and subjective aesthetic characterized by radical experimentation that he eventually achieved a creative breakthrough in which artist and artwork became one. Relationally Degas' aesthetic development mirrored his psychological transition from the loyal (but ambivalent) attachment to his father towards the recovery of the experience of play in the arms of the mother.

Born in 1934 Edgar Degas was the oldest of five children of a businessman and banker, Auguste, and his wife, Celestine, who died when the artist was 13 years old. Though there is little that we know about Edgar's early childhood, I would argue that he was extremely close to his mother and that her death had an enduring impact on the rest of his self-development. Strikingly, he rarely talked about her after her death (most likely a family expectation) but when he did it was clear that his grief endured, silent but unremitting. While his attachment to his mother became sequestered, his relationship to his father, especially as the oldest son, strengthened. However, there was clear ambivalence. His father wanted him to take over the family business, and while Degas did make a pretence for a time, even entering law school, he eventually admitted his compulsive sketching and copying and his decision to be an artist. Auguste was disturbed, but ultimately supported Edgar – but on the condition that his son pursue his career as an artist with the same vigor and eye to financial success that the father had as a banker.

As a young artist learning his trade, Degas submitted himself to the constraining academic strictures of the institutional artistic hierarchy of nineteenth-century Europe. This culture dictated who would be granted admission, how the student should learn and ultimately whose works would be rewarded. In fact Degas did not have to behave. He quickly dropped out of the École des Beaux-Arts and left for Italy to live with his family and study painting on his own. But his own sense of self and aesthetic sensibility was deeply tied to the conditions of the father – literally. Degas' father, a lover of art and a supporter of his son's career, was an opinionated and traditional man who idealized the Italian artists of the sixteenth century and who encouraged Edgar to copy the masters as part of his training and development as an artist. And Degas did copy, enthusiastically, literally thousands of sketches and paintings based on old master techniques. But over time, even as his skill developed in proficiency, his capacity to formulate and act on his own aesthetic was blocked and he struggled to complete several major projects upon which his budding career were based. Noting his inhibition his family would worry and frequently chide him that he risked failure in the fulfillment of his talent and ambition.

An interesting episode in Degas' young manhood occurred during his three years of study in Italy. At one point he was forced to stay at the home of his beloved aunt Laura, the wife of Gennaro Bellelli. To his dismay his aunt and cousins were delayed in Naples and unable to return home for several months. Edgar complained of the loathing he felt for his uncle and he experienced the period without his aunt as lonesome and boring. In a letter he quoted Pascal that he had "only himself in front of him, nothing but himself to look at, nothing but himself to think about . . . which recommends that we detest the self" (quoted in Loyrette, 1993, p. 27). It was also during this time that he complained to his father that he no longer wanted to paint portraits. (His father, claiming that Edgar's income depended on it, retorted that he could never give up portrait painting. Edgar was frequently ambivalent about this expectation.) However, tellingly, upon his aunt's return Edgar resumed portraits with a renewed enthusiasm; his primary interest was in his aunt, whom he sketched many times and eventually made the centerpiece of one of his greatest works, *The Bellelli Family*.

In that painting Degas created a compelling image of a family which I suggest reflects the internal struggle within Degas' own psyche. Most obviously there is the fascination and loving portrayal of the mother, rising proudly over the family, dignified, beautiful and pregnant. All of Edgar's infatuation with Laura is expressed in her image, but she is dressed fully in black, and there is strength and intense sadness in the figure – is she mourning? For whom (her self)? The husband, Gennaro, is seated facing away, almost across the room. He is shadowy, uninvolved, reflecting the artist's indifference and scorn. And in the center of the picture is a portrait of Degas' grandfather, recently deceased (in fact it was the old man's death that had delayed Laura's return home). Therefore, I would argue that the painting graphically represents Degas' inner struggle between his attachment to his living, powerful father and his longing for his lost, beloved mother. In the painting he portrays this struggle by putting the father in his place, degrading him and forcing him into the background, creating a space in which the son can give himself over to his enthrallment with the aunt/mother who is the object of his longing. Being the great artist that he was Degas' act of love is his art, his immersion in her image (which he altered and played with many times over the next ten years, much to his father's dismay). Despite the fact that the painting was a critical success, he would never part with it and it was found among his personal collection after his death.

Another work that I feel reflects Degas' aesthetic dilemma is the painting of the musician Lorenzo Pagans and Degas' Father, Auguste. It is one of the few paintings Degas completed of his father (none of which are individual portraits). Interestingly, Degas never sold the work and it hung for many years in a place of honor over his bed. Pagans is sitting very stiffly in the foreground in the act of singing and playing a Spanish guitar. The father is immediately behind him, leaning forward, his hands clasped, listening intently with a sullen look on his face. Given the father's rigid and traditional attitudes towards art and his frequent critical view of his son's performance and deviation from classical forms, I would argue that the painting can be understood to represent the repressive presence of the father in Degas' aesthetic life. Each note, each creative impulse of Pagans', is shadowed by the father's awareness and judgment. Despite this view of the work I do not believe that Auguste stifled his son's creativity – if anything the lingering discipline and academic trainings became a foundation for Degas' gradually emerging modernist aesthetic. In fact this positive viewpoint is captured by Carl Rotenberg's response to the painting (which is very different from my own). Reflecting the positive side of Degas' ambivalence, Dr. Rotenberg noted (personal communication):

> I don't see the father's expression as sullen, and I don't see Pagans as sitting particularly stiffly. If one sees the father as being in rapt attention to the artist's (musician's) production, and you want to see that as reflecting the artist's dynamics, then one might say that this is the expression of Degas' dissociated wish for his father's (mirroring) attention to the artist's productions and also the negation perhaps of some trauma/disappointment in that area. In other words, it is wish fulfillment having to do with the hope for a more optimal mirroring relationship with the father, perhaps to fend off the loss of the earlier mirroring selfobject, the mother, through her untimely death.

I think our contrasting viewpoints reflect the psychological/relational conflict embedded in the work. In this painting we see a complex aesthetic resolution of Degas' disordered self-state. The artist's tie to his father and the paternal aesthetic functioned as a compensation for the lost selfobject bond with the dead mother. At the same time the tie to the father necessitated the repression of the experience of connection to the mother and resulted in a period of inhibition in aesthetic development (evidence by the decade-long inability to complete major projects). The Pagans painting represented this dilemma in both representation and style. Degas valued his father's classicism but also rebelled. Even his later pastels, deeply personal and idiosyncratic, play with classical motifs and echo Degas' lifelong commitment to classical aesthetic values. Briefly put, his relationship with his father and his father's aesthetic was deeply ambivalent. This resulted in lifelong conflict and states of self-disorder of which there were many symptoms.

A long-suffering artist

One of Degas' best-known traits, which became worse with age, was his general sourness of mood and biting criticisms. At times he seemed to have not a good word for anyone. Even his beloved dancers, his "little rats", could become the objects of biting scorn. (However, the common misunderstanding that Degas hated everyone, especially women and dancers, is not true. He had many close women friends and was very caring and friendly to the young performers he would paint.) Of course, he reserved his most damaging criticism for his endless rounds of self-criticism and despair. As an older man, he was able to describe this conflict in an honest piece of self-reflection. In a letter he wrote to one of his oldest friends, Evariste de Valernes, Degas wrote:

> I want to ask your forgiveness for having been, in the course of our long relationship as artists – for seeming to have been *hard* on you. I am especially so on myself, you must remember that, since you even reproached me for it and expressed some surprise that I had so little confidence in myself. I was, or seemed, hard on everyone, out of a kind of inurnment to brutality which came from my doubt and my bad humor. I felt so poorly constituted, so ill equipped, so flabby, while it seemed to me that my *calculations* as an artist were so accurate. I resented everyone, and myself most of all.
>
> (quoted in Gordon, 1988, p. 401)

In fact, throughout his life Degas was enormously self-critical, anxious and preoccupied with loss. Valéry called him "the anxious figure of the tragic-comedy of Modern Art . . . divided against himself . . ." (McMullen, 1984, p. 399). Vollard recalled the following story: "One day he said to me, 'I have a terrible invincible enemy.' 'Who is that?' 'You old fool,' he said, pounding his chest 'you should know better than anyone else, my enemy is myself!'" (McMullen, 1984, p. 401). Even his father recognized these self-attitudes in his young son, and tried to boost the boy's self-esteem by exhortation: "You have made tremendous strides in art." Auguste wrote the young artist studying in Italy: "Your drawing is strong, your colors are true. You have rid yourself of that trivial Falndrinian-Lamothian line work, of that gray, leaden color. There is no need to keep tormenting yourself, my dear Edgar; you have set an excellent course" (quoted in Loyrette, 1988, p. 27). In an insightful statement regarding Edgar's dilemma, Auguste wrote in 1864: "What is fermenting in that head is frightening. I for one maintain, and am even convinced, that he has not only talent, but genius; only, will he express what he is feeling?" (quoted in Meyers, 2005, p. 137). But what Degas was "feeling" was impossible for the artist to integrate, let alone safely represent in his art.

Edgar Degas saw himself as a man much put upon by fate. Throughout his life he bemoaned the gradual loss of his vision although the accounts at times contradict his claims and it is quite possible that the problem was all in his head. He always feared the disabilities of age (even at the age of 50) as if in fantasy age represented the deterioration and depletion of self, and its ultimate annihilation. I suggest that these fantasies are symptoms of self-disorder, in which a split-off grandiosity (linked to the loving but lost mother) and a damaged self (overtly attached, ambivalently, to the demanding father) are precariously maintained. Wholeness and vitality are tenuous. There is instability in mood, uncertain self-esteem and a defensive avoidance of close contact with others.

Not surprisingly, Degas never had an intimate committed relationship and the common assumption is that he never had sex. This was apparently well known at the time and became a part of his persona, even, for some, a source of his aesthetic. Van Gogh said provocatively:

> Degas' painting is virile and impersonal, precisely because he personally has acquiesced to being nothing but a little notary who shudders at the thought of debauchery. He watched human animals that are stronger than he is, animals that [have sex] and [have more sex], and he paints them well precisely because he himself has no such pretensions about [having sex].
>
> (quoted in Loyrette, 1993, p. 111)

Sex, intimacy and, most importantly, selfobject longings were just too dangerous for Degas. So he defended his vulnerability by avoiding the first two and putting on a gruff, ornery exterior, which would frighten and repel others, thus allowing some feeling of control and distance in a threatening world. So how did Degas obtain experiences of self-confirmation, mirroring and closeness to an ideal other? I suggest that his self-experience was sustained and enhanced through the creative process itself and the thrill of aesthetic experience. It was only through the enjoyment and creation of art that Degas could feel whole and alive, as precarious and transitory as that experience may have been. Unconsciously, I suggest that it was in giving himself over to aesthetic experience that Degas was able to recapture the distant and lost sense of involvement with his loving mother. And despite the fact that we have no way to know what the actual relationship was like,

I would hypothesise that as an adult, unconsciously he remained preoccupied with fantasies of connection and playful engagement, which came to infuse the experience of his art. In fact, some authors have argued that as a general principle the aesthetic experience at its unconscious core has its roots in the playful and loving security of the mother's embrace. Terry Eagleton wrote:

> The beautiful representation, like the body of the mother, is an idealized material form safely diffused of sensuality and desire, with which, in free play of its faculties, the subject can happily sport. The bliss of the aesthetic subject is the felicity of the small child playing in the bosom of the mother, enthralled by an utterly indivisible object which is at once intimate and indeterminate, brimming with purposive life, yet plastic enough to put up no resistance to the subject's own ends.
> (Eagleton, 1990, p. 91)

I would conjecture that psychologically Degas was caught between two opposing forces: 1) The desire to become immersed and enthralled by the aesthetic experience, to give himself over to the medium, to play in the arms of the idealized maternal environment and become whole and vital again; and 2) His loyalty to and fear of the only surviving parent, his father, whose demands required the constriction of spontaneity and the confinement of imagination to the replication of the images of idealized males – thus the drives to work and to play became both delimited and linked, making his creative process both desirable and fearful – a lifelong dilemma for Degas.

However, to return to Degas' letter quoted above, though he despaired about his psychological worthiness, it was his capacity for aesthetic experience that he never questions: "I felt so poorly constituted, so ill equipped, so flabby, while it seemed to me that my calculations as an artist were so accurate" (quoted in Gordon, 1988, pp. 39–40). This awareness of his talent, and his confidence in the vitality and cohesion of his artistic self, became the means by which Degas sought to transcend his experience of fragmentation, depletion and self-injury. Specifically, it was by means of his art that Degas sought to resolve the inner conflict between the maternal and paternal aesthetics – the classical and modernist edges of his self. And these personal struggles were the private correlative to his very public effort to break through the strictures of classical standards and values, and create a new aesthetic, which would eventually be called modernism.

The transition to modernism

As noted above, Degas' early career was consistent with the institutional training that was standard at that time in France. His early masterpieces were variations on the themes and techniques that were common to the

Academy and which he hoped would gain him the approval of both father and mentors. The classicism of Ingres was considered the height of aesthetic excellence. But Degas' interest in Delacroix and Moreau indicated his growing fascination with forms of aesthetics that would challenge the accepted culture. Delacroix, the passionate colorist, and Moreau, the promoter of subjective symbolism, by capturing the young artist's imagination opened Degas to an aesthetic that was very different, if not antithetical, to his father's classicism. Sensuality, spontaneity, and the subjective sources of creativity became increasingly important to Degas. Over time, he began to experiment with new subjects, new mediums and a radical approach to color and line.

Degas' increasing professional success was accompanied by breakthroughs in his artwork. From 1890 he retreated further into a solitary life, where he worked furiously at his art. He abandoned oil paints almost entirely and concentrated on pastels (which he would use on very thin and transparent tracing paper) and sculpture (which he never exhibited during his lifetime). His subject matter became increasingly intimate (bathers and dancers) as well as formally experimental. He used composition and line in idiosyncratic ways with little concern for verisimilitude. Color virtually exploded from some canvasses and was no longer restrained by reality. During this period the discipline of the copyist was transformed into the commitment to a personal, powerful aesthetic revolution. Degas gave himself over entirely to this process. He drew and drew. If he copied anything it was his own work as he sought the right form, the right color, the right line, all to capture a private, fresh vision of artistic beauty.

In particular it was his many depictions of bathers that became the primary occasion for his most radical experiments. Examining these paintings and pastels the first thing we are struck with is the wild use of color. No longer constrained by reality (and often working from memory photo or prior sketches), Degas has completely abandoned the classical expectations. Color after color is piled on, spread over and jumbled together. The model is at the same time familiar and normal in build and shape, but she stretches out, bent into odd, uncomfortable poses. Degas seems to love the feel of the woman's body, not sexually, but as flesh and muscle. His women are real and durable. They push and bend as they struggle against their own bone and sinew. Although we rarely see their faces, we confront people who are truly "there", flesh and blood and pure, unselfconscious nakedness. One striking thing is the importance of the back in these works. It is as if we have walked into a bath or bedroom to observe, unnoticed, the private rituals of a woman washing, drying, and grooming herself. Degas (we) comes on her often from behind, her back a gorgeous broad landscape of muscles, flesh and color. I would suggest that we, with Degas, rediscover in fantasy the mother, alive and vital in her bedroom, far from the father; but we don't want to seduce her, we simply want to watch and enjoy her living presence.

Indeed Degas was enthralled with these women. Sketching with pastels he repeated the images over and over, varying the combinations of color, the quality of line and composition, adding strips of paper, making impressions onto other sheets and reworking the image, it's opposite now, searching for the perfect image and then moving on quickly to the next. Contrary to his meticulous work habits in his early career, the older Degas cultivated a spontaneous, unrestricted attitude towards every aspect of his art – the medium, the subject, his personal vision. Over the years in which he produced these works he must have studied and then imagined every inch of flesh, every knot of muscle, each length of bone, as well as the state of mind and body of these wonderful women. Interestingly, some of the poses he chose to concentrate on were derived from classical statues or paintings, but his approach to them is contemporary, reflecting the radical transformation he underwent between his father's aesthetic and the renewed playfulness of his later art. But these late works could never have happened unless Edgar had thrown off the old man's restrictions and standards. Even where the classical remains, Degas is the master, thoroughly integrating tradition into a fantastic new aesthetic, which would become one of the guiding beacons for generations of twentieth-century artists.

Chapter 6

Pierre Bonnard: The seduction of beauty

> The arts cannot escape their sensuous basis: their whole purpose is to extract perfection from experience, but they can do this only be using the organs of perception, which convey and communicate human feeling and emotion. A living contemporary art differs from the dead art of the past, not in its exclusion of subjective feeling, but by the concreteness and directness of the means used to express such feeling.
>
> (Read, 1963, p. 164)

When Pierre Bonnard was on his deathbed in 1947 at the age of 80 he completed his last work, a dazzling image of an almond tree in bloom. His nephew Charles was by the bedside when Bonnard, still dissatisfied with the painting, said: "The green on the patch of ground to the left is wrong... what it needs is yellow" (Hyman, 1998, p. 208). He asked Charles to help him add a final touch of golden paint.

After his death a leading art magazine published an article titled: "Pierre Bonnard: Is he a great painter?" The writer questioned the artist's status, asserting that real artists know the great difficulties of art and don't cling to the facile and agreeable (a prejudice shared by many towards Bonnard's work). Matisse (who should know) became enraged when he read the article and scrawled across the top: "Yes! I certify that Pierre Bonnard is a great painter, for today and for the future. [signed] Henri Matisse" (quoted in Groom, 2001, p. 25).

Throughout his long life Pierre Bonnard was a consummate artist and (to those who knew and cared) one of the great painters of the twentieth century. He was born into a comfortable middle-class family in 1867 (biographical information on Bonnard is from Hyman, 1998; Whitfield and Elderfield, 1998; and Turner, 2002). As a young man, seeking to escape the restrictions and values of his father's life, he rejected a career as a lawyer and civil servant. He began his artistic life in the early 1890s upon the heels of the impressionist movement that was (at least among the avant-garde) in the process of decline. Bonnard was a member of the Nabis group of artists.

Taking their name from the Hebrew word for prophet, the Nabis promulgated a new aesthetic. In 1890 Maurice Denis summed up the movement's approach to painting: "Remember that a painting – before being a battle horse, a nude, or some anecdote – is essentially a flat surface covered with colors arranged in a certain order" (Hyman, 1998, p. 20). Rather than seeing a painting as a special object standing out from the world, a representation of observed reality, the Nabis asserted the primary function of art as decoration. To them the intimate world of the interior of parlors and living rooms became a total aesthetic environment in which every component – furniture, wallpaper, paintings, even teacups – were beautiful creations surrounding the inhabitants with pleasurable, soothing forms. They wanted to aestheticize everyday life, so they often chose family tableaus, street scenes and portraits of attractive middle-class people as subjects. They were also preoccupied with creating an art of emotion and subjectivity. Art would no longer focus on simply portraying the real world, nor the inner world of fantasy; art would capture and explore the emotions and sentiments of daily life (Groom, 2001).

As a Nabis Bonnard cultivated his ability to capture the special, transient beauties of everyday life. He walked the streets of Paris collecting social "snapshots" that became the basis of paintings and prints. He was accomplished at capturing the gesture, an unexpected interaction, and the movement of daily life. He did this not as illusion, but through flat surfaces of color – suggesting the experience of reality rather than a representation of it. Bonnard enjoyed the beauty of color, of form and gesture. Along with his fellow Nabis he moved gradually towards abstraction, and pioneered an aesthetics of intimism – the art of the world of our internal and social lives. Lush cultivated gardens, dark drawing rooms with somber adults, fields populated with playing children, and busy Paris street scenes captured in large, patterned panels of rich colors conveyed moments of feeling rather than the truth of observation.

It was during these years that Bonnard began to hone his personal creative sensibility. The most important factor in his work was his search for the unexpected moment of beauty in which he overcame the obstacle of self and achieved a naive, seemingly childlike perception of the world around him. Bonnard wanted, he said, to "show what one sees on first entering a room, what the eye takes in at one glance; one sees everything, and at the same time nothing" (Hyman, 1998, p. 136). It was this startling and moving encounter that he came to call the "primary conception", a psychological state of inspiration – in which the heightened self-state, not the actual object, was the creative spark. Bonnard wrote regarding this process:

> Through attraction or primary conception the painter achieves universality. It is attraction which determines the choice of motif and which conforms exactly to the picture. If this attraction, this primary

conception, fades away, the painter becomes dominated solely by the motif, the object before him. From that moment he ceases to create his own painting. In certain painters – Titian, for example – this conception is so strong that it never abandons them, even if they remain for a long time in direct contact with the object. But I am very weak; it is difficult for me to keep myself under control in the presence of the object. I often see interesting things around me, but for me to want to paint them they must have a particular attraction – what may be called beauty. When I paint them I try not to lose control of the primary conception; I am weak, and if I let myself go, in a moment I have lost my primary vision, I no longer know where I am going. The presence of the object, the motif, is very disturbing to the painter at the time he is painting. Since the staring point of a picture is an idea, if the object is there at the moment he is working, the artist is always in danger of allowing himself to be distracted by the effect of direct and immediate vision, and to lose the primary idea along the way. Thus after a certain period of work, the painter can no longer recover his original idea and depends on accidental qualities, he reproduces the shadow he sees ... and such details as did not strike him at the beginning.

(quoted in Protter, 1997, p. 178)

You can be sure Renoir would never have made such a statement.

This quote captures the psychological dilemma of Bonnard's art: the moment of attraction that inspired the aesthetic experience does not survive the object. This led to Bonnard's development of a special strategy that represented a unique relation to the subject of his art. The quick sketch captured the moment, followed by a retreat to the studio where, far from the object's oppressive reality, the artist reconstituted the subjective dimension of the experience of beauty. Bonnard pointed out that artists like Titian did not have to avoid the object, their primary conception survived the full recognition of the object's reality. I would add that this was also true of Renoir, and despite the shared love of color, this was a fundamental difference between Bonnard and Renoir's art. As I will argue later the heightened moment of the primary conception was of crucial importance to Bonnard but due to the nature of his self-disorder (what he referred to as his "weakness") he experienced these moments as fragile and prone to collapse when the needs of the object world intruded.

Let us imagine the routine Bonnard might have followed in order to induce and cultivate such a state of inspiration:

Bonnard wanders about his country house, drawing pad in hand, waiting for an encounter. He passes through the kitchen, past the wide circular table set for lunch, and out the doors onto the terrace. He observes the trees and the sunlight on the stone walkway, the blue of the Mediterranean in the distance. He steps back into the house. Marthe is there. She leans over next to the kitchen table to give milk to the cat. Unexpectedly the light, color, shapes all come together and he feels it. An image locks into place accompanied by a sudden unexpected sensation of excitement, fascination and confidence. He quickly captures this heightened state with a sketch. He is not worried about visual accuracy; he wants only to hold the sensation. Then Bonnard takes the sketch into his studio. The prior day he had unrolled a bolt of canvas. The long strip hangs pinned, primed and unstretched across the wall. He begins by sketching the basic composition of the painting with charcoal. He glances back at the drawing pad but is not interested in reproducing the image captured there; he is trying to recapture that fleeting moment of excited attraction. After sketching for a while he begins to add color. He seems to ignore reality; the colors accumulate in a strange and "unrealistic manner". He builds the painting from masses of color, surrounded by clouds of sharp blotches of paint. A human figure, distinct in the drawing, gradually succumbs to the rising tide of gold and amber, flecked with red, becoming ghostlike. After a few hours he moves down the canvas and begins another version, following the same procedure; from the sketched image a different painting crystallizes. He carefully mixes his paints creating burning hues which he applies to the one painting, and then moving to the other he applies it there as well; with still some left he wanders into the parlor, where he dabs onto a landscape he "completed" several years before. He is building a world of color.

Bonnard once claimed that "to begin a painting there must be an empty space in the center" (Hyman, 1998, p. 181). I suggest that he is referring to an experience of defect in self-experience combined with an absence of connection. Through the creative process he tried to recover something essential which had been lost – the primary conception – which he only snared in his sketch. He must build on his notes and elaborate the residue of the past by means of memory and color. Gradually he fills the empty space with aesthetic experience – the sensation of beauty.

Bonnard once wrote: *"Represent nature when it is beautiful. Everything has its moments of beauty. Beauty is the satisfaction of sight. Sight is satisfied by simplicity and order. Simplicity and order are produced by the legible divisions of surface, the grouping of sympathetic colour, etc"* (Hyman, 1998, p. 188). It was beauty that he was missing and it was beauty that Bonnard longed to recapture and preserve through his art.

Although the psychoanalyst and self psychologist Heinz Kohut never addressed the problem of beauty directly, the concept is implicit in his description of the experience of idealization that characterizes selfobject experience. What is idealized is felt to be perfect, and what is perfect is beautiful. The self psychologist Charles Kligerman (1980) in his discussion of the psychology of the artist directly linked idealization and beauty, describing how the artist's experience of loss of perfection leads to the development of his or her lifelong efforts to recapture beauty. One of the important qualities of idealization is the sense of "formal" perfection and value known as beauty. The idealized object or the grandiose self is experienced as possessing in its essence a perfection of form and mode of being which is beautiful. Therefore the sense of beauty is an aspect of the experience of idealization. In his formulation Kligerman speculated that the artist is someone who experienced consistent mirroring of his or her grandiosity in childhood. Inevitably this archaic selfobject experience at some point failed and the artist-to-be was cast out from this state of perfection. He wrote:

> The ensuing fall from grace is followed by a passionate need to recover the original beauty and perfection and later on to present the world with a work of beauty (really the artist himself) that will evoke universal awe and admiration. There are thus at least three main currents to the creative drive.
>
> 1. An intrinsic joy in creating, related to what has been termed "functional" pleasure. This is perhaps the most important factor, but the one we know least about.
> 2. The exhibitionistic grandiose ecstasy of being regarded as the acme of beauty and perfection and the nearly insatiable need to repeat and confirm this feeling.
> 3. The need to regain a lost paradise – the original bliss of perfection – to overcome the empty feeling of self-depletion and to recover self-esteem. In the metapsychology of the self this would amount to healing the threatened fragmentation and restoring firm self-cohesion through a merger with the selfobject – the work of art – and a bid for mirroring approval of the world. We can also add a fourth current to the creative drive – the need to regain perfection by merging with the ideals of the powerful selfobjects, first the parents, and then later revered models that represent the highest standards of some great artistic tradition.
>
> (Kligerman, 1980, pp. 387–388)

Central to Kligerman's psychology of the artist was the notion that archaic idealization involves the experience of the object's beauty. The sense of beauty throughout life recaptures "the original beauty and perfection" of our original archaic selfobject ties, which inevitably and appropriately succumbed to disillusionment and, perhaps, failure. Thus, the mature sense of beauty is an effort to recover the perfection of the archaic selfobject tie.

What Bonnard was searching for as he scanned the world around him was a sensation of beauty, a subjective state in which inner experience (excitement, vitality and self-cohesion) was seduced by an image of perfection. The image could be anything, especially anything – for Bonnard it was the beauty of the everyday that he was most attracted to. I would argue that these moments of attraction were unconscious experiences of the recovery of an idealized selfobject tie. Bonnard recognized that due to his "weakness" this selfobject experience was fragile and easily lost. The reality of the separateness of the object quickly lead to the failure and collapse of the selfobject tie. So he sketched quickly to capture some aspect of the experience – his "primary conception". As Kligerman described, the process of painting was an effort to recover and preserve the original self-selfobject relationship. The actual object or objects were merely opportunities (as well as impediments); Bonnard was primarily interested in the self-state of that first encounter with beauty, before reality asserted itself.

As an artist Bonnard was continually involved in a process of recovery of archaic experiences of his "lost paradise" – the early sense of connection with the idealized objects of childhood. These selfobject experiences would involve states of heightened excitement and well-being. Given the lifelong issues related to self-esteem and efficacy – his "weaknesses" – it makes sense that given his talent Bonnard was compulsively drawn to his search to recreate these selfobject experiences through his art.

If we look at Bonnard's creative process we can see how elusive this selfobject tie remained for him. As he worked to recreate the primary conception he reassessed and reworked the image. He would feel that he got it right and then despair with a sudden recognition that this or that color was improperly placed, or not of the right hue. Sometimes years would pass as he reworked the painting, intent on accomplishing the perfect feeling, and over time the painting crystallized not into a representation of that first encounter, but the perfect visual equivalent of the memory of that primary conception.

As in many instances of narcissistic disorder, Bonnard could not sustain the longed-for selfobject experience in the face of the object's separate existence – he was always in danger of losing that primary idea and being left only with the shadow of what he saw. The fragility of beauty and the inevitability of loss are Bonnard's central themes. Why Bonnard was so driven to explore these areas is hard to say. As far as we know, his childhood was secure and affectionate. There were no traumas, no abuses and no abandonment. The closest thing to a manifestation of Oedipal conflict was his father's desire for him to become a lawyer and civil servant – and Bonnard's eventual defiance of his father's wishes and lifestyle. But this conflict was mild compared with most, and when Bonnard began to make an income from art early in his career, his father acceded with pleasure to his son's wishes. And Bonnard's defiance was not especially strong or long-standing; he would eventually become the artist of middle-class life, with nothing more than a mild ironic perspective on the bourgeois life to reflect his defiance. So the conflicts within Bonnard and within his family were either minimal or suppressed. On the other hand, I wonder how extensive Bonnard's alienation from his father was; after all, his initial attraction to art was the opportunity it offered to escape from the lifestyle which his father held dear. He also disliked painting portraits of men, noting that they always appeared like calamities. Women and the aesthetics of beauty had a compelling value to him, which makes you wonder at the function of his mother and later of Marthe in the maintenance of his self-experience.

There are several things about Bonnard which point strongly to a deeper and enduring character pathology. Many friends and colleagues noted Bonnard's passivity and obsequious manner. As we saw in the earlier quote, his self-image was denigrating and he saw himself as weak and tentative. His lack of self-assertion and his vulnerability to influence supports the idea that he struggled with a mild character disorder – his narcissistic vulnerabilities being evident in his self-image and social life.

However, the most apparent area of disorder was his relationship with Marthe. The story goes that Bonnard became immediately attracted to this strange woman on the street in Paris and pursued her to her place of work. This was in 1895, the same year his father died. From the start Marthe was a reclusive and even paranoid person. She rarely participated in his social life and at times was morbidly reclusive. Over the years she became more so. Eventually she developed some type of infection for which she had to take long baths several times a day, sequestered in the bathroom. Bonnard and Marthe's lifestyle was transient; for some years they would travel about France, staying in hotels and rented houses. They were vagabonds. Bonnard rolled up his paintings and strapped them to the top of the car, unpacking them in some third-class anonymous hotel room where he would resume work. During the 1920s and 1930s they lived away from Paris with reduced contact with friends. Marthe was continually sick and a burden to Bonnard. Despite several serious affairs (one of which led to suicide when he cut it off), Bonnard clung to Marthe and increasingly shared her pathological life. Through all of this she appears to have been his muse and the most frequent subject of his art. At the same time the period of most intense isolation and merger also facilitated the development of Bonnard's glorious mature style. He sketched and sketched. Eventually he achieved a technique free of influence, where the power of impressionist color could be used for the authentic exploration of his subjective world.

It is reasonable to assume that Bonnard's relationship with Marthe and their reclusive lifestyle caused him quite a bit of suffering. He must have become identified with her ongoing state of self-fragmentation, self-depletion and vulnerability. Given this, the importance of his art and his talent, especially the attraction that these intense moments of aesthetic passion and subsequent obsession with recreating and preserving them, must have exerted a powerful appeal for Bonnard. In the midst of their isolation and suffering he found through art fleeting "golden moments" in which his "quest for the absolute" must have felt close to fulfillment. Like Marthe in the tub, he wrapped himself in an enclosure of vibrant colors, restoring some ancient, lost state of unity through images of perfection and beauty.

For Heinz Kohut (1971) the quintessential selfobject experience is a momentary sensation, similar to Bonnard's aesthetic moment, in which the child encounters the "gleam in the mother's eye". The child experiences a sudden sense of pleasure, excitement and self-confirmation. There is not just a sense of connection but also a fragile and ephemeral recognition of beauty and love (that infuses the self with value). In most cases the child shares the love and excitement by looking back with a responsive gleam of his own. There is a moment of reciprocal valuation, of engrossing and passionate mutual enthrallment. Both participants give themselves over to the wonderful, shared celebration of themselves – a selfobject experience. There is also frequent and inevitable failure and loss.

In his moments of primary conception Bonnard re-discovered the gleam in the mother's eye – that special instant where self and other are united in valuing each other. He found that special moment of beauty (often in the common objects about the house); he internalized it, created a subjective memory and then conjured the moment through paint. For Bonnard the act of creation was a relationship in which selfobject experience was found, refined and made permanent.

For Bonnard this aesthetic selfobject experience became more and more important with time. As Marthe sickened the couple became isolative. Bonnard's life became more and more centered on caring for her, and he sought these moments of beauty in the hours of isolation. Several of his most exquisite paintings were in fact of Marthe submerged in radiant color (the greatest of which was completed several years after her death). He would seek to convert what must have been painful and disintegrative experiences into moments of idealized encounter made permanent and unassailable. His anxiety about whether a painting was finished supports the idea of how fragile he considered this experience to be.

Bonnard was not as interested in the mother as in how it feels to be with her. And he was not interested in the experience of the day-to-day grind, but the ephemeral, sudden overwhelming sensation of rapture at that first encounter, in which her beauty was almost painful and the feelings rapturous.

Bonnard worked to create moments of finding and recognition of the ideal other. He tried to eliminate the secondary elaboration of vision into perspective and evokes a broad, diffuse sense of surprise and heightened sensation. There was a sustained experience of wonder at the beauty of the moment. The accompanying affects were conveyed in the flood of color, texture and light.

I believe that what Bonnard was seeking was the child's moment of finding and recognizing the ideal mother. He would feel joy and rapture at her beauty. There would have been (he fantasized) a powerful sense of safety and rightness. His life work was an exploration of this encounter – especially of how it makes one feel. In the midst of isolation, anxiety and depression, an instant of rapture is found and held. The moment of coming into sight of beauty was made permanent. The wish was for it not to be lost.

In the bather paintings he takes the aged and sick body of his wife and encases her in a fantastic robe of color. She is made ideal even at a time of illness and isolation. Bonnard transcends the moment even as he dwells on it. His subjectivity makes it transcendent and eternally beautiful.

Bonnard did not seek to achieve relatedness. He did not give himself over to love of the object, nor did he submit himself to become an object of love for the other. He sought that indeterminate moment of the archaic self-object experience in which self and object are fused and subjectivity is flooded with the sensation of perfection and vitality. In his old age, alone, forgotten, he nonetheless conjured out of pure memory a primal state of transcendent absolute perfection. Let us look at how he did this through his use of color.

The impressionists approached light and color as phenomena of perception – they viewed themselves as ocular scientists. Subjectivity was secondary to the desire to convey the experience of looking. On the other hand, Bonnard explored not looking but the glance, the experience of what you see upon walking into a room. But then he would add to this spontaneous experience, reflection; ultimately his paintings were fantasies based on memories of perceptions. "I have all my subjects at hand," he said, "I go and look at them. I take notes. Then I go home. And before I start painting I reflect, I dream" (Whitfield and Elderfield, 1998, p. 9). Bonnard fled the light of the real world, which was oppressive, and he feared the way it tended to threaten his subjectivity. From the safety of his studio Bonnard explored the memory of light (or more precisely the "dream" of light). In this way he conjured light sources more fantastic than real. This manifold reflection of light was especially of interest to him. He was very resourceful in discovering numerous ways in which looking was, once again, fresh, spontaneous and surprising.

Light/color was also the medium of emotion and feeling. Color unbounded by form indicates primitive affect. This certainly applies to Bonnard; masses of light and color embodying archaic, passionate affect. Color after all is light. Light is affect. Bonnard explored the affective dimension of light. He cultivated the experience of primordial affect, non-differentiated and arousing, in which self and other are merged – or, rather, the other is merged into the self, enraptured by the memory of light. He loved the light of the mind in seclusion, not the light of the sun – light imagined or remembered, conjured out of the unconscious as a psychic residue of a fantasized primordial paradise.

Perhaps it was Bonnard's unguarded, spontaneous immersion in color that led to his condemnation by other modern artists. After all, as Lesley Higgins (2002) pointed out in her book *The Cult of Ugliness*, in the modern world color was seen as unstable, even dangerous (like women). Drawing, and especially form, were the more serious and legitimate focus of the contemporary (largely male) artist. She pointed out that artists like Seurat proved that instinct and passion could be removed from the experience of color perception, replaced by science – in other words, the masculine authority that modern aesthetics idealized. Bonnard, on the other hand, was unassertive and even passive. He loved women and rather than blustering through his life exploiting them for self-aggrandizement and sexual power, he invested himself in a close mutually dependent relationship with a woman. I think that there is a relation between Bonnard's fascination with women and his infatuation with the sensuous nature of color. It is no accident that his greatest experiments with color involve the simultaneous study of women's bodies and feminine subjectivity.

It was Bonnard's relationship to paint and color that was different and new. Rather than approaching vision as a scientist (as the impressionists claimed to do) or for its symbolic value (as his fellow Nabis did), Bonnard progressively approached color and paint for the purpose of indulging in their sensuousness and inherent excitement. When we view a Bonnard there is nothing between the paint and us; the impact is immediate and stirring, we are dazzled and perhaps even turned on. When Bonnard talked about his art as devoted to "the adventures of the optic nerve" he was referring to a passionate enthrallment, abandonment to the erotics of pigment. We are left challenged and breathless. We burn more brightly. As Walter Pater pointed out in the conclusion to his study of the Renaissance:

> To burn always with this hard, gem-like flame, to maintain ecstasy, is success in life. In a sense it might even be said that our failure is to form habits; for after all habit is relative to a stereotyped world, and meantime it is only the roughness of the eye that makes any two persons, things and situations seem alike. Great passions may give us this quickened sense of life, ecstasy and sorrow of love, the various forms of enthusiastic activity, disinterested or otherwise, which come naturally to many of us. Only be sure it is passion – that it does yield you this fruit of a quickened, multiplied consciousness. Of such wisdom, the poetic passion, the desire for beauty, the love of art for its own sake, has most. For art comes to you proposing frankly to giving nothing but the highest quality to your moments as they pass, and simply for the moment's sake.
>
> (Pater, 1886, p. 153)

In fact, Bonnard was a creature of habits in his day-to-day life, and to this extent his life failed completely to burn with the intensity Pater described. But paradoxically as his life became more and more restricted, still and deadened, his creativity burned harder and brighter. Beauty and art became the gem-like passions of his later life and, as we have seen, he searched relentlessly for those moments of highest quality and held to them, sustaining the flame not just for himself but also for all of us, for today and for the future.

Chapter 7

The creative anxiety of Henri Matisse

> Matisse the anxious, the Madly anxious
> (Henri-Edmund Cross, 1904, quoted in Flam, 1995, p. 114)

Sometime around 1888, Henri Matisse, then a relatively unknown, no longer young artist, joined the aesthetic revolution that would transform western art. His efforts led to the development of entirely new forms of painting and sculpture which would shock and challenge audiences and critics across several continents. Interestingly, Matisse's artwork was perturbing not only to his audience but to himself as well. In fact, as we shall see in his art, he purposefully and relentlessly challenged his own aesthetic values, creating works which at times he himself found to be ugly, confusing and incompetent. For years, as he pursued artistic breakthroughs, he was filled with self-doubt and anxiety about his work. When he exhibited new paintings they were often objects of scorn and derision. At times he was tormented with shame for what he was doing.

This chapter is a psychoanalytic study of Matisse's creative process and its disruptive impact on his self-experience, focusing on his most aesthetically innovative years, from 1888 until 1908. It examines Matisse's affective response to his own artworks – specifically the intense anxiety that he experienced during the years of his first major breakthrough into modernist aesthetics – and it will show how creative anxiety can be an essential part of the creative process for some artists, especially when they challenge their own internal aesthetic value systems. The complex portrait of Matisse that is presented is a new one. As Hilary Spurling (2005b) stated, despite the acknowledgement of Matisse's greatness, for many years he was not considered to possess the psychological richness and depth to warrant much biographical effort. More recently this attitude has changed, as evidenced by the publication of Spurling's biography, the first volume of which was titled *The Unknown Matisse* (1998). Spurling offers a convincing portrait of Matisse as a complex man torn between the traditional values of his father's world and the revolutionary ambitions within his own tortured self. To my mind the most intriguing of Spurling's discoveries is the conflicted relationship between the artist and the seemingly unstoppable force of his own creative insights and ambitions. Threatened, even terrified, by his own iconoclasm, he nonetheless pursued his goals with untiring energy and ambition, a project challenging the aesthetic values at the heart of western culture.

The myth of the artist as a tormented revolutionary is a familiar narrative in modern western culture. However, Matisse's psychological struggle and pain was very different from the psychosis of Van Gogh or the pathological narcissism of Gauguin (in fact, Matisse, affectionately called "the Doctor", was seen as a notoriously sane man). The source of his anxiety was not in his personal demons (at least not purely so), rather it arose as a direct result of his commitment to being an artist and the creative processes in which he became engaged. This chapter will examine the nature of Matisse's creative anxiety; the sources of his conflict and the aesthetic challenges that provoked his anxiety; and the aesthetic innovations by which he sought to resolve them. Matisse always said that he was seeking through his art to communicate a state of calm (at the time, to many, an absurd claim given the provocative nature of his art), but his work towards that goal was anything but calm. I will argue that Matisse was seeking the calm that accompanies the experience of self-cohesion, self-actualization and vitality and is associated with a successful creative process. He found this calm when he was able to reconcile within himself a number of powerful tensions and conflicts, which he feared would defeat, perhaps even annihilate, him.

Artists are anxious for many reasons. In fact, I would argue that anxiety may be essential to a successful creative process – whether it is a fear of beginning, worry about one's ability to bring order to the chaotic marks on a canvas, the periodic confusion the artist feels regarding where the work is going, or the sense of failure when the finished work does not live up to one's ideal. It is the artist's ability to manage anxiety, make sense of it and resolve the problem through artistic effort, that is at the heart of creativity. In Matisse's case his anxiety was directly connected to the innovative work he was doing. He was venturing into unknown aesthetic realms, moving outside traditional conventions in his use of paint, line, color, imagery and, most significantly (as we will see), establishing a profoundly new relationship between the artist's subjectivity and the artwork. To understand what this meant for Matisse we need to start with a discussion of his psychological and professional development.

The artistic self

Matisse grew up in northern France, close to the Belgian border in the town of Bohain (biographical information about Matisse is from *The Unknown*

Matisse by Spurling, 1998). Once set in a lush wooded countryside, during Matisse's childhood the rapidly industrializing town was increasingly surrounded by factories, the trees chopped down, the field cleared for building. It was a grim, hardworking, middle-class community characterized by a strict work ethic, an emphasis on financial success and a hierarchical, paternalistic social and familial structure. Matisse's father, Hippolyte Henri Matisse, was a tough, ambitious businessman who became very prosperous as a seed merchant. He assumed that his eldest son, Henri, would follow in his footsteps as a lawyer or a businessman.

Matisse followed the normal developmental course of a middle-class boy in his newly middle-class hometown. He suffered the loss of a younger brother when he was four years old, which may have contributed to his mother's attachment to him. His father worked long hours and was a stern, rough presence, but from what we know, he loved his son and maintained high hopes for his future. (Interestingly, Hippolyte Matisse was himself a revolutionary as he and his peers challenged the traditional economic assumptions of life in their town, contributing to a transformation of the French economy.) Matisse's mother, Anna, was a loving and loyal wife and mother. Her support for Henri was unquestionable, even when he would act up or challenge the authorities. The plan was for Henri to take over his father's business, continuing the economic advancement of the Matisse family. However, when the time came for him to begin to obtain schooling and training specific to this expectation, he became seriously ill and was bedridden for some months. The recognition of Henri's supposed frailty led to the decision to bypass him and begin to groom his younger brother as successor. Most importantly and fatefully it was towards the end of his convalescence that the most important event in Henri's life occurred. His mother gave him a box of colored crayons to entertain himself. From that moment on Matisse felt drawn towards color and art, "like an animal that plunges headlong towards what it loves," he would later recall (Spurling, 1998, p. 44).

Having explored and rejected professional training in law, Matisse enrolled in a Parisian art school, to test his talent and ambition to be an artist. Over the next five years he began to elaborate and articulate his artistic self. In time art would become the primary focus of his self-experience, self-esteem and mode of relatedness to others. In 2002, Alan Roland, in his book *Dreams and Drama: Psychoanalytic Criticism, Creativity and the Artist*, discussed the multiplicity of selves which make up the human sense of self. For some people the artistic self comes to take precedence over all others, becoming the organizing principle of their life. Roland wrote:

> In an artistic self there is an inborn aesthetic sensibility and resonance as well as talent in one or more fields of art. This not only draws the person into the field(s) of art but perhaps more important, to a

particular tradition within the field. For every field has a number of traditions. Almost all of a particular artist's selfobjects and transformational objects, whether it be idealized figures, mentors, or fellow artists, are within the particular tradition of the field of art with which an artist is involved. The artist then spends his of her life in a dialogue with the tradition: trying to live up to the best of it while creatively modifying it.

(Roland, 2002, p. 31)

Matisse was totally committed to his artistic self. Every day became centered on the creation of art. His family life revolved around his work, with his children and wife being his most frequent models. His family would later talk about the importance of art in the household and the enduring influence that art and the art world would have on their lives. (Matisse's paintings stood untouchable in the center of the household. His children were in awe of him and never lost their sense of closeness and commitment to their father's art.) All of Matisse's friends were either artists or consumers of art. Every aspect of his private and social life was organized around his vocation, with the goal being the production of art. Even as an old man, an invalid confined to his bed, he continued to be energetic and innovative, producing some of his most spectacular "cut-outs" in his sickbed. It is important to note as well that unlike some of his fellow artists his total commitment to art did not lead to a disruption of his motivation for intimate relations or social responsibilities. He was one of the few modern artists who maintained a stable and "normal" middle-class family life despite his almost fanatical devotion to his art.

The choice of a career as an artist was an enormously risky and provocative one for the young Matisse, coming from the "no nonsense" community in which he grew up. Spurling stated:

It would be hard to exaggerate the shock of Matisse's defection in a community, which dismissed any form of art as an irrelevant, probably seditious, and essentially contemptible occupation indulged in by layabouts, of whom the most successful might at best be regarded as a kind of clown. Henri was already well known in Bohain as an invalid, a failure who had proved unfit to take over his father's shop. Now he was a failed lawyer, too, and he was about to become a public laughing stock.

(Spurling, 1998, p. 59)

Matisse's decision to be an artist did not just reflect on him but was also a source of intense shame for his family, especially his father. In his rejection of all that his father had worked for, and the life which he had built in the Bohain community, Matisse was "throwing down the gauntlet" to his father, precipitating a conflict which would persist with great bitterness for many years. As Matisse himself noted years later regarding his father's reaction to his decision to be an artist: "When I said, 'I want to be a painter' it was the equivalent of saying to the man, 'Everything you do is pointless and leads nowhere'" (Spurling, 1998, p. 59).

Matisse's relationship with his mother was another thing entirely: "My mother loved everything I did" (Spurling, 1998, p. 14). Unlike with his father, he felt understood by her and met with her approval. In fact, for his first few years as an artist he would show his work to his mother, whose judgment mattered greatly to him. When she disapproved he was devastated – as he was even as late as 1905 when he showed her his new painting, Le Port d'Abaill, a work he had been struggling for some months to complete (he was experimenting unsuccessfully with a pointillist style). Anna's response was: "That's not painting." In his distress, Matisse slashed the painting with a knife. He then hurriedly painted another painting, "putting into it, out of tenderness to her, everything that theory could not give him" (quoted by Spurling, 1998, p. 330).

The work that Matisse rushed to create as an offering to his mother was Woman in a Hat, which became one of the most notorious of the fauve paintings, a radical piece and, at the time, bizarre creation of clashing colors and rough, violent brushwork. The fact that this painting was executed for his mother so as to undo her earlier rejection speaks to the way in which his mother's aesthetic (at least in Matisse's mind) supported the highly subjective methods which he had been engaged in, rather than the theoretically based, scientific technique which the pointillist school had been promoting.

Matisse's mother played an important part in his decision to be an artist, not just because she was the first to introduce him to art, but also because she supported his pursuit of non-traditional approaches to his artwork. It was her family, after all, that had a long history of involvement in the Bohain textile industry, producing glorious fabrics for the clothing business in Paris. Bohain textile workers were famous for innovative and colorful silk fabrics, dominating a highly competitive and lucrative market. This family background influenced Matisse, who collected fabrics and surrounded himself with beautiful textiles throughout his life. In addition, more personally, Matisse would often seek his mother's approval of his work and, as we saw above his desire to please her, this motivated some of his most revolutionary efforts. It is also safe to assume that Matisse shared his aesthetic ideas with Anna; she understood them, and encouraged him to pursue his innovation ideas. In other words, as Matisse struggled to maintain his sense of self in the face of his own "discoveries", it may have been the knowledge of Anna's support and encouragement that helped sustain him.

Matisse's artistic self and its function in his self-experience

> Before I had no interest in anything. I felt a great indifference to everything they tried to make me do. From the moment I held the box of colors in my hand, I knew this was my life. I dived in, to the understandable despair of my father, who had made me study quite different subjects. It was a tremendous attraction, a sort of Paradise Found in which I was completely free, alone, at peace.
>
> (Spurling, 1998, p. 46)

For Matisse the paradise of art was a psychological state in which the experience of self was felt to be cohesive, vital and affectively positively charged – a selfobject experience. But he would find this self-state elusive, requiring hard work and risk to achieve. For it was not just artwork that attracted Matisse (he could not be satisfied with being just an artist), he sought also to alter his own relationship to his culture and his profession with work that would be radically new, not just an affront to his father's way of life, but an all out assault on the aesthetic values of western civilization itself. Hence, to find his paradise, and to keep it, would require effort, risk and a persistent state of anxiety regarding the possibility of failure and, perhaps even more importantly, the consequences of success.

Henri Matisse's artistic self was protean, an unfolding set of skills, ambitions and values, which were continually reworked and reconciled in the light of often dramatically conflicting psychological and aesthetic demands. For an artist such as Matisse, creativity was a means to strive towards an objectification and perfection of his subjectivity. If successful, this would bring about the longed-for achievement of self-cohesion, vitality and idealization. But as we will see, the process of articulating the artistic self ended up requiring the disruption and repair of the selfobject ties that Matisse most deeply longed for.

Creating an art of subjectivity

> Matisse was not simply discarding perspective, abolishing shadows, and repudiating the academic distinction between line and color. He was attempting to overturn a way of seeing evolved and accepted by the Western world for centuries. He was substituting for the illusion of objectivity a conscious subjectivity, a twentieth-century art that would draw its validity essentially from the painter's own visual and emotional responses.
>
> (Spurling, 1998, p. 325)

Until Matisse's time, western artists expressed subjectivity (at least overtly) by means of symbol and narrative. Whether the image was of a coronation, a biblical event, a nude, or a country abbey, the expressive element was primarily what was represented, and the story was implied by the image. Some nineteenth-century painters, such as Eugene Delacroix, augmented their narratives with a vigorous and rough use of pigment and color, thus moving towards a more direct painterly expressiveness. However, even for Delacroix, the medium only supported the feelings evoked by the representation, it was never the sole or primary point. On the other hand, Matisse saw the tradition of symbolism and representation as a restriction of the expressive potential of painting. He came to believe that the meaning of a painting was in the way in which color and line embodied the subjectivity of the artist, not through illusion, but directly and concretely as pigment arranged on a flat canvas surface.

At the same time Matisse was fascinated by visual experience and always claimed that he was not an abstract artist, but an artist/scientist studying his own relation to reality. It was not the obvious visual elements that interested him but the emotional engagement he felt with the world. So, rather than constructing his painting out of already existing elements, he painted the evanescent, subjective response to the object or person he was painting. This is why in many cases he preferred the portrait, because the emotional engagement was more immediate and powerful, and thus his inspiration was more compelling.

Matisse possessed a highly refined sensibility and a disciplined creative mind. He was fully aware of western and non-western artistic traditions and had copied hundreds of the masters during his training. He possessed a deeply personal understanding of many different forms of artistic expression, all of which might play a part in his creative effort. However, in practice much of this understanding may have been outside his conscious awareness, and this may have contributed to the artist's surprise (and dismay) at many of the decisions he made in the course of his work. The aesthetic unconscious is a concept that I believe captures those aspects of aesthetic experience that over the course of a lifetime become the deepest psychological sources of line, form, color and rhythm, which the artist draws on in the process of creation. These internalizations, which are co-constructed in interaction with early caretakers, become the templates for later, higher-level aesthetic organizations and motivations. For Matisse the strength of the aesthetic unconscious can be seen in his powerful reaction to his mother's gift of crayons during his convalescence at age 18. However, over time, and especially when an artist receives the type of intensive training as Matisse did, the aesthetic unconscious is elaborated and sculpted, taking on the mature forms and values of the artist's culture and familial and academic relationships.

One important aspect of Matisse's training was making many copies of old masters. This was a central method that the Academy used to instill proper technique and respect for tradition. In Matisse's mind his immersion in traditional aesthetics would become the internal value system that he would relentlessly challenge and deconstruct in his creative project. Matisse's painting methods were designed to allow for the richest expression of the aesthetic unconscious. He did this by combining two approaches: one was to resist the use of a traditional symbolic language – which was not an easy task for an artist trained in the Academy system of that time, molded as he had been by years of rigorous study and stern mentoring; the second was to free himself from loyalty to appearances. Matisse argued that the true representation of reality did not result from precise depiction of what was seen, but from what the artist felt. Thus, although he frequently started with a visually "realistic" image, he would gradually simplify and transform the image, which took on the character of his emotional relation to the subject. "I paint how the world makes me feel," was a statement that he made in many forms over the years. In this way Matisse would "kick himself free" from traditional modes of perception and symbolic narrative, setting the conditions for the emergence of an as yet unknown aesthetic system.

Matisse's creative process

Donald Kuspit has argued that at the dawn of the twentieth century aesthetics took on a more personal, subjective function than it had for artists of prior generations (Kuspit, 1993). For the modern artist the creation of art was therapeutic, according to Kuspit, permitting the alleviation of psychological conflict through the elaboration and resolution of aesthetic problems. If for the modern artist art became a means to resolve self-crisis and restore self-experience, then I hypothesize that it may have been the case that Matisse's motivation to create was accompanied by some degree of self-crisis. In support of this idea, it is important to note the emotional state that Matisse claimed was necessary for the initiation of work on a new picture. He told the actor Edward G. Robinson that he could only begin a new canvas when he "felt like throttling someone" (Spurling, 2005a). He told another, Aragon, that his state of arousal in front of his models was something more like a rape (Spurling, 2005a, p. 24). Thus, for Matisse the motivation to create is accompanied by an increase in aggression. What was this about? Why was he so aroused and how did these feelings motivate him to create?

There were many indications that Matisse, far from the joyful, sensual man of myth, was depressed and highly neurotic, "an unhappy creature", as he himself put it, "tormented day and night" (Spurling, 2005a, p. 405). As an adolescent he was plagued by psychosomatic symptoms, which blocked his assumed transition to his father's work (this was obviously an unconscious intention). Later in life, after he began his project to challenge the aesthetic establishment, he was an insomniac. Tormented by doubt and self-loathing, he immersed himself more and more into work, seeking to "relieve himself of his passions in his pictures" (Spurling, 2005a, p. 427). Heinz Kohut claimed that such forms of anxiety, somatization, and hostility were tied to narcissistic injury or, as he later saw it, selfobject failure. These feelings rather than being primary motivators were symptomatic of a state of self-crisis. I believe that the need to create is motivated by the desire to objectify this inner state and manipulate the externalized subjectivity (the artwork) to resolve the inner conflict and restore self-experience through the aesthetic selfobject tie. Matisse had to create the emotional conditions, as well as a relation to reality, that would allow for the interpenetration of internal and external realities. In this way the internal would be made external and thus available for (re) construction. Significantly, it was the directing of aggression into creative action that set the psychological conditions for innovation.

Over time Matisse worked less and less from nature. He would typically construct highly structured arrangements of flowers, textiles and models. (A recent exhibit at the Metropolitan Museum in New York displays selections from Matisse's large collection of fabrics, which he would use to create exotic, colorful environments for his models.) Hence the subjects of his paintings were already constructions that reflected Matisse's aesthetic interests and values. His first marks on the canvas were made hurriedly "like flashes of revelation – the result of an analysis made initially without fully grasping the nature not the subject to be treated: a sort of meditation." He turned his aesthetic unconscious "like a receptive organ", or rather an analytical organ, to understand and respond to the visual world in a fully subjective fashion (Spurling, 2005a, p. 440).

However, it has been noted that even some of the most innovative paintings were begun as fairly conventional sketches. In fact, Matisse often, initially at least, responded to his subject with a traditional aesthetic approach – this first image would never satisfy him, it simply existed as the first point of attack. He would then dismantle these conventions, pushing the organization of the painting towards simpler, more subjectively determined forms. He would purposely go against his own aesthetic tendencies and submitted his work to relentless and at time ruthless deconstruction, or more precisely and disturbingly, destruction. Once he had managed to free himself of the restraints of conventional aesthetics, he had to struggle with the new organization of the painting, attempting to reconcile his own often powerful emotions to the sometimes unintelligible nature of the painting. Matisse explained: "I work without a theory. I am conscious above all of the forces involved, and find myself driven forward by an idea that I can really only grasp bit by bit as it grows into a picture" (Spurling, 1998, p. ix).

A painting grew for Matisse as a group of relations between fields of color and lines. He experienced the developing structure as a reflection of his own subjective state, not so much isolated and internal, but engaged dynamically with the subject of the work. His emotionally aroused state would continue as the relations in the picture continued to feel unresolved – the crisis of his self would ebb and flow, creating at times a vortex of doubt and anxiety.

In addition, since Matisse would encourage the emergence of unexpected new forms, his picture would frequently challenge his own earlier creations as well as the prevailing cultural standards. As the paintings appeared under his brush, the artist himself was frequently surprised, shocked, and even dismayed. Matisse wrote: "No one is more surprised that I am at the results, for I can never tell what a work will reveal to me" (quoted in Flam, 1986, p. 374). This was the biggest source of Matisse's anxiety. He could never know what to expect, yet that was also his intention. By giving up conscious control of the process, he created the conditions for uncertainty, confusion, fear – and innovation. Some analysts have argued that regression is an essential aspect of the creative process. The idea was that it might be necessary to allow for the emergence of unconscious fantasy to facilitate inspiration and innovation. The expression of these unconscious fantasies would then be subjected to a secondary process in which order was imposed on raw, inchoate materials. Matisse's achievement was not to impose traditional formal organizations on his developing work but to seek and discover a new set of relationships (expressed through color, line and form), building on previously unknown (or unexpressed) formal relations – these relations, though always retaining some tie to traditional aesthetic organizations, were not, however, constrained by them. With this method Matisse wrested out of his deeply divided self something altogether unpredictable and profoundly new. Hence each painting was a potential revolution. Aesthetic danger and professional risk shadowed his every brushstroke.

Some analysts have argued that for many artists there is a desire (need) to challenge and disrupt traditional aesthetic forms and values. For example, Carl Rotenberg in his article "Optimal Operative Perversity" (1992) discussed how many modern artists, such as Matisse, intentionally pursued disorder and chaos in their work so as to work through and discover a fresh aesthetic organization. Rotenberg wrote:

> The artist engages in perverse expression because it is essential to the process of creativity. The artist's goal is to incorporate information that will transform or expand existing assumptions and structures by changing the rules. He achieves this goal within a context of evolving artistic knowledge that has its own traditions and does so in some form that is readily observable. In the course of this activity he creates problems to which he must respond. Hopefully, this series of initiatives and subsequent responses will result in an integrated aesthetic that expresses the artist's individual style.
>
> (Rotenberg, 1992, p. 174)

Rotenberg stated later in the article:

> In each artwork, noise, disorder, chaos, or disorganization is introduced by the perverse expression. As a consequence there arises a struggle between the organizing and disorganizing principles as seen at that point in time. Artworks are felt to be successful insofar as these struggles are resolved in the work, both individually and in relationship to each other.
>
> (Rotenberg, 1992, p. 178)

This process of disruption and repair can be an emotional ordeal, especially given that the new aesthetic organization remains by its very nature to be created (discovered). When Matisse successfully evaded the cultural assumptions which restricted his vision by violating almost every commonly held painterly value and method, he also set himself adrift, purposefully abandoning all known reference points and guides. Often he had no way to know even when the work was finished, since the "resolution", the new organizing principles, would appear at first meaningless, or ugly, unintelligible from the point of view of existing perspectives and values. In many instances the quality of the new aesthetic discovery would emerge with time and after a good deal of argument, recrimination and despair – all this happening not just in the artistic community but within the mind of the artist himself. As Spurling noted regarding the psychological effects of such innovation:

> Matisse's fierce, unrelenting interrogation of his own darkest moods and instincts felt at times like madness. It took all of his resources of nerve and imagination to impose a previously unimagined equilibrium on what seemed like fevered images of a disordered brain. Sometimes he feared that the blazing colors he had let loose would end by making him go blind.
>
> (Spurling, 1998, p. 325)

Spurling quotes Matisse's son-in-law:

> The obvious forebodings experienced by the painter – who at the same time was so prudent and so orderly that people call him "the doctor" – made him tremble. During the few years when he was able to endure this vision, Matisse spent whole nights without sleep, nights of desperation and panic.
>
> (Spurling, 1998, p. 324)

How did Matisse maintain his artistic self in the midst of such a chronic state of self-crisis? As we discussed earlier, I believe that Matisse's mother,

Anna, played an important role in supporting her son's ambitions and encouraging his aesthetic goals. In addition there was his wife of many years, Amelia, who passionately believed in her husband and supported his work even in the face of decades of poverty, struggle and rejection. There were also fellow painters who joined with him in the revolution: John Peter Russell (whose experiments with color inspired Matisse to fundamentally change his palette); André Derain and Maurice de Vlaminck (his fellow Fauves); and the sculptor Aristide Maillol. And finally there were his collectors, prominent among whom were the Stein family, the Cone sisters from Baltimore and Sergei Shchukin, the Russian industrialist. All of these people (and many others) provided Matisse with a selfobject milieu without which he probably would have been unable to sustain his work. They cared for his living and work environment. They admired his creations and at times joined him through their own aesthetic ambitions. And most importantly, his collectors gave him money for his work, even at times when the public and the art world were the most harshly critical and rejecting of him.

Matisse endured the suffering of his creative revolt because of a greater, more important need. He harbored a fantasy of renewal and transformation, of victory over the stifling restrictions of tradition (his father's world) and the victorious creation of a new aesthetic universe. As a result of his efforts, nothing would be the same again. He believed (desperately) in the logic of his theory and methods and, most importantly, his ability to bring order into the chaos that he had wrought.

Synthesis and originality

Jack Flam wrote: "Matisse's ability to synthesize what he took from his predecessors and his capacity to use these borrowings in order to invent his own visual language are crucial aspects of his originality" (Flam, 1986, p. 138). In an interview with Apollinaire in 1907, Matisse stated: "I have never avoided the influence of others, I would have considered this a cowardice and a lack of sincerity towards myself. I believe that the personality of the artist develops and asserts itself through the struggles it has to go through when pitted against other personalities" (quoted in Flam, 1986, p. 209).

Matisse's desire was to free himself from the constraints of tradition (a powerful force both in his familial and professional life) through the creation and perfection of an aesthetic of authentic self-expression. But unlike later painters, such as Jackson Pollock, whose action paintings embodied raw, primitive emotion, Matisse could only express himself by attempting to work through and out of the traditional forms and values with which he has been completely and deeply indoctrinated. He repeatedly emphasized to other artists the importance of "unlearning". Thus his originality was always in reference to other aesthetic projects of his time (most importantly Cézanne and later Picasso). He would immerse himself in their aesthetic, make it his own and then work his way out, discovering his own solutions to the aesthetic problems posed by these idealized mentors. This work of individuation and rebellion had its emotional, psychological and spiritual costs. Despite the persistent anxiety, which Matisse experienced in response to his creative process, his ultimate goal was always to seek a state of "calm" which would accompany the resolution of the difficult aesthetic problems that he presented to himself.

Matisse and color

> 'Where did I take this red color come from?' Matisse mused to Goldschmidt. 'My goodness, I don't know'.
> (Flam, 1985, p. 56)

As a student Matisse was known for his subdued palette and limited, often somber emotional range. He succeeded in utilizing the color aesthetic of the Academy with competence and was praised by his fellow students and teachers for his skill. He knew very well what he was doing and the choice of color and tone was very consciously chosen to create a certain look. However, the impressionists had already assaulted the Academy's color values and, while far from mainstream, the free use of color was in the air. But Matisse's accomplishment was not just in what colors he chose or how he used them, rather he transformed the artist's entire relationship to color. He allowed his unconscious to resonate with the paint and image to drive his decision making. He worked in such a way as to allow the color to reveal itself, to happen, and he would then be confronted by an often shocking, unsettling new color or color relation with which he would then have to contend.

Matisse also experimented for a short time with the deliberate, scientific approach of pointillism. In pointillism each drop of color is carefully chosen to construct through rational decision making and observation the authentic color of the representational image. But his relationship with pointillism was short-lived and ambivalent. He never seemed able to side with one or the other side of this problem. Matisse noted this within himself: "I know that Seurat is altogether the opposite of a romantic," he wrote, "and that I am one, a Romantic, but a good half of me is a scientist, a rationalist, and that's what causes the struggle from which I sometimes emerge the victor, but exhausted" (quoted in Flam, 1986, p. 397). The rational methods of pointillism resulted in sterile and mechanical images, but the purely expressive and abstract approach which was developing in the art world around him also left him uninspired and unmotivated. For Matisse, color was not just to be studied as an aspect of objects in the world, nor was it just a mode of imagination, it was an essential and passionate mode of engaging reality – it was through color that the artist's emotional response to his subject was felt and expressed. Thus the aesthetic investigation of color had to be carried out in a transitional space within which objectivity and subjectivity are engaged and reconciled.

Matisse and the line

Another central aesthetic concern to Matisse was his innovation in line. Throughout his paintings he played with a changing relation between straight and curved lines, in particular he was interested in the arabesque, a dramatically curved complex unit that decorated his canvasses periodically throughout his career. Matisse would organize the curved line in his paintings against the straight line and, most importantly, the plumb line that invariably grounds even his most dramatic arabesques.

In Chapter 1 I distinguished between two different forms of aesthetics – the maternal and the paternal. The most basic form of the maternal aesthetic is the circle, and its derivative, the curve. The basic form of the paternal aesthetic is the straight line, and its use as a vertical, horizontal or diagonal. In Matisse's paintings he is frequently concerned with the relation between these two types of line. And I would argue that one of the primary motivators of this struggle to reconcile these contrasting aesthetic forms was the unconscious association that they invariably had with aspects of the aesthetic unconscious, which was grounded in the artist's early relations with his parents. Thus Matisse sought to maintain order within his painting even while he ventured to push the aesthetic organization into new areas. In other words, hidden within the seemingly mad disorder of his arabesque-laden images, there is an imaginary "plumb line" by which the disorder is grounded and organized.

Chapter 8

The beauty of indifference: The art of Marcel Duchamp

This chapter examines the aesthetics of Marcel Duchamp, the French-American artist whose early contributions to the Dadaist and Surrealist movements opened the way for much of the innovation of late twentieth-century art. Most importantly it was Duchamp's critique of classical western aesthetics and the mystique of the artist that has had the most enduring impact. From the perspective of contemporary psychoanalytic theory, I will argue that much of Duchamp's aesthetics and his approach to the problem of the modern artist was derived from his relationship with his deaf and schizoid mother. Specifically, I will suggest that she failed to provide a responsive parental relationship to confirm her son's vitality, self-esteem and sense of interpersonal engagement. Duchamp attempted to compensate for these deficits through artistic activity and the articulation of an aesthetics that both reflected the experience of failure while at the same time embodying beauty and perfection. I believe that this "artistic self" (Roland, 2002) had an important function for Duchamp. It offered an opportunity for a healing process to occur in which early developmental failure and self-deficits could be compensated for through engagement in the creative process and the production of art. It also recapitulated aspects of the mother–child relationship that remained unresolved and highly conflicted for Duchamp.

At the core of Duchamp's aesthetics was a profound ambivalence towards his mother that was given expression towards and through his art. He was an artist who eschewed traditional standards of beauty, who attempted to bypass the normal turmoil of creativity, and who cultivated indifference and emotional coldness in an age that idealized emotionality and the subjectivity of the artist. He was a great artist who treated art with a casual and at time dismissive attitude. For many years he seemed to reject art, devoting himself to chess and inactivity. Just breathing and thinking became for him an aesthetic act. Perhaps his most influential innovation was art as idea, as conceptual as opposed to productive and expressive.

Duchamp was a member of a talented artistic family. His grandfather and father were amateur artists, and his two older brothers and his younger sister were accomplished artists in their own right. Art was Marcel's first career choice, and though he did not attend the normal academies of his day, he learned his art through various mentorships and self-study. His early artwork was in the post-impressionist and early cubist style. He was recognized as a talented colorist and his portraits of people seemed to capture the alienation of modern relationships. One of his earliest works, *Nude Descending a Staircase*, was one of the most scandalous paintings of its day; it transformed an unambitious and unproductive young artist into an international art celebrity. As a result Duchamp would become known for his iconoclasm and unpredictability. He refused to allow himself to find his niche and continually pushed the definition of art and aesthetic standards. He created artworks of wire, wax and paint encased in glass. He displayed common objects as "readymade" artworks. He stressed the central importance of ideas in art, and cultivated an approach that stressed language and ambiguity, forcing his viewers to think and struggle with the "meaning" behind the work. At the same time, he would intentionally avoid fixed meanings and he loved to undermine expectations and create unanswerable questions and dilemmas. He lived his life according to a new aesthetics that emphasized experimental mediums, expansion of the notion of what constitutes an artwork (most importantly the notion of conceptual art), and the cultivation of an aesthetic lifestyle (many would view his style of living as his greatest aesthetic accomplishment). Duchamp influenced many areas of modern art: music, dance, sculpture and literature. More than other great modernists, such as Picasso and Matisse, Duchamp's influence has touched broad areas of cultural life from the most refined to the most popular.

The deaf mother: The impact of a failed maternal environment

Marcel Duchamp was born in northern France in 1887 (biographical information about Duchamp is from *Duchamp: A Biography* by Tomkins, 1996). His family life was generally happy and there is no record of major developmental problems or traumas. However, his mother suffered from progressive degeneration of her hearing and was most likely deaf at the time of his birth (Tomkins, 1996). Complicating this was the fact that Mme. Duchamp in response to her illness withdrew emotionally from her family. This resulted in what Duchamp later described as a generalized indifference, an attitude that the artist would elaborate into an aesthetic principle. Late in life he reported that he had always harbored angry feelings towards his mother because of her indifference, claiming that his lack of a relationship with her was a dark spot in an otherwise "sunny" childhood. There is no evidence to discredit this view of Duchamp's family. His relationship with his siblings was good and his father, a prosperous notary in the small provincial city in which they lived, supported his four oldest children's choice of art as a profession and provided them with financial assistance to help them during their early adult years. Despite this support, as we will discuss later, Duchamp showed a pronounced ambivalence towards art and his vocation as an artist. To understand this, I believe it is essential to look at the early developmental context, the matrix of aesthetic experience.

In his biography of Duchamp Calvin Tomkins (1996) described the auditory disorder that resulted in Lucie Duchamp's complete hearing loss:

> Lucie Nicolle Duchamp suffered from a progressive hearing disorder that made her almost completely deaf by the time Marcel was born, and she dealt with this by withdrawing more and more into a private world of her own. Duchamp described her as "placid and indifferent".
> (Tomkins, 1996, p. 19)

Madame Duchamp appeared to have adapted poorly to her hearing loss. Rather than attempting to develop ways to compensate she appeared to have responded by withdrawal and suppression of affect. "Indifference" is the term most used by her son to describe her attitude. On the other hand, Duchamp was not indifferent to his mother's withdrawal. He often expressed his hatred of her for her coldness. Since, as Tomkins noted, Madame Duchamp had become deaf by the time of his birth we must ask the question: what may have been the impact of her deafness, withdrawal and emotional suppression on her relationship with her baby son, and what might have been the developmental sequelae for Duchamp in terms of his psychological, emotional and social life? Specifically, given the importance of Duchamp the artist, we will extend the discussion to the important area of his aesthetic life: the function of his artistic self, his ambivalence towards beauty, his struggles with creativity, and his invention of new aesthetic forms.

Hearing impairment or deafness in a parent does not inevitably have a negative impact on child development. In fact, in many cases the parent's reliance on other means of communication can result in heightened capacities in these areas and when the parent is highly motivated, development can be enhanced in the children of deaf parents (Singleton & Tittle, 2000, pp. 226–227; Rutter & Taylor, 2002, pp. 849–850). The problem is more the parent's reaction to their illness and the way in which this attitude affects their relationship to their children. Although the loss of hearing must always be difficult, it was Mme. Duchamp's indifference that was the problem. In thinking about Duchamp's early childhood experiences and their developmental impact, the most important single factor is the chronic indifference of his mother. This indifference may have always been associated with her deafness, but it is the effect of her indifference on Duchamp's development that we must try to explain. That being said, there are few details available about the actual experience of his relationship with his mother, thus we are stuck with generally vague and global statements about her indifference and withdrawal. However, given his mature statements about Lucie and the significant references to indifference in Duchamp's own self assessment as well as in his art, I think we need to make a leap of faith to explore the possible impact of this relationship on his mature aesthetic life. To begin, let us survey some of what we know about the role of the maternal relationship in early development.

Healthy normal development occurs in the context of an ongoing reciprocal interaction between parent and child (Beebe & Lachmann, 2002). From the earliest moments of life the child is hardwired to engage with others, and to respond to their facial expressions, sounds and smells. Parents actively try to stimulate the child with cooing, smiles, singing, rocking and combinations of the above, all of which the child responds to, mirrors and encourages in return. Facial matching is one of the most common capacities. Along with these external processes the child's internal world is forming also in dynamic relation to the person and people who he interacts with. Bodily feelings and affects are stimulated and linked to interactions. The regulation and modulation of feelings is made possible through the internalization and structuralization of functions of these interactions. For example, the child who gradually gains the ability to sooth him or herself autonomously takes in the mother's soothing singing and rocking. It is through interaction that the child gains confidence and motivation to engage the world, to invest emotion and desire in others, and to actualize self-experience through a vital creative dialogue with the world.

In some instances the mother fails to provide the child with such an opportunity. When a mother is withdrawn, as was the case with Mme. Duchamp, she is much less responsive to her child. Facial blankness, lethargy, and subdued affect are all signs withdrawal. These symptoms impact on the parent's motivation and ability to engage with and stimulate the child. When there is also a sensory loss (which is not dealt with) there is an additional level of non-responsiveness. In other words, emotional withdrawal and sensory loss impact on the parent's ability to provide the interactive context for normal development. Although it is not clear if Mme. Duchamp was depressed, recent studies of depressed mothers may help in our analysis. Interestingly, in many cases maternal depression is not usually traumatic; in other words, the disruption to the child's development does not necessarily result in psychosis or severe developmental disorder. As Beatrice Beebe argues, the child of a depressed mother often adapts to the depression and accepts the low level of interaction that he or she becomes familiar with. The withdrawn mother is "just the way it is" and the child adjusts expectations to suit the context (Beebe & Lachmann, 2002, pp. 161–162). The child will also look to other people in the environment for interaction; for Duchamp there was an otherwise engaged family that would have provided ample opportunities for contact. Psychological development is inevitably effected but the person may be able to adapt and achieve a fair level of functioning as an adult; this may be accomplished through internalization, identification and enduring ambivalence.

Duchamp must have learned at an early age to internalize his feelings about his mother – indifference, after all, would become one of his guiding principles. Duchamp once said that he had "intensely disliked" his mother and that his two older brothers had felt the same way about her. For someone as reticent as Duchamp on the subject of personal relationships, this was a startling admission (Tomkins, 1996, p. 19).

Calvin Tomkins in his biography of Duchamp also notes that he harbored a lifelong resentment towards his "cold and distant" mother (Tomkins, 1996, p. 112). Importantly, the very characteristics for which he blamed her he also admitted to in himself (emotional coldness, indifference, a tendency for social withdrawal). Paradoxically, these became the values that he held to in his professional life – indifference, emotional coolness, intellectuality – suggesting that Lucie Duchamp's relationship with her son had a significant effect on the formation of his adult aesthetic and artistic career. Duchamp may have elaborated into his personal and revolutionary aesthetic values his memories of his mother's pathological adaptation to hearing loss.

Aesthetic sequelae of developmental failures

Aesthetic experience crystallizes as a result of the rhythms, forms, sounds and other sensations of the mother–infant interaction. In particular it is the liveliness, symmetry, responsiveness and music associated with the mother's body (her face, her voice, her shape, her rhythms, warmth and touch) that become the complex template for later aesthetics (Hagman, 2005). Having had a good enough mother, most people take aesthetic experience for granted and may never appreciate how the sense of the formal organization of sensations is perfected and sculpted in this early relationship. In instances where this early aesthetic bond is deficient or lacking there may be developmental problems and the child may rely on compensatory strategies to make up for archaic aesthetic failures. As with Duchamp the pathology of the mother may have broad ramifications.

In Marcel Duchamp's case his mother's indifference and unresponsiveness may have resulted in a general absence of pleasing aesthetic experiences in the interaction with her. This may have led to an intensification of Duchamp's interest in and psychological dependency on aesthetic experiences that could compensate for the early failures. As with many such failures, Duchamp turned to an overdeveloped aesthetic sense to cope. In fact there was a good deal of support for Marcel's choice of art as a career. His grandfather was an artist, his father a supporter of the arts and his two brothers and a sister chose artistic careers. Given this, art helped Duchamp to compensate for selfobject failures and self-deficits. Alan Roland (2002) argued that the support and encouragement of family and peers is an important part of the development and elaboration of the artistic self. I would say that it was his identification with the aesthetic values of his father and siblings that provided Duchamp with opportunities for the selfobject experience that had been absent in his relationship with his mother.

The failure of the mother also contributed to Duchamp's conscious repudiation of beauty. I believe that the early failure of the maternal attachment may have resulted in a suppression of the drive to idealize. Idealization is an essential component of the motivation for and experience of attachment (Hagman, 2005). The sense of valuation – of the other as special, even ideal – is communicated between parent and child by means of multiple modalities. Eye contact, smiling, vocalization, touch and a variety of non-specific ways in which affect is shared. The augmentation of these value affects occurs as each member of the dyad responds to the communication of the other, in a reciprocal process of increasing idealization. If one member of the dyad is not adequately responsive due, for instance, to sensory impairment and emotional indifference, this process of idealization can remain undeveloped resulting in a suppression of idealization and impoverishment of attachment. However, though an indifferent response may lead to the suppression of idealization and ambivalence towards the parent, in most cases the child retains a motivation to idealize, which can be manifest later in life through activities such as art. Paradoxically, Duchamp attempted to merge ambivalence and idealization in his aesthetic. "The beauty of indifference" became a touchstone principle for Duchampian aesthetics (Tomkins, 1996, p. 16). Art was a means to externalize and refine subjectivity without effort or longing. Duchamp's cultivated disinterest may have been a means of suppressing selfobject needs and protecting the self from the disruptions of failure and disappointment. We will talk more about this below.

The artistic self

A number of analysts (Mitchell, 1993; Bromberg, 1996) have asserted that the concept of a normal unitary self has given way to a more complex model. They argue that people tend to organize themselves around multiple selves, which are structured according to differing needs and contexts. In his book *Dreams and Drama* psychoanalyst Alan Roland argued that one type of self-organization, the artistic self, is a frequent occurrence "that may exist in a fair number of persons but is only developed in relatively few" (Roland, 2002, p. 30). Roland explained that the successful development of an artistic self depends on a number of factors: parental encouragement, identifications and counter-identifications with a parent who is an artist, inborn aesthetic sensibilities and resonance, as well as talent.

As we discussed in Chapter 3, the artist creates/finds opportunities for aesthetic selfobject experience. He externalizes his subjectivity by acting to alter something so that it reflects a personal vision. In the hands of the artist this work comes to embody his self-experience, as well as the experience of self in relation to the world. The creative process involves an effort to refine the artwork and elaborate on it. Gradually the refinement and perfection of the artwork results in an increasingly idealized but inevitably failing object. Successful creativity results in a work that perfectly expresses the artist's subjectivity, which has become both objectified and highly personal. Thus this process is highly relational; it is not just about self-expression but the embodying of the artist's relation to his or her reality.

The paradox of Marcel Duchamp is that he was one of the most talented and innovative artists of his time and yet he also repudiated the title, for years even seeming to give up working on art. It was as if the identification of himself as an artist would confine his identity, force him to comply with expectations and destroy him. Therefore he continually defied expectations, changing styles and methods, cultivating an indifference towards his work, and devoting large amounts of time and energy to non-artistic pursuits.

Despite his ambivalence, his artistic self was crucial to his psychological stability and functioned to provide opportunities for selfobject experience that helped him to sustain and to repair narcissistic equilibrium despite significant vulnerabilities and deficits. Duchamp's hunger for art and aesthetic experience was so powerful that he sought to reduce vulnerability by dissociating himself from many of the responsibilities and demands of the artist. He never let himself depend on his art as a livelihood. He never would cooperate with expectations of what his art should be. He told everyone how "lazy" he was, as if his work habits were such that he did not care if he made art or not. He tried to depersonalize his art, going so far as to select objects with no relationship to his personal subjectivity. Most importantly, Duchamp refused to repeat himself and would intentionally produce works radically different in medium, image and method, so as to prevent any tendency he might have to "fix" his identity as an artist.

Why would Duchamp fear the idea of a fixed identity? He felt a lifelong need to avoid committing himself to a vocation, a home, or a relationship. He denied his intent to be an artist, he was unwilling to repeat himself, he changed medium and styles frequently, and he made a way of life out of ambiguity, paradox and obfuscation.

Behind Duchamp's claim to have devoted his career to destabilizing his personality, countering the pull of taste and habit with an aesthetic of indifference and avoiding the trap of fixed identity by his various strategies of self-contradiction, there lurked an uncompromising exaltation of the self. All Duchamp's modes of seemingly undermining his own coherence as a consciousness were actually ways to assure his detachment from things that might draw him into conditions or relations he could not control; they freed him to live wholly in the world of his imagination (Siegel, 1995, p. 207).

Contemporary psychoanalysis locates one of the earliest sources of the self in the experience of the parent's gaze. Kohut (1971, p. 116) referred to this many times as the "gleam in the parent's eye". As infant and mother playfully interact the baby sees himself mirrored in the responsive eyes of the other. From this mirroring he comes to believe "I exist. I am whole and alive. I am a person who has a unique personality and value." It is through this experience of mirroring that the self is gradually structured and given life in the mind of the child. But what if the mirror is devitalized and blank; suppose what is reflected back by the mirrored gaze is indifference. What then? The child may come to fear the self that is reflected in the mother's dead eyes. In Duchamp's case it was as if he feared the fixed gaze of the other. Thinking once again of his mother's indifference, perhaps he was trying to manage that which he both longed for and feared – recognition and responsiveness from the parent – while at the same time dreading to identify himself with his mother's deadness and indifference. Faced with an unresponsive and devitalized parent, might not the child fear that the parent would be unable to engage in a lively exchange; with their vision dull and mechanical what would it mean to be seen and known? I believe that Duchamp feared this recognition – that what would be mirrored back, the self as she saw him, would not be vitalizing or self-confirming, but draining, devitalizing and confining. He kept on the move to stay alive.

He also needed to preserve the selfobject function of his art – this meant never allowing his creativity to fall into patterns, or his identity as an artist to be confirmed by expectations and needs. Paradoxically, to nurture his creativity he had to deny it. But this meant that when he did engage the world creatively it was a surprise, a new experience which for that very reason would feel more alive and responsive. This meant that he would have to bypass certain parts of the creative process – especially anything having to do with longing, frustration and self-aggrandizement.

Coping with creativity

As I noted above creativity involves a search for a selfobject experience through the externalization and perfection of aesthetic form. Aesthetic form is the objectification of subjectivity; through the affective engagement with the art-object, the artist alters the object in such a way as to shape it according to inspiration (the immediate subjective response to an experience). The object, the artwork, is altered and made to reflect the inner life of the artist. Reality and subjectivity become one. The perfection and refinement of this transitional phenomenon, in which the subjective possession of reality becomes increasingly clarified and ideal, leads to the creation of beauty. The recognition of this perfection, when the artwork and inner subjective experience are not only the same but also ideal, results in a sense of inner perfection and vitality that I call the aesthetic selfobject experience.

However, this process is not easy and there are real psychological risks: 1) The longing for an aesthetic selfobject experience can result in anxiety when failure is expected. The artist accepts and even gives him or herself over to vulnerability, which can lead to disappointment and self-injury; 2) The perfecting of the artwork also involves vulnerability because the artist is manipulating external manifestations of his or her own feelings, thus the distortion or inadequacy of the depiction may be painful and disconcerting; 3) In fact, self-crisis is an essential part of creativity because until it is finished the artwork always fails to satisfy the artist's longings; selfobject failure, hopefully followed by restoration, is virtually inevitable; 4) The finished work is presented for public display and judgment. Understandably this opens the artist up to potential ridicule as well as praise. The desire for a positive mirroring from the selfobject milieu can be traumatically disappointed.

The failure of Duchamp's mother, whose deafness and indifferences resulted in affective blankness and unresponsiveness, seems to have resulted in the development of a schizoid defense in her son. Although subtle in many ways it nonetheless resulted in pervasive characterological traits, such as emotional suppression that resulted in a lifelong tendency to shallowness in emotional relations, lack of motivation for intimacy and commitment, an attitude of indifference, reluctance to invest in reality and an overemphasis of the cognitive and rational side of psychological life. Duchamp could not be disappointed or hurt because he did not care. He could easily be charming and clever, because he would never allow himself to be truly vulnerable to an other.

The beauty of indifference

In response to these developmental failures and their sequelae, Duchamp cultivated an aesthetics of indifference that was characterized by a denial that art was subjectively based, that argued that beauty was peripheral to art, that separated the artist from the work, that rationalized art and converted in into a joke or puzzle, that denigrated art through the promotion of a urinal as artwork.

> By purging his images of direct affect, while at the same time distancing himself from the subjects he had taken on while still trying to work in the orbit of cubism, Duchamp found a position of detachment that allowed him to evoke a much cooler and more intellectualistic – yet at the same time more deeply personal – way of being an artist.
>
> (Seigel, 1995, p. 39)

But what does Duchamp mean by "the beauty of indifference"? Even Calvin Tomkins noted that this aesthetic might be tied to Duchamp's identification with his mother. After all, indifference is the primary attitude that characterized her after her hearing loss, and Duchamp conspicuously complained about her in this regard. If we take the phrase "as is" it is not hard to see how the mother's indifference (the source of failure in responsiveness to her child) was converted by the son into a type of virtue. As an artist this conversion was an aesthetic one – indifference, rather than the source of anger and frustration, becomes aestheticized, the experience formalized as a type of gesture or attitude which is carried out with grace, or formal perfection. I assume that the idea of "the beauty of indifference" is intentionally ironic and is meant to provoke an intellectual response in the audience. But it is also accurate – many of Duchamp's works are cool, even cold, mechanical and densely obscure. They hold back more than they give. Thus a dimension of the attitude of indifference is how it functions as a defense against the reoccurrence of selfobject failure. Those who do not care, who are emotionally detached, who do not seek passionate engagement, are not vulnerable and cannot suffer loss or abandonment. I suggest that Duchamp did not just identify with the mother's symptom of indifference but also its use to contain and protect self-experience in the face of actual or threatened loss. Aesthetically this leads to the possibility of removing all subjectivity from art.

The empty object: Readymades

One afternoon Duchamp was walking down Broadway with a friend. He stopped at a hardware store and bought a snow shovel. When he returned home he painted on the handle "In Advance of the Broken Arm" and then hung the shovel from the ceiling. This was his first American readymade; an item chosen on the basis of "visual indifference, and, at the same time, on the total absence of good or bad taste" (Tomkins, 1996, p. 157). Most importantly, it was not "made" by the artist, nor was it bound by other aesthetic conventions – it was not even created – it was selected not as an artwork but as an idea, a purely mental object. Throughout his career Duchamp would "create" a number of these readymades: bottle racks, bicycle wheels mounted on chairs, an inscribed urinal. The aesthetic implications of these selections would be felt for decades afterwards, in the works of Cornell, Warhol, Rauschenberg and many others.

In promoting the "readymades" Duchamp was able to avoid the turmoil of creativity. The object is not intrinsically meaningful except to the extent that it is given a title as an artwork. But the objects are interchangeable and any version of the object will serve the purpose. Therefore, the artist does not have to care for the object, nor is he vulnerable since it in no way reflects his subjectivity; like the wheel on the chair it only exists to amuse – it is not art.

The readymade is a "found object" and as such it is aesthetically deaf and dumb. Rather than exuding beauty it must be provided with aesthetic value, which it lacks (it may even lack awareness of itself). It is unresponsive as it sits out of its natural context – essentially useless. If we had to imagine into the "readymade" a subjectivity it would be feeling alienated, its identity a blank. It is not so much an object as an idea, an idea about negation and lack. But it is also important to note that the readymades are not depressing, they are playful and even humorous. They celebrate the perverse and some of the pleasure they give is in the optimal way in which they violate some of society's most cherished values (Rotenberg, 1992). The playfulness of the readymades suggests the joy behind the artist's indifference. If Duchamp was just indifferent to art he would not have created it (and in fact for 20 years he appeared to do just that) but in the end Duchamp was enthralled by art and attempted to cultivate an aesthetics of living that was pervasive. But his longing for art was expressed through absence – through the beauty of unrequited anticipation.

An aesthetic of "delay"

With the creation of his greatest (and most notorious) single work The Bride Stripped Bare by the Bachelors Even (or The Large Glass), Duchamp invented a new modality for art – "the delay". This odd notion implies that the aesthetic experience associated with an encounter with an artwork is withheld, the moment is "stretched out" (Siegel, 1995, p. 94) as we wait for the experience of recognition and response. With The Large Glass there are many reasons for this delay: the barrier of the plate glass, the unintelligibility of the imagery and objects, the obscurity of the notes which accompany the work, and the sense that meanings are arbitrary and intentionally nonsensical. The delay of The Large Glass never comes to a full conclusion – one is always left waiting. The aesthetic experience is inevitably (and intentionally) incomplete and dissatisfying.

The interpersonal world of The Large Glass is also empty of humanness. The forms are mechanical and two-dimensional, they lack color, they do not appear to be functional (or at least the function is not self-evident), the bride and the bachelors are separated by a metal frame that cuts across the glass horizontally, creating two separate zones. Most importantly, the contents of the work are locked between heavy sheets of glass – entombed and silent, they can be observed, but they are forever sealed off from the viewer, untouchable and silent.

The Large Glass is the clearest expression of Duchamp's experience of his deaf mother. The normal tie between mother and child is based on interaction – gesture and response in an endless vitalizing sequence. When the parent is withdrawn the child's natural gesture, the attempt to elicit response from the parent, is met with a delay. She is unresponsive, immobile or blank – the child waits for the expected response, which does not occur. She is unresponsive and cut off from the child. As if a sheet of glass encased her, she can be seen but not engaged. Her gestures, lacking vitality, are mechanical and do not convey warmth. There is a sense of separation, a blockage that stands between child and mother preventing engagement. The experience of self and self-with-other is fragmented and depleted of feeling. The child does not feel a human connection, yet there remains a fascination, a longing for contact. But there is no way to satisfy the desire. Over time the affects felt towards the mother are suppressed – hope is lost – the delay in response as the child attempts to get a reaction from the mother extends throughout childhood and becomes the way in which life is experienced.

Duchamp's construction of the "delay" is an attempt to capture through art this childhood experience of relational failure. He intentionally provokes a state of crisis in the viewer similar to that experienced by the child with the withdrawn parent. In this way the provocatively distorted work of art forces recognition of primordial contradiction upon the viewer. Such recognition is inevitably traumatizing for it implies intuition of one's own incompleteness, "unwholesomeness", self-contradictoriness – intuition of the deep, permanent split within oneself. Recognition of one's inner distortion evokes disintegration anxiety. This threatens the complete collapse of the self. At the same time, the intense awareness of internal contradictoriness catalyzed by the explicitly distorted work of art has an abreactive effect, ultimately emancipating and maturing. One spontaneously coheres again and acquires fresh self-possession, greater ego strength. One has a sense, however short-lived, of being whole (Kuspit, 1993, p. 32).

The Large Glass is just such a provocation, as Kuspit described, but on a more intersubjective level. The primordial contradiction is both within the self as well as in the relationship between self and artwork/mother. The trauma of delay accompanies the anxiety that the response will never come, that one will remain adrift and incomplete. The environment of indifference leaves all experience incomplete, feelings are uncontained (unwholesome), presence and absence are unresolved – the split between the mother and the self, and within the self, results in a permanent state of disintegration potential, which in Duchamp's case also never came. A primary, needed relationship remains permanently incomplete and distorted – meaning is elusive and perhaps nonexistent.

But as Kuspit noted, the function of this provocation is that it hopefully leads to healing – if the person viewing the glass for the first time can feel both the turmoil and the search for resolution which takes place. However, like with any aesthetic process, Duchamp does not allow for full resolution. Although the potential for healing may exist, it is never fully possible; the viewer can never, ever fully resolve the meaning (or lack of meaning) of The

Glass. Human life exists at best in a suspension between existence and non-existence, between frustration and satisfaction, between indifference and love, between a solitary self left alone by a withdrawn parent and the fact that the parent is nevertheless physically present and alive. The delay is the best that one can achieve – the moment of waiting in which potential exists but satisfaction never arrives.

The breather

Later in his life Duchamp claimed that his aesthetics could best be expressed through breathing. Simple existence was all that was necessary, the gentle back and forth, in and out, of breath. By this means he would reduce aesthetic longing to its most primordial form. It would no longer be necessary to engage the world, to actualize the self, to express feeling, or communicate. For "the breather" aesthetic experience is refined to its most exquisite and minimal form, the rhythmic gesture of respiration. To practice his art, Duchamp would sit in his apartment on 14th Street in Manhattan by himself. The furnishings were minimal and since he had supposedly given up art there was nothing to do in the apartment. He would sit and breathe, hours would pass, uneventfully it seemed, but for the artist the beauty was found in thought, imagination, conceptualizing.

Duchamp's persona, the "Respirateur", is the ultimate reduction of aesthetic experience, as well as the perfect expression of narcissistic self-sufficiency (Tomkins, 1996, p. 408). Interaction and responsiveness are reduced to the most basic and minimalist level. It doesn't even involve will, just the rhythmical contraction and release of the autonomic nervous system. Interestingly, the affect which Duchamp associated with breathing was elation. It was only when the longing for the world was abandoned that the "delay" ceased – the pain and disintegration which plagued him no longer mattered.

In the end Duchamp's accomplishment was the seeming elimination of the relational and personal from aesthetics. However, the reason his art is so compelling is the way in which absence evokes presence; during the delay desire and fantasy flourish, during the process of breathing thought is given full and unrestricted opportunity and fantasy can be elaborated and enjoyed without restraint.

During the last 20 years of his life Duchamp worked secretly on one of his most ambitious and strange works. Having rented a small apartment in his building in New York he constructed a type of diorama, a display called Given: 1) The Waterfall, 2) The Illuminating Glass. The work was constructed with an old wooden door, which he had acquired during a trip to southern Spain, through which two holes were bored, so that a single person could step up and view the display within. Peering through the holes the viewer sees a naked woman lying on her back on piles of brush with her legs spread apart, her genitals fully in view. Her face is partly obscured by her hair, is not in view. In her left hand she holds aloft an oil lamp. Beyond the lamp are a river, a wooded glade and a waterfall. Upon Duchamp's death the existence of the work was revealed. Duchamp had also left a manual for the work's construction. It was eventually dismantled and installed permanently at the Philadelphia Museum of Art.

Many things are remarkable about the work. First, the initial impression on approaching the work is the door as a barrier; heavy wood, tall and wide, it appears impregnable and gives no hint of what is beyond. The room itself is dark and initially, unless the viewer is aware, he or she might turn away, not knowing what was beyond the door. The door itself is not without character: the wood is weathered and worn, the boards bound together in a rustic and primitive fashion. But nothing prepares the viewer for the image beyond the peepholes.

The glum, impassive door gives way to a brilliantly lit fantasy world. There are shattered bricks to the left as if you are looking through the wall of a bombed out building. The woman is lying back, her legs wide apart, exposing her genitals. She is lying on a bed of twigs and branches. Is she dead? The pale skin makes one think of a corpse. Why would anyone lie naked on a bed of branches? But she is clearly alive for in her left hand a lantern is held up in the middle of the scene – it is burning. Beyond are a glade, fir trees and a stream with a waterfall, seeming to be spilling water from a plateau in the distance. It is a carefully constructed illusion, similar to the dioramas you would find in a natural history museum. It is also a traditional allegorical image, filled with apparent symbols – the lamp, the branches and the waterfall. Having appeared to abandon art, Duchamp had secretly been constructing an admittedly provocative but in many ways traditional artwork. I believe that this hidden, secret quality is its essential element. Beyond the immobile and dense facade – unseen to the casual viewer – is a bizarre world of sexuality, imagination and archaic meanings. The female, inert, her face turned away, is once again the unresponsive mother – instead of eyes and mouth, there is the labia and vagina, the only passage to communication a sexual one. Then there are the rough branches, the harsh condition of her emotional life, and the lamp, a beacon, a hopeful illuminator of a restored and plentiful Eden.

So as with the experience of the deaf and withdrawn mother, the viewer of this work, at first confronted by blankness, gazes through the facade and encounters affect, fantasy and hope. As with all of Duchamp's works, you never know. There is ultimately no definitive meaning to be "found" in the work. The sylvan scene is also distinctly artificial, even kitschy. The woman turns indifferently away from the lamp. There remains a strong ambivalence and cynicism, typical of Duchamp's work.

But I think the most provocative aspect of the work is the way in which Duchamp controls access and structures the way in which it can be seen.

Most importantly, it is not possible for more than one person to view the work at a time and since the room in which it is displayed is off to the side and unmarked as well as dimly lit, the viewing of it feels markedly solitary, the aesthetics fostering a state of vulnerability and regression. One views the work alone; there is no sharing it. It is interesting that in this last work Duchamp emphasizes the activity of "seeing" in the most obvious way, by forcing us to "peep", to "look" – and the shock is in what we "see". One can imagine no better way to create an experience of alienation and isolation; one is confronted by a disturbing and confusing image. But it is only artifice, a contrivance of pigskin and lighting and simulated motion. The interior world of The Waterfall assaults our visual sense, but there is also silence and isolation. It is a visually stunning creation but, as we have noted all along, in Duchamp's aesthetic universe it exists – in all its glory – in silence.

Chapter 9

Modern art in America

In the next three chapters I will focus on modernism in the United States during the first half of the twentieth century. In particular I will discuss the impact of modern art on several Americans: Frank Lloyd Wright, Joseph Cornell and Jackson Pollock. I hope to show through a discussion of the lives and works of these three men how modernist art spoke to the psychological and aesthetic dilemmas of the American people and especially American artists during the decades up to the mid twentieth century, at which time the development of modernist values and beliefs about the artist came to a dramatic, violent end with Pollock's death.

Prior to the twentieth century modernism had no direct influence on art in the United States. Gradually, in the new century, artists such as the young Thomas Hart Benton, Arthur Dove, Frank Sheeler, and Joseph Stella began to experiment with the abstractions and other artistic innovations of the modern Europeans. Gradually, with the arrival of Marcel Duchamp and Picabia in New York, some of the provocativeness and rebelliousness of the young Europeans began to disrupt the staid art world of America. Despite the beachhead made by modernism during the initial decades of the century, the predominant art forms remained traditional, representational, and even regional depictions of scenes of American life. However, over time there were clear reasons why American society and the American art world (which expanded exponentially over the next decades) would find both opportunity and liberation in the new aesthetic world of modern art.

Modernism – as did psychoanalysis – appealed to twentieth-century America in a number of ways. First, by deliberately deconstructing, if not attacking, the aesthetic standards of prior generations, modern art opened the door to artistic ambitions outside the traditional American obsession with European artistic institutions and standards. As the American economy expanded in both productivity and diversity, the natural American tendency for self-reliance and rebelliousness could thrive in the iconoclastic culture of modernism. Second, the notion of the modern artist as a special, inspired aesthetic hero, bringing new art forms into being out of the Self, free of controls and at times even influence itself, also appealed to the long American tradition of primitive and naïve art. With the coming of modern art American artists no longer had to travel to Europe to attend the schools of the French Academy or mingle with the society of European artists. American artists could be modern, and perhaps create great art, without leaving home (in Cornell's case) or by waiting to learn from Europeans (as Pollock did) as some of the best artists sought refuge in New York during the Second World War. Third, the modern psychologizing of art, especially as promoted by the surrealists, attracted a new type of artist who sought in art and artistic success a solution to inner conflicts and demons which traditional art could not have provided. This notion appealed to Americans who were also fascinated with the idea that inner exploration of forbidden and hidden parts of the mind would lead to success and happiness. In other words, Americans during the twentieth century continually sought means of self-improvement and personal enhancement, whether through the new technology of psychoanalysis, or the authentic and innovative art forms of modernism. Fourth, the expansion of new art forms and the loosening of aesthetic standards led to an explosion of artworks as products and commodities. No longer were Americans dependent on the sale and purchase of old European masters (or imitations); rather, modern art led to an interest in a new, home-grown art, created by "authentic Americans". And finally, there was the rise of New York City. By the middle of the century New York had become an international center not only of art, but also of finance and the new media and service industries. During the war years educated middle-class people and successful artists from all over Europe flooded into the city, changing its culture in fundamental ways. It was a relatively cheap, cosmopolitan and economically expanding new American city like no place the world had ever seen. And this new city, and new country, sought a new form of art that would be just as unique, just as free, and just as successful as New York, and America, felt it had become. Modern art provided the means to this end, and the city was full of striving young artists, eager to exploit modernism in pursuit of fame and riches.

Frank Lloyd Wright, Joseph Cornell and Jackson Pollock were born into American middle-class families and all three became artists outside the European tradition – or, for that matter, any sort of institutional milieu – but in a new artistic culture influenced by modern European art. Each artist would transform aspects of modern European art (for Wright, the aesthetics of the arts and craft movement; for Cornell and Pollock, surrealism) and create exceptionally individual and revolutionary art forms. Most importantly, they were products of the modern idea of creativity rising out of a personal aesthetic vision which could express and realize idiosyncratic yet powerful truths. All three sought from art a type of transcendent self-experience in which beauty would be personally grounded.

Of these three American artists Frank Lloyd Wright had the longest, most aesthetically complex and highly public career. As an architect and artist, his art was fundamentally different from the small shadowboxes of Cornell or the broad, paint-splashed canvases of Pollock, but his conception of the nature of art, the role of the artist and the personal nature of the creative process were the same. Art for Wright was embedded in the present, with traditional standards of beauty and aesthetic judgment held at a distance. He believed that art was a means by which man could transcend mortality and create a universe of beauty and idealization. He promoted the idea that the artist was a type of heroic figure, as he "shakes new ideas out of his sleeve" and brings forth perfection and joy. Wright was the quintessential modern artist: virtually unschooled, iconoclastic, grandiose and fully in tune with the changing economic and cultural rhythms of his time.

Joseph Cornell, a reclusive man, most likely with an autistic or schizoid personality, discovered that through surrealistic art he could create artworks that could express and contain his extraordinarily personal and idiosyncratic fantasy life. He found that the notion of the source of the artist's creativity being in the unconscious, and the varieties of art forms and imagery of the surrealists, provided him with an idiom for the expression of his peculiar obsessions and also permitted the construction of an aesthetic lifestyle that aided him in regulating and containing a fragile self-organization. A quiet, gentle man, Cornell just as much as Pollock saw the opportunity which modern art offered for an untrained artist seeking an artistic career. But true to his nature, he found success through the methodical exploration of his rich fantasy life in the basement of his family's home in Queens, New York. However, Cornell – as Pollock would later – found in modern art an opportunity for self-repair and self-enhancement which led to the production of exquisite artworks. Cornell's private and personal art would impact the art world for many decades to come.

Jackson Pollock also found inspiration and aesthetic liberation from the surrealists, but he took it in the opposite direction. While Cornell worked to contain his subjective life in carefully crafted and organized shadow boxes, Pollock sought to explode the limits of his canvas and to destroy the last vestiges of traditional formal representation. Rather than containing and regulating, Pollock sought to release his emotion and created canvases that would overcome the viewer and the artist in their raw intensity and formlessness. As a result Pollock seemed to embody the essence of modern America in his apparent power, ambition and independence from foreign influence. He represented America, self-made and new, producing artworks which seemed to sum up the whole of modern life with extraordinary imaginativeness and power, and without precedent – he was brand new, the perfect American modern artist.

All three of these artists represented the limits of modernism. Each, in their idiosyncratic and fundamentally personal aesthetic, allowed for no tradition to develop and no place to go but imitation. The modern artist in these extreme instances is so restricted to his or her own psychological sources that they come to a dead end. As with Pollock, if the artist *is* nature, then he is doomed to repeat himself. The modern artist in these extreme instances, abandoning the surrounding culture, eschewing the influence of other artists, teachers and even the audience, is ultimately alone, cut off from sources of inspiration and influence.

A significant part of the problem for modern American artists was the tension between the very personal (and often private) nature of their artwork and creative processes, and the hunger and fascination of the media and public for information about the new artistic heroes. Cornell dealt with this by not getting involved. He was famous for his reclusiveness and didn't attend major exhibitions of his work even when his artistic reputation was secure. On the other hand, Pollock was destroyed by his fame and the exceptional pressures that living up to his reputation as the tormented genius exerted on him both socially and internally as self-loathing and drunkenness fed doubts about his worthiness as a person and as an artist.

In the end, as we will see in the rise of Andy Warhol and postmodernism, the cult of the modern artist and of modern art had to give way to an entirely new art form, artist and art world. But that will be the subject of Chapter 13.

Chapter 10

Joseph Cornell's quest for beauty

> Creative filing
> Creative arranging
> as poetics
> as technique
> as joyous creation
>
> (Diary entry from 1959, Cornell, 1993)

Joseph Cornell was one of the great American artists, and despite his simple life and eccentric character, one of the most prolific and successful as well. His career spanned five decades and during that time his work never went out of critical favor. He had shows at major New York galleries and the most prestigious museums and private collections in the world. The vast majority of his artworks were "shadow boxes" within which he constructed compositions of such exquisite expressiveness and aesthetic refinement that, even given the capricious tastes of the art community, he became an inspiration for several generations of artists.

As well as being a thoroughly American artist, Cornell was also a quintessentially "Modern" one. He worked in assemblage, a modernist art form in which found objects, printed matter, photographs (in fact anything that could be put to use) were arranged on a picture plane or as a sculpture. Typically the resulting form or image had a surreal quality – often reconfiguring components of familiar reality in surprising, even shocking ways. The first and perhaps greatest artist of assemblage was the Dadaist Kurt Schwiters, who also pioneered collage. Many other major twentieth-century artists, including Pablo Picasso, Marcel Duchamp and Alexander Calder, worked in assemblage. However, it was probably the association of assemblage to surrealism and that movement's focus on fantasy and the exploration of the unconscious that appealed to Cornell. As we will see, Cornell's mission as an artist was the relentless and passionate examination of his own subjectivity and it was in his shadow box assemblages that he found a versatile medium for the expression of his self-experience.

Assemblage is rich in symbolism – another connection to the surrealistic aesthetic. This has made the art form an ideal area for psychoanalytic study. This interpretive approach, where unconscious meanings are revealed through the analysis of symbols, is the bedrock of classical analytic aesthetics. However, recent theorists have shifted the psychoanalytic focus from the symbolic content of artwork to the aesthetic experience itself and the psychology of the creative process. This is not to say that symbolism is not important, rather it is only one part of a multidimensional view of the artist, his artwork and his audience. Consistent with these contemporary analytic theories of art, specifically object relations theory and self psychology, I will explore Cornell's use of the medium of the shadow box. We will discuss the meaning of the constructions (boxes), the nature of the creative process by which he produced them, the psychological function of the boxes as containers of self-experience, and, their role in Cornell's lifelong search for beauty.

A brief life history

Joseph Cornell was born in 1903 in Nyack, a northern suburb of New York City (this history is based on D. Solomon's *Utopia Parkway*, 1997). He was the oldest son of an artistically inclined middle-class family. His younger brother had cerebral palsy and was cared for by the family. There was also a sister, who was able to establish her own family as an adult but remained close and supportive. Cornell's childhood was happy, stable and generally unremarkable. Given his adult vocation, as a child he showed little artistic gift or inclination. He later looked back at his childhood as idyllic and protected. Tragically, when he was 14, his father died of leukemia, an event that dramatically altered his life.

At 15 Cornell attended boarding school in Massachusetts but returned home after several undistinguished years. Eventually he moved with his mother and invalid brother to a modest house in Queens, New York, where he resided for the remainder of his life. From 1921 to 1931 he sold woolen samples in the garment district. During this time Cornell was psychologically adrift. He wandered about the city foraging in bookstores and second-hand shops. He collected books, records, theatrical memorabilia and prints of old movies. He grew introspective and preoccupied with personal interests. But most importantly it was during this decade that Cornell developed his fascination with modern art, cinema and the theatre. He attended numerous gallery openings, Broadway shows and concerts, where he began to cultivate relationships with many important figures in the modern art movement. But it was the attitude of spontaneity and the naturalness of surrealism that resonated most strongly with Cornell's interest in his own thoughts, fantasies and feelings.

One day in 1931 Cornell discovered the progressive Julien Levy Gallery. He watched as they unpacked the surrealist art objects and paintings that had been shipped from France. Inspired, he went home and created his own collages in imitation of the surrealist style. With encouragement from Levy, Cornell made more of these "montages" and was soon included in an exhibition. Eventually he moved from two-dimensional collages to his signature box constructions. At first they were ready-made but with time he began to build the boxes himself, making the actual container an essential part of the artwork. These boxes were relatively small and composed of wood that he selected for its character. He arranged objects, photographs and simple mechanical contraptions within the box. Viewed through a glass window these constructions embodied ineffable associations and ambiguous meanings. Cornell also created box series in which he dwelled on certain themes and images seeking deeper and often more obscure associations. His works were greatly admired and many were included in major exhibitions at the Museum of Modern Art and the Metropolitan Museum of Art in New York City, and eventually in collections and exhibitions worldwide. Despite his success Cornell maintained a reclusive and modest lifestyle devoted largely to his family. His primary indulgence was his wanderings – his "wanderlust" as he sometimes called it (Solomon, 1997, p. 231) – through Manhattan neighborhoods, searching second-hand shops, lingering long hours in coffee shops and exciting himself with vivid fantasies of young women whom he watched from a distance or followed through the city streets. During these wanderings Cornell's imagination worked feverishly, and much of his inspiration for his art was nurtured by these reveries. His studio was in the basement of his Utopia Parkway house, where he developed an intricate filing system for his burgeoning collection of found objects and other items. There he labored, often late into the night, typically on several works at the same time. He continued throughout his life to construct his boxes and collages from these found objects and photographs that he collected.

Beginning in 1940 Cornell kept a detailed journal of his daily life, observations, feelings and self-state. Many of these were spontaneous, colorful reactions to sudden observations or stream of consciousness associations to his artworks, his found objects, his memories or often his dreams. Since these writings are rich in personal detail and self-observation I will quote from some of them in the pages that follow.

Cornell's inner life was split between his commitment to his mother and brother and his private, solitary absorption in his mental life and his artwork. From what we can tell his mother showed little interest in his vocation and was often critical of his messiness and lack of ambition. He was very close to his brother who was his main emotional tie and the only member of the family who seemed to support Cornell's artistic activities and interests. The relationship between these two men was a source of companionship for both.

In the final decade of his life Cornell's production declined even as his reputation grew both in the United States and abroad. His brother died in 1965 and his mother in 1966. He lived alone and continued to work. Despite his fame within the art world and his rising income, he continued to be reclusive and preoccupied with his interests: music, the cinema and theater. However, there is evidence that he was ambivalent about his approach to life. The day he died of heart failure in 1972 he called his sister and told her: "I wish I had not been so reserved" (McShine, 1995, p. 115).

Discussion

It is clear that the major determining event of Cornell's life was the loss of his father when he was 14 years old. Prior to the father's death the Cornell family was stable, social, at times prosperous and joyful. Afterwards, the family, grief stricken and financially strapped, became dislocated from their home and friends. Cornell was traumatized and may even have suffered from pathologic grief or, given the loss of his father in late childhood, a developmental disorder. Not surprisingly the family's fortunes were devastated and the relationships within the family forever transformed. Soon after the death, he was sent away to school. His sister recalled the following memories of Cornell during that time:

> Before Daddy died – that was when he had a full sense of security. As soon as Daddy died then he felt that he should be the man of the house. And that's when all his dreams and terrible nightmares started. You know, in Andover he had a terrible time. He used to have these terrible nightmares and he'd yell for me. I would find myself running up the stairs, not even awake, saying "I'm coming. I'm coming." At one time he was cowering in the corner and he said, "It's a white antelope, it's a white antelope, and I didn't turn the light on, you know. I had learnt not to startle him. So I said, "It's alright Joe, it's just the sheet." It was hard to convince him because he was in the grip of terror.
>
> (From an interview quoted in Blair, 1998, p. 63)

The death of a parent in childhood may have serious effects on psychological development (Hagman, 1996). Most importantly, the child's experience of self and self-in-relation, still in a formative state, may be disrupted. The feeling of security and continuity in life, especially family life, can be shattered. The freedom to engage creatively and spontaneously in the world of people and objects is often curtailed as the child retreats into his or her inner object world, clinging to memories and fantasies of the people, and perhaps the world, that has been lost. As we see in the sister's account, Cornell at age 14 suffered a severe psychic wound. Anxiety, even terror, and the eruption of primitive aggressive fantasies, overwhelmed him and precipitated (at least in this one instance) psychotic states. We can only speculate, but it is highly probable that the traumatic impact of his father's death resulted in a profound psychic vulnerability and proneness to self-fragmentation and annihilation anxiety. Understandably, he came to develop emergency strategies to ensure self-continuity, self-cohesion and a feeling of security. As we shall see, one dimension of this strategy involved the elaboration of a lifestyle and an ongoing tendency to self-preoccupation that emphasized the stimulation of ecstatic emotions and positive self-experiences. This reduced his feeling of vulnerability, heightened his creative drive, and assured the availability of selfobject experience. In everyday terms, he became as a result of his losses an odd, reclusive and self-protective man with an intense commitment to art.

Behaviorally this led to his increasing devotion to his widowed mother and brother, and his assumption of the dead father's role as breadwinner and caretaker. Gradually Cornell's life became socially restricted, resulting in isolation and developmental fixation. In addition he became schizoid, his internal world of fears and desires being increasingly channeled into imagination and ultimately into his art. It was Cornell's genius that he converted this strange and often perverse self-preoccupation into evocative and profound artworks.

Potential space, the creative process and self-experience

As a foundation for the discussion that will follow, I will briefly review some of the psychoanalytic concepts regarding creativity and art that are especially relevant to Cornell's work. In particular I will discuss the notion of potential space, the transitional area of subjective experience in which subject and object merge and create new realities.

It is the artist's readiness to play with the world within this potential space and engage in a dialectic between inner and outer that characterizes the creative process; and it is the elusive goal of objectifying self-experience in an ideal, meaningful and self-confirming fashion that is the artist's primary challenge.

As I discussed in Chapter 3, it was British object relations theorists Marion Milner (1957) and D. W. Winnicott (1971) who first examined creativity's link to individual subjectivity and environment, especially in a developmental context. While the classical analytic model viewed mental life and reality as separate and to some extent adversarial domains, Milner and Winnicott were interested in the complex embeddedness of the developing self in the early environment (which to them was synonymous with the mother). They believed that the adult artist retains the capability for a fluid, undifferentiated engagement of self with the world. Unconscious fantasy and the experience of real objects and events are merged, and the distinction between inner and outer breaks down. Rather than going crazy the artist is resourceful, disciplined and skilled enough to elaborate out of this non-differentiated state fresh imagery and unforeseen meanings. Winnicott conceptualized this process as occurring in a type of transitional zone or potential space in which the separation of self and object does not matter, and a playful engagement between psyche and reality results in creation. The artist has a special ability and willingness to work in this potential space; in fact, he or she may be compelled to because it is in this psychological activity that he or she feels most alive. Milner describes several patients whose severely impaired self-structure resulted in a creative drive to bring about self-healing through art.

Milner's (1957) discussion of the function of the frame in painting is especially relevant to our understanding of Cornell's use of the shadow box as an art form. For Milner the frame served several functions in regards to the creation and use of potential space. First the frame marks off a zone of reality – in a sense creates it – as a space in which subjectivity and the object world interact to create something new. It offers defining boundaries as well as protection for the vulnerable state of the creative mind at work. The frame concentrates attention and raises the significance of the contents, the aesthetic imagery or structures, to a special status. Cornell literally gave depth to the frame. His boxes created three-dimensional coordinates in which illusion gave way to new arrangements of a highly subjectivized reality, pushing the limits of psyche and substance to new levels of evocativeness.

Wilfred Bion (1965), another British analyst, developed a related idea that is helpful in understanding Cornell. This was the concept of the "container". Bion described how the infant or the psychologically ill adult often struggled with terrifying and primitive thoughts and phantasies which they seek to get rid of through projection into another person's mind, most importantly the mother or analyst. If properly prepared the other person accepts the projections and works to understand them and communicate their meaning back to the child/patient through words, thus helping the other person organize and manage their inner world. This model works best to address issues of parenting and the treatment of severe mental illness in which the relationship between infant and parent and patient and analyst accentuates the separate subjectivities of the dyad. But if we combine the notion of potential space with that of Bion's container, we can see that potential space does act to contain, protect and give meaning to unconscious experience. The container is at times within the analyst, or between people, but it is within the psychic container (think Cornell's boxes) that the creative elaboration of an intertwined subjectivity and objectivity stimulates new forms of perception and even newer realities. As we will see later, Cornell's boxes acted as this type of psychic container – a space constructed to facilitate the metabolization and reordering of his self-experience.

As discussed in Chapter 3, self psychology describes an additional dimension of this process. Heinz Kohut (1985) believed that artists have a special ability to merge with the world, self-boundaries being fluid and responsive. He believed that the function of the artwork was as a selfobject, meaning that the artist experienced the created art object as part of him or herself. This selfobject, which was either idealized or experienced as a mirror of the artist's "grandiose self", enhanced, confirmed and vitalized the artist's self-experience in a way which intensified the motivation to create. Artists such as Cornell create in order to bring about opportunities for these selfobject experiences, and when successful they feel enlivened and more cohesive (Hagman, 2005). This experience is especially meaningful to someone with a fragile and vulnerable sense of self. Given sufficient talent and opportunity, an artist like Cornell (a highly self-protective and schizoid man) could obtain enormous personal validation and comfort from creative work. At the same time, art can never substitute for flesh-and-blood relationships, and therefore it can never eliminate the feeling of vulnerability and pain completely; rather, art becomes almost a compulsion as the artist repeatedly seeks an ultimate cure for his or her self-deficits.

Bringing together these disparate models we can say that the artist's creative work occurs in a realm between reality and fantasy. For Cornell this psychological zone, constructed within the box-frame, is a potential space in which inner and outer realities merge; meanings and images are played with and elaborated in surprising ways. This space can be described metaphorically as a psychological container, which is both inside and outside the self, into which the artist projects their thoughts, feelings and fantasies, bringing them together with the outer world in new configurations, meanings and even new forms of reality. The artist's primary motivation to engage in this work is to enhance and vitalize self-experience as well as the quality of his or her sense of relatedness to others. He does this by constructing within the container an ideal representation of his or her subjectivity and experience of being.

The psychological meanings of Cornell's boxes

For most of his career Cornell personally constructed each box. The selection of materials and the preparation of the box-frame was one of the most important concerns of Cornell's creative process. The boxes varied in size; a typical one was 12 inches in width, 18 inches in height and 4 inches in depth. The front of the box was sealed by a glass window, which acted to both close off the interior and allow viewing. Cornell constructed an arrangement of objects usually in three dimensions, but he sometimes added flat cut-outs, maps, and pictures of birds, stars and landscapes. His first self-made box contains a large, two-dimensional moon, a stem-glass, a clay pipe, a doll's head and a row of cylinders that appear to float in a line across the upper interior space of the box.

Within each box Cornell created a private world with its own physical laws and idiosyncratic associations. Objects were placed into strange even contradictory associations. Space was broken up and/or twisted. The laws of physics were irrelevant within the box – at times even gravity appeared suspended or made irrelevant. Objects and images appeared to mean more than what they normally are assumed to mean. Seemingly unrelated things were juxtaposed as if linked by some hidden logic. In other words, through the construction and artistic use of his boxes, Cornell created a slice of an alternate universe which had the characteristics of unconscious reality, where the primary process ruled. Within the box he was radically free to transform specific objects of his selection into a structure of subjective objects.

Cornell's creative work was first and foremost a type of playing (and I don't mean this in any trivial sense). He combined and recombined objects within the box using a process that Anton Ehrenzweig (1967) called *unconscious scanning* to determine their content and arrangement. Rather than regressing in the service of his ego – a process Ernst Kris (1952) described creative inspiration – Cornell's psychic topography was fluid and undifferentiated. From his frequent remarks about being surprised by the outcome of some of his works we can assume that his approach was playful, allowing for unpredictability and chance to have a free hand. In this playing Cornell felt most fully alive and engaged with life. The boxes were infinitely malleable, as is the unconscious. Anything could be placed inside and combined in different arrangements. The boxes were totally determined by the subjectivity of their creator. Cornell was confined by gravity and the limits imposed by the three dimensions, but by nothing else. In some of his descriptions of his work he seemed unbound even by time as his associations slipped back and forth between early experiences such as a childhood mountain vacation, his discovery of music as a young man, or yesterday's recollection of a book in a shop window – all linked by Cornell's unique aesthetic sense.

Unlike other art forms such as painting, more than simply framing the object or image, the box-frame created a three-dimensional space in which Cornell could work. This meant that rather than simply conjuring an image or an illusion, he could play with a new, home-made reality. His boxes contain actual things, often playful and childlike objects, which are not meant to represent something else, as symbols do; rather, we are asked to experience these things in a new subjectivized reality, in which Cornell's unconscious life is made concrete before our gaze. But it is no humdrum subjectivity that is contained in the box. The box grants a high level of significance to the new reality. Each box is a unique and special construction. Objects that may have been discarded as worthless in another setting are displayed as precious and deeply meaningful. The boxes both evoked and heightened a feeling of unique perfection. Most importantly, this perfection involves the recovery of lost time.

In her book *Joseph Cornell's Vision of Spiritual Order* Lindsay Blair (1998) quotes a sentence from Proust that Cornell heard spoken by André Maurois on the radio:

> Time as it flows is so much time wasted and nothing can ever truly be possessed save under the aspect of eternity which is also the aspect of art . . . Yes, art because it gives the past a form, saves it from change and disintegration.
>
> (Blair, 1998, p. 67)

The cloistered perfection of the box stops time – even as its imagery suggests longing for the past and the recognition of loss. At the same time age, decay and loss are absent from the box's reality. The Bébé Marie doll glares out from among the surrounding twigs, forever young and untouched by age. A youthful Lauren Bacall remains cool and beautiful, as she was when she was enclosed within the box dedicated to her in 1947. Behind the glass barriers the contents of the boxes are untouchable and protected. The wooden board frame and cool glass are the only things we can make contact with. The rich, erotic and dramatic inner contents of the box are permanently beyond our grasp. They exist, forever cut off in their private, silent and still world. Given Cornell's experiences of loss, his tenuous sense of connection to others and his lifelong terror of death, this quality of the boxes is especially important. His tendency to hold onto the boxes or take them back from friends or clients also speaks of the way in which Cornell sought to prevent or undo the loss associated with the passage of time.

In terms of content and imagery, the meaning of the boxes often involved the stimulation and exploration of memory – they were tools for the recovery of lost time. Regarding one 1958 box Cornell wrote:

> another surprise burst of working on *long* dormant COCKATOO for PASTA #3 – large blonde box hanging heavy after original burst of energy about 2 or 3 years ago – but – again – endless "byproduct" concerning it – elusive – escaping – astonishing tie-in – or correspondence in the realization of relationship to Adirondack mountains 1921 vacation – discovery of music – Russian overture "Barber of Seville" in Richard Jessup lodge house – and all the precious memories that evoked by this especially now at this time of year – in remembering street browsing in city same time of life – faded sepia Pasta in Alfred Goldsmith book shop – 24th + Lexington Ave. – however, working on box alone would have been enough – simple, uncluttered

> mood – simplicity of working all but finished – irksome aspects of material dissolved – but this was a full blown working spell of extravagant energies.
>
> (Cornell, 1993, p. 245)

Ultimately the box provided security and protection. Many were not thin lattice frames but solid, thick wood, at times appearing rustic or heavy. For Cornell this protection was essential to his creativity. Being a fragile and vulnerable man he continually sought means to structure his experience and nurture his isolation in such a way as to allow the greatest opportunities for self-relating and the elaborating and actualization of his inner life.

The box not only protects its contents from the outside world, but also the outside world from its contents. The box is a type of cage in which primitive and uncontrolled fantasy can be acted upon and given concrete form. The thick walls of the box and the hard glass protect the viewer from direct contact with the outrageous imagination of the artist. The safety found in the box allows an opportunity to give vent to unconscious contents and passions.

Yet, on the other hand, the box was exhibitionistic. It displayed a dramatic scene. But it did so in a controlled way. It revealed only what Cornell wanted the viewer to see – a slice of fantasy, a glimpse of some secret drama. Hence, the Box also functioned to protect and limit Cornell's contact with his audience. It was an armored and hermetically sealed capsule that he sent out into the world.

Finally, Cornell's art functioned as his means of entry into society. After all, he took up art as a result of his fascination with a surrealist exhibition, not purely from private interest. From the start he sought recognition and early on was granted access to an audience for his work. Despite his privacy these works were for display. He longed for relationships, but often his real relationships were disillusioning shadows of his vivid, passionate fantasy of them. In his boxes he could create the ideal other, imbued with wild imaginings and deep emotional resonance, without the risk of real intimacy and potential failure and disillusionment. When these boxes were put on display Cornell could additionally engage in a form of connection as he seduced and challenged the audience into his web of meanings, images and sexual longings.

Cornell's creative process

> Joseph's mind worked by association and by passionate identification with specific things, and a very acute feeling of connections between specific things, but I don't think by intellectual theory.
>
> (Donald Windham, quoted in Blair, 1998, p. 80)

For Cornell the creative process started long before he entered his basement to begin building a box. From his journals we know that he continually cultivated an aesthetic sensibility with which he was preoccupied for much of his waking hours, most significantly during his wanderings far from the demands of his studio. His creativity was stimulated by solitude that was emotional and psychological more than social. Cornell's attitude towards the world and his own thought processes was associative, fluid and undifferentiated. He was not only intensely introspective but also cultivated a state of transitional experience in which unconscious fantasy and real objects intermingled in his reactions to people, objects, music, etc. Milner refers to how "relating ourselves to our own perceiving" (1987, p. 250) makes our perceptions come alive. This clearly applies to Cornell, who felt more vitally alive in his own passionate relating to his own experience, thoughts, and feelings.

Cornell's preparative activities included foraging and collecting. He frequented the book stalls and second-hand shops in the downtown Manhattan area around Union Square. He searched bins and small stores for objects, maps and books that caught his interest. During the Thirties and Forties these places must have been treasure houses of nostalgia and bric-a-brac. In a sense this rummaging was the first stage of the creative process. Scanning the shops, Cornell selected, often inexplicably, things that interested or amused him. He took these things home and filed them away in his basement studio for later use. These were his paints and his marble, to use as a medium for creating his boxes.

Cornell often noted in his diary the chaotic condition of his basement studio, where his found objects, papers and photos were scattered about – a "rat's nest" he once called it. This environment, Cornell's cellar, cluttered with objects rich with personal meaning, a fragmented, inchoate morass, was quite literally and concretely the artist's unconscious – a potential space, an area of play. Creating often involved a cleaning out or ordering of the basement. For example, he noted regarding the "rat's nest": "Instead of yielding to the wanderlust too often disillusioning and instead suddenly see the collage framing come to life (new glass) and the whole rat's nest in cellar reviewed, framed, varnished and lined up" (Cornell, 1993, p. 235).

Then he would build a box by hand, thus creating the container for his imagination. While the viewer may focus on the content of the box, to Cornell the construction of the box itself was inseparable from it's aesthetic. He noted in his journal regarding a day of working on a box:

> working with old wood for BOXES – plus introspection – constant experiments resulting in CHOCOLATE MENIER (Egan) without realizing "What I had" – the problem to work with fresh wood and still catch the *elusive something* to work on ART NOTES appreciation of doing own work vs. helper with carpentry – but a good physical

working is the thing (spells of inertia maddening) old wood – very personal feeling – especially reclaiming aspects.

(Cornell, 1993, p. 247)

Bion's ideas are relevant here, especially the artwork as a psychic container that takes the fragmented and obscure contents of the unconscious and metabolizes them, giving them order and meaning. Bion saw this as the function of the parent or analyst. Cornell did it himself, constructing his own external psychic space in which his unconscious could be projected, contained and transformed.

Cornell worked for long hours selecting the contents of the box, deciding on its theme. For example, many of his boxes are offerings, gifts to movie stars and others with whom he was infatuated. He then arranged and rearranged the objects and images in the interior. Typically a box was not completed in one sitting. Often months, even years passed as he lived with and ruminated over his unfinished work. As noted earlier, he engaged in *unconscious scanning*, subliminally working over the content of each piece, his dissatisfaction and frustration with the work's incompleteness nagging at him and stimulating his imagination to take action. It was the dialectic between his objectified subjectivity (the artwork) and his unconscious reassessment, between resonance and disjunction, between feelings of dullness and elation, which fueled his effort to achieve resolution and to create an aesthetic selfobject experience. At times the completion of a box occurred spontaneously, surprising even the artist with the results.

One question about Cornell's creativity was the extent to which he was conscious in his choices of objects and arrangements. Was he unaware, acting on instinct, impulse or whim? It appears that Cornell's decisions about the contents and arrangements of the boxes' interiors was deeply associative; he cultivated a spontaneous and passionate engagement with nature and valued his own capacity for self-surprise. Given this, it is reliable to say that Cornell's work was not consciously symbolic, because the classical notion of the symbol implies a clear distinction between self and reality – and it was states of psychic non-differentiation which Cornell valued. Heinz Kohut would have emphasized the fluidity between Cornell's sense of self and the world. Ehrenzweig, from an object relations perspective, would have argued that there is a hidden order connecting the meanings of the objects, an order found within Cornell's unconscious mind. Thus any interpretation of the symbolic meaning of the boxes can only be uncertain and overdetermined.

Rather than representing a meaning or a feeling, the boxes created a concrete reality that was infused with the artist's subjectivity – a private universe. Cornell was creating his own subjectivity not simply representing it. His subjectivity was concretized, given real form. At the same time the box contents were also found objects, only slightly altered, if at all, in the process of inclusion. We are meant to take them as they are, and perhaps to question our entire preconceptions about what art is. These things obviously have private meanings for Cornell, but that is true of everything at all times. The box forces us to respond to objects that are dislocated and brought into provocative association. We can no longer deny the presence of the unconscious when we view a Cornell box. We experience the unconscious not just in its derivative symbols, but also as a vital presence, a part of our experience of everyday things.

In this way Cornell shatters our assumptions about our own being as well as about our reality. He combines disparate objects and images; he splits and fragments our assumptive world, but at the same time transforms the world so that it has a radically fresh and transcendent order. Even in his most inexplicable juxtapositions, the beauty and sense of perfection is undeniable. In object relational terms the rhythm between the fragmentation of the paranoid-schizoid position and the integration of the depressive position are quite evident in Cornell's work. He broke apart to bring together. He re-enacted the experience of loss and then sought restoration and renewal. But what he renewed was not just the same old thing; it was something perfect, an enchanted fragment of a magic world.

In summary, Cornell's creative process involved a deep, ongoing immersion of his subjectivity in a deeply associative engagement with his own experience. Rather than regressing he cultivated an intermingling of his conscious and unconscious self-experience and sense of being in the world. Out of the myriad objects that he collected he constructed an associative structure, linking objects, breaking those links, and then reintegrating until he had a sense that the box was "complete". This dialectic between internal and objectified aspects of the self led to an ideal embodiment of Cornell's being. Thus it is shortsighted to see just the symbolism in his work; the boxes are a transcendent, ideal form of experience and their perfection of form expresses both self-crisis and personal salvation through the creation of beauty.

Self in a box

In a conversation with Cornell, the gallery owner David Mann once expressed admiration for one of the artist's works. Mann reported that Cornell had the following reaction:

> I once praised a new group of things that he was working on and he said, "I'm glad you find them beautiful" and then he became very sort of depressed. I said well that's a funny way to take a compliment and he said you don't know how terrible it is to be locked into boxes all your life, you have no idea what a terrible thing it is.
>
> (quoted in Blair, 1998, p. 19)

Cornell was a man of deep vulnerabilities with a tendency to depression and anxiety. In a world of loss and disillusionment, he constructed a series of small worlds in which self-experience and self-in-relation could be contained, expressed and exhibited. Cornell's reaction to Mann's admiration is symptomatic of his plight. When faced with the experience of mirroring of his subjectivity, he is depressed. He cannot accept the direct experience of intimacy and connection with his friend. His subjective beauty can only be made real when it is contained, bounded and locked inside the box, forever set apart, forever silent and untouchable – despite its frequent seductiveness and erotic intensity. Cornell's great talent was his capacity to express the private, unknowable aspects of his self-experience within a dazzling aesthetic display.

It is this tragic duality that is at the heart of our fascination with the boxes. We have never seen anything like them, these strange dramas locked up in their small, silent world. However, we immediately sense that Cornell's confinement paradoxically results in and amplifies the beauty of the work. These objects were the artist's primary medium of self-expression and self-actualization. It was through them that Cornell gave full expression to his self-experience. These tiny, hermetically sealed stages were capable of packing all of Cornell's vast imagination and being into their contents. And it speaks to Cornell's enormous talent that he succeeded time and again to craft a perfect, elegant embodiment of his self.

On one level, as per Mann's recollection, Cornell experienced his creative preoccupation with the boxes as a terrible confinement. But he also treasured his work and continued to hold on to many of the best boxes, keeping them to himself despite their increasing value. (He was even prone to reclaim boxes that he had given as gifts or sold.) His sadness as he described it to Mann doesn't tell the whole story. In fact, Cornell lived vitally and expansively through his work. Through his work he conducted an all-out pursuit of selfobject experience through the creation of beauty.

Conclusion: Joseph Cornell's quest for beauty

> Tues. 6:15 dawn
> Crescent moon thru top of bare branches
> Star above it clear, fresh beauty
> Night blue
> Gently faded
> Fresh beauty the way Delacroix saw it.
> (Diary entry from 1956, Cornell, 1993, p. 224)

Joseph Cornell cultivated an aesthetic sensibility in which his every waking moment seemed to be charged with a readiness for beauty. He often rose early in the morning and his journals frequently describe the morning sunlight, the birds in the neighbors' yards, and the fresh dawn air. During his afternoon wanderings in the city he was always on the lookout for special objects, books or magazines that stimulated his aesthetic sense. In his journals Cornell frequently described the elation and rich fascination of his aesthetic experiences. For example, he sat for hours over a cup of coffee in a cheap automat, lost in passionate reverie about a young girl working the register, dwelling not on her sex, but her perfection and the web of aesthetic associations for which she was the catalyst. It was the sense of beauty he was after, and he was always ready to grab at any event or sensation that satisfied this need for passionate perfection.

The sense of beauty is an aspect of our experience of the ideal (see Chapter 1). Most commonly we find something beautiful when we feel that it is perfect, that it has qualities (such as its appearance) that we consider transcendent, of a quality far above the ordinary. Psychologically the sense of beauty is a selfobject experience. In the presence of beauty we feel more alive, vitalized and whole; our mood lifts and we become optimistic even when the message or subject of the beautiful thing is tragic or fearful. This is the most important part of the sense of beauty; it paradoxically embodies aspects of human experience that are painful or evocative of anxiety in a manner or form which results in a positive selfobject experience merged with a full recognition of loss and tragedy. Hence, proximity to beauty is a fundamental human desire, and universally functions to help us endure life.

Cornell was hungry for beauty. His wanderlust was not an attempt to avoid his work (something which he often claimed) but a search to find beautiful things or people. Cornell was a good example of the psychological basis of beauty; he often fell under the spell of some beautiful girl, only to experience a sad disillusionment when he learned something about who she really was. It certainly appears that in his creative work he found beauty elusive. His working and reworking of his boxes involved a continual search for a more precise and compelling beauty, for in his art Cornell was perfecting himself, his own subjectivity, his own experience of his being, idealized and exquisitely embodied within the special universes of his boxes. These boxes were also for people to see and admire, to join in creative association with his vision, and to encounter beauty as if for the first time.

Cornell's work compels us to yield to our imagination, to permit (perhaps indulge in) the emergence of the hidden ordering ability of our unconscious. But I am not referring to the type of regression we experience on an analyst's couch. Standing before a Cornell box one feels as if one is taken by the hand and gently guided though a web of one's own associations. While the boxes frame our fantasies with their formal perfection, we encounter the ineffable source of our own sense of beauty that always seems beyond our grasp. Using the terms of self psychology, a Cornell box is an opportunity for selfobject experience, an ideal mirror of our inner life where we also encounter and recognize the artist's self. Our self-experience is elevated, brought together and enlivened by the beauty of the object and it's perfect embodiment of our intertwining subjectivities. This explains why many people who encounter Cornell for the first time claim to have discovered him for themselves. In the aesthetic moment we see in the mirror of the idealized box our own perfection, and for a moment our imagination is set free, just as Cornell himself was as he sat reading in the sunny backyard of his perfect quarter acre of nature on Utopia Parkway in Queens, New York.

Chapter 11

Form follows function: The selfobject function of Frank Lloyd Wright's art and architecture

> Architecture is man's great sense of himself embodied in a world of his creation.
>
> (Frank Lloyd Wright, 1955, p. 44)

This chapter explores the psychological function that the practice of architecture served for Frank Lloyd Wright. In this regard Wright was very different from the most prominent modern architects, most notably those of the Bauhaus School, who attempted to rid their designs of subjectivity, creating a stark, machine-like aesthetic free of affective expression. As a result modern architecture, as represented by the Bauhaus architects, had a fundamentally different psychological and aesthetic world-view to modern artists working in other art forms. On the other hand, Wright, because he saw himself as equal part artist and architect, was the most modernist of these architects in that for him architectural design became a means for expression and perfection of self. Specifically I will argue that Wright sought through the design and construction of his "organic" architecture (most importantly homes) to create opportunities for selfobject experience that not only shored up a precarious and fragmented self-structure, but also enhanced his self-experience to such an extent that he was able to actualize his role as the most respected and successful architect of his time. As he noted in the epigraph that begins this chapter, Frank Lloyd Wright designed not just buildings but entire self-created aesthetic worlds of such beauty that he transformed the physical and psychological landscape in which he and his clients lived, and along the way profoundly altered our modern social landscape.

Architecture is the concrete expression and perfection of human subjectivity through the alteration of the environment. This transformation can be of geography and vegetation, such as in landscape architecture, or the construction of new, artificial environments, as in the construction of homes and other buildings. Through architecture people express or externalizes subjectivity by changing the environment in such a way as to reflect inner experience. They then further elaborate this altered environment until the externalized subjectivity is perfectly embodied in it. This of course is at the heart of all art, but in this chapter this definition is important in the sense that it differentiates building or engineering from architecture.

I will offer a self-psychological perspective on Louis Sullivan's claim that in architecture "form ever follows function" (Carlson, 1999, p. 206). Of course Sullivan was referring to function in regards to the use or purpose to which a building is put. This "rule" leads to the repudiation of ornament and the simplification of architectural design to the point of an almost mechanistic minimalism. However, I am using the term "function" in a different sense. As a psychoanalyst I am interested in the psychological function of architecture, and as we shall see, when we identify how a building functions psychologically we also want to understand how its form plays a part in making this happen (and of course vice versa).

Over time the psychology of art and architecture changes with the evolution of cultural life and the changing function of the arts both for individuals and for society. In the next section I will sketch the life story of Frank Lloyd Wright, setting the stage for a discussion of the dynamics of creativity and art for the artist/architect of the modern era, Frank Lloyd Wright being one of the most important examples of the architect as modern artist.

Frank Lloyd Wright: Genius and the vulnerable self

Frank Lloyd Wright was born in 1867 in Wisconsin. His mother, Anna Lloyd Jones, was of a large, immigrant Welsh family with a long history of liberal politics, religion and an enduring sense of both specialness and persecution. His father, William Carey Wright, a widower with three children, was a charming, charismatic musician, lawyer and minister. During Wright's childhood the family moved many times throughout the Midwest and New England. His father, always starting a job with great energy and enthusiasm, would after several years fail and the family would move on. Money was tight and economic advancement was stagnant. Anna, ambitious for herself and her young son, became bitter and angry towards her husband, and the Wright family life was filled with recrimination and resentment. Anna's hope became increasingly centered on Frank as her marriage gradually failed. Eventually the couple divorced and William left with the stepchildren.

In 1884, when Wright was 17 years old, his parents divorced. Wright never saw his father again, a fact that supports Wright's claim that (speaking of himself in the third person) "the father never loved the son at any time" (Secrest, 1998, p. 77). On the other hand, Wright was always aware of his mother's intense love and ambition for him, as well as the damaging impact that her need for him had on his self-experience. James

William Anderson in his 2006 paper Frank Lloyd Wright: A Psychobiographical Exploration, argues that as a result of these two radically different relationships Wright struggled with the management of a radically split self-structure characterized by "an exalted self" and "a denigrated self". Anderson states:

> His father's way of viewing him was very different from his mother's. His father saw him as a nonentity, as someone who was not special. Many of the children in school also looked down at Frank; they saw him as a mama's boy with long golden curls. Frank was always threatened by what I call the denigrated self, by a self-image that reflected his understanding of his father's way of seeing him. One should also keep in mind that his exalted self was never secure. His mother doted on him and supported him, but the expectation was that he would achieve great things, and if he did not, he feared, she would be disappointed and would give up on him as she had given up on her husband.
> (quoted in Winer, Anderson & Danze, 2006, p. 165)

After several semesters in College, where Wright studied engineering, he moved to Chicago and eventually joined the architecture firm of Louis Sullivan. At that time Chicago was a center of architectural innovation and Sullivan's firm was one of the leaders. Over the next few years Wright learned his craft, and began to learn about many of the new ideas. Most importantly, Wright encountered Louis Sullivan's notion of "form follows functions", eventually espousing what he considered a more radical approach that he called "organic architecture". He applied this most successfully to the design of his prairie style homes, many of which were built from 1890 through 1908.

Up to this time, American homes were at best a hodgepodge of different local styles and imitations of European architecture. They (as Wright often complained) were constructed as an assortment of boxes that were arranged together often with no notion of the total design. Wright argued that these houses were artificial, ugly and had no relationship to the environment in which they were built. Organic architecture, as exemplified in the Wright's prairie style, had a unity of design, an organization of interior space attuned to the physical needs of the residents, and a sense of place, attuned to the physical environment of which the home was an essential part. Wright opened up his interiors with lofted ceilings, wide banks of windows and a prodigious use of natural materials, often found locally in the woods and quarries about the neighborhood. His roofs were low and wide, with eaves cantilevered far beyond the walls of the house to keep out the sun and prying eyes. The most important thing about Wright's designs was their artfulness. Wright was a truly modern artist of architecture, seeing himself as not just a builder, but also a poet of space, creating opportunities for aesthetic pleasure that would transform the lives of his clients.

By 1908 Wright was a prosperous professional man with a large family and a bright future. However, with so much demanded from him by others and a wife distracted by childrearing, Wright entered a period of crisis which led to an affair and eventually the abandonment of his family (unlike his own father he would remain involved with his children). He fled to Europe but eventually returned to construct one of his finest homes, his own, which he called Taliesin, translated from Welsh as Shining Brow. This was a period of both personal and creative crisis for Wright, and over the next few years a number of scandals and losses further impacted on this state of affairs. At the same time, however, some of his greatest projects were realized – the Hollyhock House and the Imperial Hotel to name a few of the most famous.

In the mid 1930s, after a period of eclipse, Wright designed his masterpiece, Falling Water, as well as the Johnson Wax Building and Taliesin West; each inspired designs that attracted worldwide attention. It was also during the 1930s – and to the end of his life – that Wright aggressively cultivated his reputation as a provocative genius, with his biography going through several editions, national magazine articles and radio interviews – whatever might bring attention to him. Perhaps this showmanship is as important to Wright's success as his architecture. He became one of the most sought after architects in the world, and his ambition seemed boundless, with designs for entire cities coming from his drafting table. With the help of the members of the Taliesin Fellowship, his shop produced hundreds of new designs, most importantly the Guggenheim Museum and the Civic Center of Marin County.

Discussion

In his biography of Wright Brendon Gill (1988) described the great architect as a resilient, confident man. In his single-minded quest for success and admiration, Wright would say anything and do anything to achieve his goal. He manipulated and took advantage of people. He was unable to maintain mutuality in relationships. Quick to take offense from those closest to him he could be cruel and blaming, inflicting the same type of damage he suffered from his parents on his own children. He was also plagued with anxiety and fear of failure, even as he worked furiously to succeed. In other words, he was from our perspective a narcissistic character. Let us review some of what we know about Wright's early relational experiences and self-development to try to develop an intrapsychic model that might be useful in understanding the function of his work.

The relationships that Frank Lloyd Wright had with each of his parents were radically different. His father, William, appeared to have ignored his son, perhaps at times using the child in an abusive manner. His attitude towards Frank was "disconfirming", and the result was massive and ongoing empathic failure, if not an experience of cumulative relational trauma. Frank must have felt unrecognized by his father, his existence as a person eventually negated by the father's abandonment. The result was the formation of a self-state characterized by low self-esteem, isolation, vulnerability and a sense of psychological precariousness. On the other hand, he was always the idol of his mother. She saw him as the genius, the son whose future was boundless and talents unsurpassed. He saw in her gaze both admiration and powerful ambitions and came to depend on this fantasy and the need to actualize it: he must be "the greatest". The result was a self-state characterized by grandiosity, intense ambition, power and supreme confidence in his greatness. Of course there would always be the danger of disappointing her (and himself), and thus the foundation of his self-worth might collapse, implode into the black hole of his father's disconfirmation.

Thus Wright maintained through dissociative processes split-off self-organizations of a denigrated self on the one hand and a grandiose self on the other. In order to keep these two self-states apart and to avoid the feared disruptive conflict, he needed to succeed, to realize his mother's ambitions and to become in actuality the great man she wanted him to be. Failure was not an option. He also needed the constant admiration and encouragement of those close to him, and he was driven to seek the support of wives and students for this purpose. The need to sustain these fantasies also resulted in financial chaos and debt, as he borrowed profligately from anyone who was available in order to maintain the lifestyle that he felt he, as a great man, deserved.

Wright's grandiose self took the form of fantasies of being the greatest of architects and artists. This self-organization was split off from the more vulnerable and denigrated self which frequently affected his intimate relationships, but regardless of what the personal struggled might have been the pursuit of his ambitions was relentless and his confidence in his artistic self was incredibly resilient. There follows a discussion of the issue of the multiple self and the structuralization of the artistic self within talented personalities.

The psychological functions of the artistic self

A number of analysts (Mitchell, 1993; Bromberg, 1996) have asserted that the concept of a normal unitary self has given way to a more complex model. They argue that people tend to organize themselves around multiple selves, which are structured according to differing needs and contexts. Alan Roland argued that one type of self-organization, the artistic self, is a frequent occurrence "that may exist in a fair number of persons but is only developed in relatively few" (Roland, 2002, p. 30). Roland explained that the successful development of an artistic self depends on a number of factors: parental encouragement, identifications and counter-identifications with a parent who is an artist, inborn aesthetic sensibilities and resonance, as well as talent. These factors draw the person towards the arts but the full potential of the artistic self is only realized within an artistic tradition and culture. Much of the ongoing encouragement and support, according to Roland, comes from idealized figures, mentors or fellow artists – feeling confirmed and validated as an artist and having heroes to model oneself on is important to the elaboration of an artistic self. "When artists have teachers or others who are not attuned to the sensibility of their artistic self, it can be very painful" (Roland, 2002, p. 31). Roland adds that in western societies the artistic self is highly individualized, often alienated from the social group and oriented towards self-promotion.

It was claimed that even when her son was in her womb Frank Lloyd Wright's mother had ambitions that her oldest son was destined to be a great architect. As a girl Anna grew up in the shadows of a male-dominated household. She was encouraged to idealize her overbearing, grandiose father, grandfather and uncles, and the Welsh immigrant story of the family's triumph over persecution and poverty. She herself was neglected; while her older sisters were given an education (they were eventually to become successful school teachers), she was made to work in the home and her view of herself as tainted and flawed was confirmed continually by her second-class role in the family. Hence I believe that Anna's self-injury arose from the convergence of two factors: 1) The strong tendency in the Lloyd Jones family towards self-aggrandizement and idealization of the family; 2) Experience of being treated as unequal to her siblings and relegated to a role as a failed child with little or no potential. Given this it is understandable that she looked to people outside her self who might fulfill her need for affirmation and mirroring. Initially she found this in her relation to the family myth, but later she would turn to her husband (who soon failed her) and then her first-born son (who would ultimately succeed in realizing her dream, albeit in an at times fragile and precarious fashion). Thus Wright's lifelong ambition to be a great architect became permanently structured into the central organizing principles of his self-experience.

As a result of these developmental experiences and the dynamics of his relationship to his mother, Frank Lloyd Wright possessed a narcissistic character structure with specific vulnerabilities that can help us explain the psychological function that he sought from the practice of architecture.

Wright worked hard to create a persona of self-confidence. However, at times he admitted to a depth of despair and struggled which belied his carefully cultivated grandiosity. Meryle Secrest (1992) in her biography of Wright summarizes a letter that the architect wrote to his wife during a period of separation in 1924. In that letter his description of his own character gives startling support to the self-disorder behind his defensively organized grandiose self. Secrest wrote:

> When she had left him in Tokyo, the letter he wrote then gave a vivid description of the ruthless Old Testament conscience lurking behind his apparent veneer of breezy self-confidence. This inner censor weighed his acts and found them wanting; it believed he had "no personal culture"; that he was selfish and made everyone else suffer; that he was self-deceptive; that he would always "slip, slide, and cheat" to escape sensor; that he would not hesitate to "slay or betray or desert"; that he was "crooked"; that he was weak; that he had pet vanities; that he was a hypocrite. This lengthy accounting is further evidence of the insecurity behind the shield that Wright had successfully erected between himself and the world, one that also kept at bay his personal conviction that "this inner chamber I call my heart has been very long neglected – the prospects are not beautiful, the air is not sweet".
>
> (Secrest, 1992, p. 281)

Secrest quotes from an earlier letter that Wright wrote to his mother from Europe, where he had fled in 1910 during the months after his abandonment of his wife and children. The most un-self-aware of men, Wright nonetheless experienced during that time extreme states of self-conflict, depression and self-fragmentation. He wrote:

> I am a house divided against itself by circumstances I can not control... I can face them and down them or go down with them trying to get whole again within – but again is not the word – I have always as you know lived a divided life, but always with a hope – undefined – but a hope. Now I will be without hope.
>
> (quoted in Secrest, 1992, p. 201)

Wright sought to repair these acute states of distress and his ongoing vulnerabilities to self-crisis through his work. In fact, I would argue that the use of artistic creativity to heal the self was a common practice among artists of the modern era given the enormous power they believed art has over self-experience, in particular through the transcendent effect of aesthetic experience.

Modern architecture and modern art: The healing function of aesthetic experience

The notion of aesthetic experience as an individual, even private, psychological state, combined with the ideal of the artist as a type of aesthetic hero, whose ultimate goal is to challenge artistic standards and produce original works of art and fresh aesthetic modes of experience, has resulted in fundamental changes in the function of art in western culture. Most importantly, people have come to view art as an opportunity for transcendent states of mind in which self-experience is heightened and, at least temporarily, enhanced if not restored to a form of perfection. The nature of this perfect self-state is tied to the way in which art and aesthetic experience evokes early relational experiences of child with parent, but we will be discussing that later. For now the important point is that in the modern world art has come to service functions in the individual psychological life which it did not have previously. But what are those functions?

Donald Kuspit (1993) has argued that at the dawn of the twentieth century aesthetics took on a more personal, subjective function than it had for artists of prior generations. For the modern artist the creation of art was therapeutic, according to Kuspit, permitting the alleviation of psychological conflict through the elaboration and resolution of aesthetic problems.

The architect Richard Neutra, a one-time student of Wright's, viewed his own work as quite literally therapeutic comparing the architect's function to that of a therapist:

> The therapeutic "situation" is a creative situation and will one day be physiologically illuminated to show what happens between a patient in general and a therapist. The anticipation of being helped in a need or an aspiration towards satisfaction is physiologically an analogous probably an identical situation. An architect producing by proper rapport with the client's aspirations and expressed or half-expressed need is actually acting very closely to the pattern of procedure of a psychiatrist. His analytical searching and retrospections into infantile precedent, conditions, trauma lead to an understanding, supplementary to empathy which so puzzlingly makes co-creativeness as affective mutual attitude and a dynamic phenomenon of the most eminent social and cultural significance.
>
> (quoted in Lavin, 2004, p. 49)

I think that the best way to use Neutra's quote is by way of comparison and contrast. Wright would have agreed with Neutra's idealization of the psychological significance of architecture. Consistent with his promotion of the total aesthetics of the arts and craft movement, Wright saw his role as the creation of highly structured and aesthetically comprehensive environments in which people would experience strong sensations of aesthetic pleasure and through which certain ideal beliefs in family life would be externalized. In the process the suffering of a disordered self could be corrected simply as a result of living within the perfect environment that the architect had conjured.

However, the biggest difference between Wright and Neutra is in the matter of empathy and the co-creative bond that Neutra refers to. Bloomer and Moore discuss the place of empathy in art and architecture in their discussion of the philosophers Robert Vischer and Theodor Lipps. They wrote:

> The philosopher Robert Vischer, who coined in 1872 the word "empathy" (Einfuhlung), spoke of it as a feeling rather than a process of formal thought. He sensed an almost mystic quality in empathy and spoke of a person forming emotional unions with an external object. Observing that feelings may be aroused by experiencing totally abstract objects (as well as storms, sunsets, and trees), he surmised that we may empathize with objects by projecting our personal emotions into them. (For our purposes the objects would be architectural settings with or without explicit functional or symbolic content.) He suggested in this way that the feelings of the artist while making the work of art could become the work of art. This was an extraordinary thought, for in the context of architecture it implied that feelings of the inner self might be projected in the walls, doorways, and domes of a building. Theodor Lipps, in his *Aesthetics of Space* was to characterize empathy as the objective enjoyment of self; for him positive empathy (beauty) is where the self is encountered in the object, and negative empathy (ugliness) is where the self is repelled.
>
> (Bloomer & Moore, 1977, p. 27)

In agreement with this concept of aesthetic empathy I would add that the feelings that are projected into the artwork by the artist are not just imagined but are in fact physically contained within the design and structure of the thing itself – through affective states evoked by particular formal aspects of the work. In addition, these feelings are not just the common feelings of daily life, they are expressed in perfected and idealized forms through which the artist has externalized the most refined expression of his or her subjectivity. So the empathy which artist and audience experience for the architectural environment is a special, transcendent form of union, a bond of beauty; and the relation between the architect and the client is also structured and affectively charged by this empathic experience. Both seek to bring about a special experience of self that in the best cases results in both parties undergoing a heightened sense of physical, psychological and social well-being.

However, while Neutra's empathy appeared to be similar to the therapist's for his patient, for Wright the bond between client and architect was between audience and performer, subject and king. Although Wright was skillful in using empathy to connect to his clients and gain their support, even alliance, the goal of the empathic tie was always the promotion of

Wright's own need for aggrandizement and self-promotion. His aim was never principally the emotional fulfillment of the client, but the realization of his fantasies of buildings of Wrightian perfection, in which everything would be designed according to fantasies of idealized spaces within which he would be proven to be creatively triumphant. As noted earlier Wright's artistic self could only be confirmed when he experienced total control over the construction of houses that reflected his vision and values, not those of his clients. Even in the matter of influence (perhaps especially in the matter of influence) Wright denied that he had any predecessors or mentors, his creativity being pure and without the taint of derivation or influence.

If Wright's work had a therapeutic function it was in regards to serving compensatory selfobject needs for himself and his clients. For Wright it was about having his grandiosity mirrored and made concretely vivid and real; for his clients it was associated with the ideal selfobject – to be the owner of a home designed and built by the "greatest architect in the world".

But what was it about Wright's homes that created these heightened aesthetic experiences that would become so psychologically powerful both for him and his clients? Are there qualities in his work that we can point to that can be said to be the "active ingredients" of the selfobject functions that Wright's buildings served?

> When we perceive a thing to be beautiful, it is because we instinctively recognize the rightness of the thing. This means that we have revealed to us a glimpse of something essential of the fiber of our own nature. The artist makes this revelation to us through his deeper insight. His power to visualize his conceptions being greater than our own, a flash of truth stimulates us, and we have a vision of harmonies not understood today, though perhaps to be tomorrow.
> (Wright quoted in in Pfeiffer, 1992, p. 104)

Wright's creative ambition was driven not only by his own psychological need for healing but also that of his mother, Anna. This would greatly complicate things for him in his career. Given this idea of the healing function of art, what were the specific injuries that Wright felt needed to be healed? The answer, based on what we know of Wright's developmental history, is the psychological split within his self between the grandiose artistic self which had been promoted and nurtured by his mother, and the depleted, worthless self that had been rejected and abandoned by his father.

In the following section we will examine the specific dimensions of architectural design that I believe are reflected in Wright's work. I will focus on those which I think are relevant to the architect's self-disorder and selfobject needs. In addition, as a result of his associated need for admiration and his drive to actualize his talent in a highly public artistic medium, we will see how his work also offered universally accessible opportunities for selfobject experience to Wright's clients and admirers.

Selfobject dimensions of the house beautiful

> The sense of beauty is the harmony between our nature and our experience. When our senses and imagination find what they crave, when the world so shapes itself or so moulds the mind that the correspondence between them is perfect, then perception is pleasure, and existence needs no apology.
> (Santayana, 1896, p. 269)

> Contrary to the old adage "beauty is but skin deep" true Beauty is always profound because it is integral. Beauty is ever individual because it is of the Soul. Beauty is never superficial – but is a joy that always satisfies the heart, the head, and hands, needing no argument, suffering no apologies: An appeal not to reason, but from Soul to Soul.
> (Wright, 1950, quoted in Pfeiffer, 1992, p. 23)

In one sense Wright was the opposite of the majority of twentieth-century artists in his infatuation with "beauty". One of the defining positions of modern art was the repudiation of beauty and the promotion of disruptive, provocative even ugly aesthetic values (see Lorraine Higgins, *The Modernist Cult of Ugliness*, 2002). But for a modern romantic such as Wright, beauty was the highest aesthetic ideal, the goal to which all great artists and great art aspired. In architecture the sense of beauty was the spiritual manifestation of a building's unity and integrity – the aesthetic dimension of an organic approach to architectural design. However, beyond the formal manifestations of beauty, Wright celebrated beauty as an affective experience and repeatedly noted the powerful integrative effect which it had on the inner life.

Beauty involves powerful affective and self-states which are of a intensely pleasurable and integrative nature. Our relation to beauty is an opportunity for an idealizing selfobject experience. The object is felt to be perfect, unsurpassed, we feel elated and whole in its presence. The sense of beauty stimulates within the viewer a heightened state of perfection arising from the viewer's proximity to the ideal thing. For Wright the most compelling and meaningful manifestations of beauty were found in his experience of nature. His was not a raw and primitive nature, but a landscape structured and organized according to a refined sensibility. This was the source of his organic architecture, a concept of beauty confirmed and supported by the universal principles of the natural world.

Wright's love of beauty and his continual search and longing for beautiful experiences in his daily life arose from the psychological function that the sense of beauty served in the maintenance of his self-experience. Thus for Wright beauty served selfobject functions not only in terms of the availability of the idealized other, but also, importantly, the mirroring provided by the successfully imagined and created artwork. The beauty of his buildings became for Wright confirmation of his greatness. Gone were all the doubts and anxieties connected with those split-off images of a failed and unwanted self – "I am the greatest" he was heard saying to himself as he stood (he thought) alone in his studio at Taliesin. In an earlier book I wrote regarding the importance of beauty for people like Wright:

> The lifelong love of beauty is an indication of the persisting importance of idealization during all phases of development. In this regard it is not primarily defensive. The sense of beauty satisfies a fundamental, healthy human need to be in relation to something or someone that is felt to be ideal. I have coined the term aesthetic resonance for the way in which this self-experience and experience of the object interact in a manner similar to a dialectic (Hagman, 2000). In this sense beauty results from this dialectic between an inner readiness for idealization and the encounter with an object that is "worthy" of the projection. By "worthy" I mean that the object resonates with unconscious, archaic sources, fantasies (memories?) of paradise. But the powerful idealization which is beauty is also fragile, often transitory, and can never be possessed. "Beauty involves a holding fast to what exists only in the slipping away" (Kirwan, 1999, p. 49). The yearning that we experience before beauty is for an experience that is ultimately unattainable, which is already lost, perhaps forever. This is what makes beauty at times unbearable: the simultaneous sense of the Ideal both recovered and lost. Fulfillment and failure, presence and absence intertwined.
>
> (Hagman, 2005, p. 93)

Thus the lover of beauty must repeatedly seek to restore the experience of idealization; it is recovered and lost repeatedly, giving it its addictive quality. For artists of great talent like Wright, the ability to conjure beauty through design and the construction of artworks becomes a compulsion. Wright sought time and again to restore his relationship to the ideal through his own abilities and effort.

I have argued that the successful artistic creative process can serve selfobject functions in and of itself, especially for the artist with talent (Hagman, 2005). Artists seek to externalize aspects of their subjective life, their self-experience, into the external world (in the case of architecture into the environment) by altering it. Then by engaging in dialectic with the now subjectivized environment (the artwork, or the building) a process of refinement characterized by a give and take between fantasy and the now subjectively structured reality takes place. Over time the object becomes increasingly resonant with the inner state of the artist until such time as there is a sense of completeness and resolution. During this process the artist is engaged not just intellectually with the work, but affectively as well. He or she experiences an alternating sense of excitement, crisis, anxiety and finally, hopefully, elation as the relationship between self and object is articulated, perfected and resolved. The driving motivation is the artist's longing for the selfobject experience, the vitalizing, confirming and idealizing self-experience which comes with creative accomplishment.

Wright, who experienced vulnerability in self-organization and the constant risk of self-fragmentation, denigration and depression, was drawn to this creative process because it offered him an opportunity for a powerful selfobject experience. For some artists (such as Henri Matisse) the experience of failure is ongoing and the creative process is rife with anxiety; not so with Wright, whose resilience even in the face of career-destroying failure was remarkable. I believe that a good part of this resilience was in his sense of an internal relationship with a fantasy of beauty, a central organizing principle which he continually nurtured and which sustained him throughout his long life.

Repose: Reconciling maternal and paternal aesthetic form

> The Ideal of beauty is simplicity and repose.
> (Wright, 1986, p. 30)

Throughout his career Wright held firmly to the values and principles of the arts and craft movement, which had been influential throughout Europe and America during the last decades of the nineteenth century. An important component of this aesthetic movement was the aesthetisizing of everyday life. People like William Morris believed that it was possible to alter a person's total environment, make it beautiful, and what would follow would be an emotional and psychological state of mind (of being) characterized by a feeling of peace, harmony and joy. Frank Lloyd Wright referred to this state as one of "repose".

I assume that the state of mind Wright is referring to is an experience of self-cohesion that follows the resolution of some state of internal disorder. Given that Wright's self-experience was grounded in his aesthetic values and experiences, the question for us is: what were the aesthetic conflicts that stirred anxiety in Wright and how were these conflicts reconciled so as to bring about this state of repose?

In my earlier book, *Aesthetic Experience: Beauty, Creativity and the Search for the Ideal* (2005), I explore the relationship between two fundamental aesthetic principles that are derived from the differing modalities of relatedness that characterize the child's relationship to his mother and father. I called these the "maternal aesthetic" and the "paternal aesthetic".

The form of the circle, and its derivatives (curves, arabesques, etc.), best represents the *maternal aesthetic*. In the circle, space is enclosed and bounded by a consistent, clear boundary. Within the circle there is a sense of containment, regulation and completeness. Affective associations are satisfaction, satiation, contentment – quiet states of joy and happiness. The earliest developmental association is with the nursing mother, her arms enclosing the child as both gaze inward at the shared experience of being together.

On the other hand, the aesthetic form of the father, the *paternal aesthetic*, is the straight line that can either be horizontal, vertical or, most significantly, diagonal. In paternal aesthetic forms space is opened up and movement is outward. Expansion and an almost centrifugal force pull the attention and the eye away from any central point. Rather than the containment and holding of maternal aesthetic forms, the paternal lets loose, releases the viewer, and the space of the artwork becomes radically open and expansive. Affectively the paternal aesthetic provokes excitement, disorientation and anxiety. In optimal cases this anxiety is experienced as manageable and non-threatening, but nonetheless exciting, invigorating and disruptive of more comfortable ways of seeing and feeling.

Importantly, Frank Lloyd Wright in the prelude to his autobiography with a memory that illustrates the tension between maternal and paternal aesthetic forms that the young architect experienced. As you will see, the sources of tension that are necessary to aesthetic experience are found in the child's engagement with important family figures. Let me quote at length from this memory of a childhood walk over snowy fields with his Uncle John:

> "Come, my boy," said Uncle John to his sister Anna's nine-year-old. "Come now, and I will show you how to go!"
>
> Taking the boy by the hand he pulled his big hat down over his shock of gray hair and started straight across and up the sloping fields toward a point upon which he had fixed his keen blue eyes.
>
> Neither to the right nor to the left, intent upon his goal, straight forward he walked – possessed.
>
> But soon the boy caught the play of naked weeds against the snow, sharp shadows laced in blue arabesque beneath. Leaving his mitten in the strong grasp, he got free.
>
> He ran first left, to gather beads on stems and then beads and tassels on more stems. Then right, to gather prettier ones. Again – left, to some darker and more brilliant – and beyond to a low-spreading kind. Farther on again to tall golden lines tipped with delicate clusters of bronze heads. Eager, trembling, he ran to and fro behind Uncle John, his arms growing full of "weeds."

A long way up the slope, arrived at that point on which he had fixed, Uncle John turned to look back.

A smile of satisfaction lit the strong Welsh face. His tracks in the snow were straight as any string could be straight.

The boy came up, arms full, face flushed, glowing.

He looked up at his Uncle – see what he had found!

A stern look came down on him. The lesson was to come. Back there was the long, straight, mindful, heedless line Uncle John's own feet had purposefully made. He pointed to it with pride. And there was the wavering, searching, heedful line embroidering the straight one like some free, engaging vine as it ran back and forth across it. He pointed to that too – with gentle reproof.

Both stood looking back. The small hand with half-frozen fingers was again in its mitten in the older, stronger hand; an indulgent, benevolent smile down now on the shamed young face.

And, somehow, there was something . . . not clear.

Uncle John's meaning was plain – NEITHER TO RIGHT NOR TO LEFT, BUT STRAIGHT, IS THE WAY.

The boy looked at his treasure and then at Uncle John's pride, comprehending more than Uncle John meant he should.

The boy was troubled. Uncle John had left out something that made all the difference.

(Wright, 1943, pp. 3–4)

Being the "prelude" to the story of his life this anecdote takes on extraordinary significance. It conveys in dramatic form a prototypical early life experience that represents Wright's essential psychological, relational and aesthetic dilemma. Uncle John, the mother's brother, and the other architect in the family, demonstrates the preferred approach to the world that characterized the history of the Lloyd Jones family (the maternal family). In that family a masculine orientation to life dominated, represented by the forward-moving, undeviating, straight-line approach. Wright, a nine-year old, and thus relatively mature and knowing, chooses to deviate from the uncle's footsteps, following a very different trajectory, characterized by loops and arabesques, as his attention darts here and there, searching for treasures (weeds) half-hidden in the snow. It is important that Wright chose to describe this interaction across a canvass of snow, on which the movements of the pair are traced, as if in an etching. This is how Wright calls attention to the fundamental aesthetic difference between the two and sets up the basic creative opportunity that he will pursue in his life story, meaning to describe that "something that made all the difference" between the curving, inward focused aesthetic (maternal) and the straight, outwardly thrusting aesthetic (paternal).

It is important to discuss the difficult affective and psychological dimensions of this memory. The Uncle, although in the end kindly, appears like a stern and expectant judge. He is teaching the young Wright a lesson as to "how to go": "neither to right nor to left, but straight is the way." Wright rebels and sets off on his own course, ignoring the uncle, and the consequence is reproof and "shame". Thus this is no neutral memory but a highly conflicted one in which the tension between stern parent and rebellious child is conveyed. Most importantly, the failure of the uncle to mirror the young boy's aesthetic, the "spontaneous gesture" to use Winnicott's term, results in selfobject failure and shame. Thus the psychological task is set: Wright must neither capitulate nor adapt to the uncle's world, nor could he just continue to pursue his own open self-expression, rather he must find another "way to go". In the meantime the boy's (and the man's) self-state is precarious. He must live between shameful empathic failure and potential disintegrative isolation. Wright used his creative life in an effort to cure this painful self-state and reconcile the dissonant aesthetic.

Wright found the "something" in his lifework as a creative artist and architect; and the "difference" would come with the possibility of "integration". The image of the circle within a square was the symbol that Wright used to represent his architectural practice (later, after 1910, he would modify this shape by blanking out its content with a field of red color). As can bee seen the symbol is a perfect expression both of the maternal and paternal aesthetic – the circle and straight line – but also the containment of both, existing one upon the other, within the limiting space defined by the square.

The symbol expressed the "something else that made all of the difference" that is the individual creative power of the artist to bring disparate and perhaps conflicting elements of aesthetic (and psychological) form and integrate them within a unified and harmonious structure. The emotional and spiritual result of such a successful integration is what Wright calls "repose."

It is important to note that simultaneously with his search for repose, Wright also cultivated a state of aesthetic tension. This tension was essential to Wright holding interest and stimulating the viewer's affects. He brings together the paternal and maternal but then never fully reconciles them; or rather the reconciliation nonetheless preserves the tension between the two, as the building seems to be suspended between containment and disintegration. A good example of this is the Robie House. Viewing the house from the street it appears to rise out of the ground and the straight lines of the road seem to break free from the house and risk escaping into space. Nonetheless there is a sense of integration of the forms, a solid, grounded sense that all parts of the house's structure are connected and firmly rooted in the earth. This sense of simultaneously flying and holding creates in the viewer a sense of fascination and excitement, and in the end a state of acceptance and resonance, repose that is typical of the enjoyment of great works of art. In the end we remain interested because the tension is never resolved, but is suspended within our selves, both stirring and calming us at once.

We can also see Wright's efforts to reconcile the maternal and paternal aesthetics in the designs of many of his other buildings, specifically the floor plans for many of the private homes that he built before 1910. In these the house pivots around a fireplace which forms the center of a cross, or a square arrangement of rooms. Within this design Wright merges a circular structure as the corridors and rooms revolve around the fireplace axis, while at the same time the ceilings and roof lines thrust outward, often breaking the edge of the square and protruding into the space around the house.

Another approach that Wright took was the use of horizontal, vertical and diagonal lines. Horizontal lines – such as in the exterior of the Robie House – since they parallel the ground are experienced as anchoring the form of the house. This is one way in which Wright links his structures firmly into the landscape. Horizontality limits the thrust of the line and holds its potential, restraining the paternal aspect by grounding the form in the plane of the earth. Wright's use of vertical lines is very different, as is most apparent in the Unity Temple design. Here the paternal aesthetic is fully expressed and restrained only by the surrounding cube of the temple interior; but within that interior space Wright allows the straight vertical line to dominate, at the same time held within a maternally organized architectural vessel. In the case of diagonal lines, Wright rarely used them as a structural form in his early homes, but you can see his play with diagonals in the stained glass windows and other interior decorative designs. I feel that this early restraint with diagonals is understandable given the disruptive power of that type of line. Diagonals reflect the paternal aesthetic in its most expressive form and are the least able to be modulated and contained by maternal forms such as the circle, square or horizontal line. Later examples of the free use of the diagonal can be seen in his Synagogue, and finally in the Guggenheim Museum where there is a perfect balance between the circular form and the overall diagonal thrust of the ziggurat shape of the building.

Architecture and the body

As we have seen, the experience of being in a building brings a sense of movement and boundary. In effect the most vital sense of self, that of being physically present in the moment, is at the heart of Wright's aesthetic. Bloomer and Moore in their book *Body, Memory, and Architecture* (1977) discuss the relation between our bodies, the environment and self-experience:

> The most fundamental organizing principle in the formation of our body image is that we unconsciously locate our bodies inside a three-

dimensional boundary. This boundary surrounds the entire body and demarcates our "inside" personal space from our "outside" extra personal space. It is an unstable boundary subject to events both inside and outside the boundary. It may be regarded as an extension of the body in the form of an imaginary envelope which modifies our perception of the forces affecting us by magnifying or suppressing the psychological effect of those forces.

(Bloomer & Moore, 1977, p. 38)

With architecture there is a powerful relationship between these experiences of body and self and the designed world about us in our buildings. Bloomer and Moore explain:

Our movements are ever subject to the same physical forces as are built forms and may be physically contained, limited and directed by these forms. Inevitably they are more intricately entwined with and dependent upon architecture than are the sound and notation expressions of conversation, song, music and writing.

(Bloomer & Moore, 1977, p. 42)

I believe that the aesthetic principles at the heart of Wright's architecture are the elaboration in physical space of the earliest modalities of self-experience and self-in-relation. The terms that I believe best characterize this physical relation to space are "holding and release" or "refuge and prospect".

Philosophers who study evolutionary aesthetics have argued that certain common features of the human enjoyment of art have their source in early experiences of danger, survival and adaptation. For example, throughout history architects have played with the relationship between the protective function of architecture, its function as a refuge, and the need to survey the surrounding landscape for danger or game. Thus we see structures that, as you move through them, create in some places experiences of closeness, seclusion and comfort (a private bedroom or bathroom, a study) and in others place openness, exposure and excitement (a balcony, a lofty hall, a grand foyer). Unlike in painting where the formal elements are visual, or music where they are aural, in architecture the aesthetics of refuge and prospect involve multiple dimensions of sensation. The proximity of wall or ceiling to your body. The changing quality and intensity of light. The muffled or open quality of sound. The feeling of temperature and air on the skin. These all play a part in creating feelings of refuge (holding) and prospect (release). The best designs move us between and among these different settings and with each encounter we experience a different affective state, a different self-state.

I believe that in addition to these evolutionary sources these experiences of refuge and prospect also recreate early relational experiences of engagement with the parent, and by extension the world. The holding of a child by the mother or father in the circle of his or her attention and the firmness of their arms is the developmental source of refuge. A child being held aloft, or swung around the parent like a carousel, or tumbled on the bed is the developmental source of prospect. Both are necessary and both are related. To be held and at the same time allowed to survey the surrounding world. To feel the strong grip of the parent as you are held aloft over the beach, suddenly thrilled by the view. These differing but related aesthetic states once again can be characterized as maternal (refuge) and paternal (prospect) and the artist's ability to express the various dimensions of these experiences in their artwork becomes the source of his or her inspiration and our enjoyment.

Consistent with what we have said so far about the function architecture served in defending and enhancing Wright's dissociative self-structure, he integrated into his architectural designs exquisitely orchestrated arrangements of space which, as a person moved through the house, blended the experience of refuge and prospect into a dazzling, harmonious whole. We feel safe and comforted but also aroused, excited and provoked. Thus Wright brings together these seemingly disparate and even conflictual elements into a unified aesthetic experience.

Order and complexity

Although Wright sought to create in his work a sense of simplicity and unity, and despite the fact that he wished to stimulate a sense of emotional repose, his aim was to do more than that. Wright didn't want to just lull people into aesthetic somnolence, far from it, he wished to thrill and excite, to challenge us with an experience so remarkable that we would never forget him. One way he did this was to embody in his buildings a state of tension between order on the one hand and a dazzling complexity on the other.

> Harmony is grace; not many things, but picturesque things. The ideals of beauty are found in the simple, restful things far oftener than in ornate things. Of two given forms for the same article – a chair, a table, a dress – the form that is least ornate is commonly the more useful, and this more useful form will commonly be the artist's eye be found the handsomer.
>
> (Wright, 1986, p. 29)

The experience of being engaged with a parent (caretaker) involves the need for consistency, familiarity and predictability ("I know you. You know me") as well as variety, surprise and mystery. These complementary experiences allow us to feel held and understood by the reliable parent, but also able to recognize and deal with changes within the parent and to respond to those changes. The most important instances of this are being able to depend on typical affect states but also to respond to new affects and self-states in the parent. These different experiences help the child in their sense of security in the world but also prepare them for the changing nature of the world and help them learn to respond to the unpredictable and mysterious events that occur in life.

The affective experiences of order and complexity are important to note. We respond to the perception of order with calmness, reassurance and a sense of resonance. Faced with complexity we are excited, perhaps somewhat anxious, and we may feel dissonant, out of sync. However, we are also challenged by complexity, and we may withdraw from the experience or seek meaning and thus order from the complexity. Part of what drives us is the tension of our own affects and the accompanying self-state. We seek some resolution, a sense of resonance with the object(s), hence we move from an internal sense of self-disorder to one of self-order. Of course complexity is usually ordered, but that order may not be known to us at first, so we may just come to see the once hidden order for what it is. Thus the child also moves from states of calm reassurance at the sight of the familiar parent to excitement and/or distress at a new complex expression or strange interaction, and he or she seeks to engage the parent and restore a sense of order and dependability. That being said, order can be boring and distressing in its own way, and the child (and parent) may seek complexity for the excitement and disruption it can create. So the relation between the two in development is not so simple or one-sided.

One of the important functions of art and especially of aesthetic experience is to embody the relationship between order and complexity, creating opportunities for self-crisis and restoration by means of the aesthetic experience of the artwork. This I see as one of the tensions between the maternal and paternal dimensions of aesthetic experience. In all art, and especially in great artworks, the conjuring of order and the disruptive, exciting power of complexity are placed into relation for the viewer to engage and respond to creatively.

Wright was a master at the orchestration of order and complexity; in fact, I see his handling of this relation as the defining quality of his greatness.

Joy

In closing I would like to consider the question of why Frank Lloyd Wright was as influential as he was. His international style was more consistently influential, as the architecture of modern urban buildings attests, but there was something about Wright and his work that was profoundly different.

I believe that it is the joy of architecture that Wright consistently captures. His buildings are exuberant and expressive. There is also a sense of fun. Wright enjoyed his performance as a provocateur and rebel genius. He was flamboyant and dramatic, and he used his art to externalize a fantasy of exuberance and ambition that, with his talent, he was able to convey with such consistence and success that his work was irresistible.

Wright is an example of a resilient and successful narcissist. He was able despite all his anxieties and inner torments to consistently hold within himself durable fantasies of grandiosity and he was able and willing to access whatever resources there were available outside of him to shore up and actualize these self states. In the end I believe it was his talent which saved him as it allowed him to transform archaic fantasy into an enduring American myth.

Chapter 12

Jackson Pollock: An American's triumph and the death of modernism

In the decade after the end of the Second World War, the center of the western art world shifted from Paris to New York City. Many of the artists who fled to the United States brought along with them the innovations and controversies over which they had argued and competed in the prior decades. Of course, the most important issue was the nature of modern art and the role of the artist in the modern world. This was particularly important given the catastrophe which had befallen art under the Nazis, but there was also the impact of an emerging global economy, the cultural ambitions of New York and Americans in general, and the need for the displaced artists to make a place for themselves (as well as a living). American artists such as Jackson Pollock, Willem de Kooning and Mark Rothko among many others had been struggling for years to find their vision, style and place in the avant-garde. In the midst of the Great Depression, with little work and virtually no viable art market, American artists had been gathering for years to discuss and argue about what they understood of the European modern artists and as a group their ambitions were at a fever pitch when many of their heroes began to flee the war, settling in a metropolitan area where culture and art were not as foreign as in the rest of the New World. One of these artists, Jackson Pollock, after many years of poverty, alcoholism, frustration and failure, was ready to make a surprising and fantastically influential next step in modern painting.

In this chapter we will examine the life and art of Jackson Pollock, the American abstract expressionist painter. In discussing Pollock what we will see is how the modernist emphasis on art as a product of individual psychological processes, relentlessly seeking new innovative forms of art and aesthetic experience, would hit a brick wall. Repudiating culture and isolating himself from the creative partnership of fellow artists, Jackson Pollock attempted to wrest a whole new art form out of his own tortured, fragile and ultimately barren inner life. His initial dramatic and aesthetically innovative paintings, characterized by flamboyant colors, richly textured application of paint and reliance on broad gesture and expressiveness (he flung or dripped his paint in his best work), captured the imagination of the art world, the media, and the American public. But, as we will see, pure self-expression, as evidenced by Pollock's desperate need to be recognized without any taint of influence, led to creative catastrophe as he increasingly, desperately failed to find inspiration or aesthetic vision within the limits of his disordered mind.

Jackson Pollock's life and art

Jackson Pollock was born in Cody, Wyoming on 28 January 1912, the fourth and last child of Roy and Stella Pollock (biographical information about Jackson Pollock is from *Jackson Pollock: An American Saga*, Naifeh & Smith, 1989). He grew up in Arizona and California. His father, an unsuccessful business owner and sometime farmer, experienced repeated financial crises, partially driven by his wife's excessive tastes and unrealistic view of the family's, and especially her own, social prospects. Roy Pollock was, for the time he was with the family, a caring but preoccupied father, always playing second fiddle to his narcissistic and nagging wife. Eventually resentful and demoralized he left the family while they were in California, and although he continued to have periodic contact with his children, essentially abandoned them to his dominating and self-centered spouse.

Pollock was an attractive and lively child, and as an infant his mother treated him as exceptional, seemingly having sown the seeds for his later precarious grandiosity. However, over time she became both overly protective and also neglectful of Pollock (and to an extent his brothers). Pollock remained a needy and insecure boy, bound to his mother, repeatedly seeking soothing and reassurance from her when he suffered from his many phobias and fears. Her response was detachment and emotional reticence. Pollock would come to believe (a belief that would be a central organizing fantasy of his adult life) that he had failed her.

Stella was a bright, ambitious and aesthetically sensitive woman. Despite the obvious limitations of her financial resources and prospects, she invested in nice homes, decorating them extravagantly and sinking into debt with little regard for the consequences. The result was constant anxiety about money, declining social status and a reactive intensification of her self-regard and fantastic sense of her importance in the social world. She neglected her children, who found little emotional nurturance in her mothering, especially her young baby son Jackson, who was often cared for by his siblings and whose immaturity and neediness were interpreted as defects. This led to low expectations from his family, all of whom, as he grew up, would view him as a partially disabled kid in need of constant support and supervision. Nonetheless, throughout his life Pollock would crave contact with his mother, especially at times of breakdown and crisis, when she would be called in to attempt to provide a fix for his troubled psyche. In her presence, without any direct interaction with her, Pollock would be soothed, even in the midst of his worst disordered rages. She would, however, continue to be unreliable, distant and ultimately unengaged with her youngest son. Later, after becoming a national celebrity, he would continually seek her approval for his success, but she seemed indifferent and uncomprehending. The emotional oases of her visits would be surrounded by drunkenness, violence and rage.

Obviously, the seeds of Pollock's adult personality can be seen in these early years: his father's failure to provide an adequate model of success and availability, so that his son might organize and elaborate a healthy idealization of the "old man" that might serve an internal structure to be identified with and from which strength might be drawn; his mother's emotional unavailability and narcissism, with the resulting failure to recognize and mirror the young boy, leading to his lifelong longing (craving) for her attention and admiration. In the end Pollock was unable to organize a stable and secure sense of self. Prone to states of depletion or self-fragmentation throughout his life, he lacked the capacity to self-regulate and care for himself. His self-cohesion, always precarious, would collapse under stress or in response to frustration, and the resulting narcissistic rage (fed by alcohol) would consume his entire world. He would always be a man starving for nurturance but unable to take it in when others offered it or to believe in them, or himself.

Heinz Kohut talked of the selfobject function of the social milieu as providing psychological oxygen to the self. In the Pollock household the oxygen of self-sustenance was all used up in Stella's hungry search for self-aggrandizement and social success. As she slipped ever further down the social ladder, she consumed more and more of the psychological resources that might have sustained and nurtured her children. By the time Jackson came along, there was virtually nothing left to do but attempt in fantasy to latch on to her bloated and precarious personality, hoping to extract some middling of nurturance or attention. Unfortunately for Jackson, he got little but indifference or ambivalence from her. As he approached maturity it became clearer that he was a failed and self-disordered person, unable to be alone, drinking too much, undisciplined and with a tendency to latch on to other people who might comfort him and take care of him. As a young man he found this comfort and caretaking from his brother, Sande.

Throughout his youth and young manhood, Pollock's psychological survival depended on his relationship with his siblings, especially his oldest brothers, both of whom entered art school and developed ambitions to succeed in the mother's largely fantastic world of the arts and culture. Pollock, a poor student with no obvious talent for the arts, imitated the older boys and eventually, after some time in an art program in Los Angeles, moved to New York City to pursue further training and, he hoped, eventual success as an artist.

In New York he attended the Art Students League, where he came under the wing of Thomas Hart Benton, a successful career artist, well known for his classically mannered regional art, which combined a mythical rural American iconography with a classical aesthetic style more characteristic of European seventeenth-century landscapes. Benton was an extremely narcissistic and misogynistic man with a big personality and a dominating and arrogant manner of relating to students and colleagues. Pollock's admiration suited the older artist and for the next few years Pollock was one of Benton's most loyal students. However, the younger artist would continually struggle with his inability to meet the strict formal standards and structured working methods of his mentor.

Benton was a methodical and fairly traditional painter. Despite the importance of gesture and movement in his paintings, he approached his work methodically, planning each composition, laying out the plan on the canvas and carefully constructing each painting in a grueling, disciplined manner. This approach to creative work was not in keeping with Pollock's emotional and physical make-up. Emotionally fragile and prone to affective disregulation, Pollock couldn't sit still unless he was sufficiently drunk. He radiated physical restlessness, and at times he could be violent.

In addition Benton's idealization of classical standards of beauty and aesthetic form filled Pollock with ambivalence, leading to virtual paralysis at times. His draftsmanship was crude and uncertain, his style cramped, rough, even ugly. Although Pollock admired Benton's work, confidence and ambition, the beauty and balance of the older man's work crippled Pollock's own aesthetic sensibility. This led to years of fumbling and searching, his work and career undeveloped, and as he got older the threat of failure was real and palpable to the increasingly desperate young painter.

What was the cause of Pollock's inhibition of talent during the first 20 years of his career as an artist? I believe that it was the specific demands of the maternal aesthetic, which confined his talent but in addition posed aesthetic demands which came up against inhibitions and anxieties associated with intimacy and probably merger with his mother. The demand for balance and classical formal elements such as line, tone and color relations, which he felt he needed to comply with according to classical standards of beauty, resonated unconsciously with archaic longings and fears associated with his early abandonment by his mother, whose narcissism precluded concern for and love for her youngest son.

Hence for the first 20 years of his career Jackson Pollock was a moderately talented albeit ambitious painter with little in the way of reputation or prospects. He was to be saved by a confluence of developments in the art world of New York City and his personal life.

With the exception of his later artistic success, Jackson Pollock's life was a relentless series of crises and experiences of failure. Unable to function on his own for much of his early adult life he was protected by and cared for by his brother, Sande. Pollock was tormented by anxiety and self-doubt. He hated himself and feared that he was a fraud. Unable to relax socially he was often insulting and sometimes violent with women. His sexuality was guilt-ridden and confused, and he was unable to actualize his desire for sex and intimacy. Alcohol was his primary tool to manage and regulate himself, but the result was usually chaos and destruction. Most likely Pollock suffered from Borderline Personality Disorder complicated by a mood disorder and alcoholism.

The impact of Pollock's mental illness on his career was substantial. He agonized over his work filled with self-doubt and self-loathing. He was often inhibited, unable to focus on his work due to either depression, drunkenness or withdrawal. When given the most important commission of his life, a mural for the foyer of Peggy Guggenheim's home, he procrastinated for months until the pressure of the deadline compelled him to break through his inhibition and create the first truly innovative painting of his career. His ability to sustain and build his career was badly crippled by his fragility, periodic alcoholic psychosis and inability to discipline himself. Most likely he would have died a failed drunk, if not for the help of his future wife and his analyst.

When Pollock was 39 years old, he met and married Lee Krasner, a talented young artist who immediately recognized Pollock's talent. She took over the caretaking of Pollock from his brother and would eventually provide structure and soothing support, allowing him some years of relative emotional stability, sobriety, and physical and emotional nurturance. Pollock came to depend on Krasner and despite his sometimes violent rages and fantastic drunken bingeing, he gradually came to accept her help and love. Eventually they moved to the relative seclusion of Suffolk County, where, under her watchful eye, in a ramshackle shed as a studio, he created some of his most important and innovative work.

Pollock also entered psychoanalysis with a Jungian therapist named Dr. Joseph Henderson, who attempted to harness Pollock's art in the exploration of the unconscious sources of his mental illness and alcoholism. The analyst encouraged Pollock to abandon objective subject matter and controlled artistic methods for a spontaneous and subjective approach. A movement towards an automatic approach allowed Pollock to shed his inhibitions and express his unconscious directly through paint. Naifeh and Smith describe the impact of Pollock's analysis on his art:

> Jackson succeeded in transforming psychological insights into artistic breakthroughs. He began to experiment with lighter strokes, more playful images, and more open compositions. Jackson began to drop the old search for the "correct" line, the representative line, the line that Charles (his older brother) could draw and he (Pollock) never could, and turned his struggle inward to discover the "right" line, the line unrelated to the outer world but perfectly expressive of the inner one.
> (Naifeh & Smith, 1989, p. 336)

Henderson encouraged Pollock to utilize Jungian imagery and forms from Native American artists. Although this approach was clearly derivative it freed Pollock from his part training and, as the images penetrated his own fantasy life, the impact on his art was to free his imagination and to create more affectively powerful paintings and drawings.

In addition the local culture of the art community changed. The war in Europe brought a flood of new artists and critics into the city. Most importantly, the surrealist artists brought with them a fascination with the unconscious and with spontaneity.

Finally, Pollock developed a relationship with the influential and ambitious critic Clement Greenberg. Greenberg had been promoting a new theory of modernism in which he argued that the progress of art history had led inevitably to the reduction of painting to its essence: paint spread over a two-dimensional canvas. Freed of the illusions and constrictions of perspective and realism, modern artists express themselves directly though the unambiguous and concrete nature of their mediums. Greenberg recognized in Pollock the potential for the realization of his vision of art (and the fulfillment of his ambitions as a major art critic). He encouraged Pollock to see the canvas as flat, to abandon imagery and depiction. With Greenberg's support Pollock began to roll out his canvases on the floor, creating large, unstructured surfaces. He bought buckets of paints and began to throw and drip the paint, making large motions, casting the liquid paint through the air. Pollock was the first western artist to embrace spontaneous gestures, full body motion and chance as part of his creative process. Naifeh and Smith described this breakthrough in their biography:

> The final breakthrough came when the long line of imagery leapt off the surface entirely and Jackson began to work in the air about the canvas, tracing the unwinding images in three-dimensional space. "Jackson told me that he wasn't just throwing the paint," recalls Nick Carone, "he was delineating some object, some real thing, from a distance above the canvas." Lee called it "working in the air," recreating "aerial forms which then landed". "Another eyewitness described how Jackson would "take his stick or brush out of the paint can and then, in a cursive sweep, pass it over the canvass high above it, so that the viscous paint would form trailing patterns which hover over the canvas before they settle upon it, and then fall into it and then leave a trace of their own passage. He is not drawing on the canvas so much as in the air above it." Jackson called his new images "memories arrested in space".
> (Naifeh & Smith, 1989, p. 540)

Pollock's transition to his mature artistic methods and aesthetic form, in particular the dripped or poured paintings that dominated his work after 1947, has its source in the long standing tensions he experienced as he struggled to fulfill the classical demands of his teachers. In fact, he was always drawn to the less formal, more expressive elements in Benton as well as Albert Pinkham Ryder.

The fact is that Pollock's aesthetic innovations, which resulted in the most individual and aesthetically innovative artworks in the history of western civilization, had their roots in many cultural and historical sources. Although our emphasis in this chapter is the inner sources of Pollock's innovations, the reality is that Pollock derived his new approach from many influences. That being said, the result was an extreme emphasis on spontaneous creation out of individual subjectivity. The question for us to consider is how Pollock's personal psychology, developmental experiences and resulting self organization resonated with the culture in which he lived, thus leading to the specific form of art he created. Pollock's work was both the outcome of an art historical process and a powerful influence on the course of that history. Based on what we know about Pollock's life and adult personality, how can we better understand the connections and outcomes?

In discussing the connection between Pollock's psychological life and his artistic innovations I will focus on two of the most important innovations. First his adoption of a new means of painting, specifically and most importantly the way in which he developed an action-based, spontaneous method of self-expression. This approach restructured the traditional notion of the creative process, removing much of the planning and contemplation. This method advanced the modernist artistic program towards a pure method of self-expression, allowing for individual artists such as Pollock to engage the artwork in an unmediated fashion, free of the influence of other relationships and of culture. In this way individual subjectivity, the most adaptable and responsive level of subjective life, was given free rein to innovate and create. Second, his cultivation of the sublime aesthetic in which chaos and power were channeled into the artwork. In particular, Pollock offered an alternative to beauty in art, offering the first modern alternative to classical standards. The promotion of the Sublime would dominate the aesthetics of Pollock and the abstract expressionists as a group. Finally, I intend to show how Pollock's innovations in these two areas contributed to the creation of a dead end for modernism; both action painting and the privileging of the Sublime would result in repetition and aesthetic depletion leading newer generations to turn their backs entirely on the modernist project in search for an alternative.

Pollock's innovations of the creative process

Let us begin by closely examining what we know about Pollock's way of working. Pollock lay his canvas out on the floor, cleared space around the sides so he could lean out over the painting and, using his entire body, he flung and dripped paint in cascading, intertwining network of ribbons and splashes of color. Here was the first important innovation: rather than mounting the canvas Pollock lay it horizontally, thus setting up a situation where gravity would play a much more central role in the process. Leaning out over the canvass resulted in dripping and pouring, so Pollock had to develop a style which took advantage of gravity and manipulated the paint's fall through more open gestures. Full control was not possible so Pollock worked with gravity and flung the paint out over the canvas. He did in fact control these gestures but out of necessity he had to be more immediate and less concerned with the plan and structure of the work. In addition, Pollock's point about drawing in the air was also important. He was literally painting in the potential space, both psychologically and concretely. The gesture in the air above the canvas was the space in which he worked, where spontaneity, feeling and gesture were allowed free expression. The painting was the residue of these actions but not equivalent to them. Thus he rarely engaged the artwork directly and so was free of constraint even from it. The making of these pictures was an act of aggression and a beautiful dance. These were both savage colorful assaults and graceful arabesques. As you watch Pollock paint he is perfectly in sync, it is like a musical performance using ribbons of color instead of music.

> When I am *in* my painting, I'm not aware of what I am doing. It is only after a sort of "get acquainted" period that I see what I have been about. I have no fears about making changes, destroying the image etc., because the painting has a life of its own. I try to let it come through. It is only when I lose contact with the painting that the result is a mess. Otherwise there is pure harmony, an easy give and take, and the painting comes out well.
>
> (Pollock, quoted in Karmel, 1999, p. 18)

In this quote Pollock describes a new relationship between an artist and his artwork. Although Pollock states that as he paints he is "not aware", if you look closely at the films of him working he is obviously keenly observant and although he works quickly, he is assessing and responding to the work as he proceeds. Although he may not be "aware" of the overall pattern or logic of the piece, he is clearly thinking through each pour and splash. In fact he seems to be feeling his way, observing, assessing, feeling and then acting as he constructs the artwork. In another quote Pollock compares his approach to painting to drawing:

> I approach painting in the same sense as one approaches drawing; that is, it's direct. I don't work from drawings, I don't make sketches and drawings and color sketches into a finished painting. Painting I think today – the more immediate, the more direct – the greater the possibilities of making a direct – of making a statement.
>
> (Pollock, quoted in Karmel, 1999, p. 22)

I think that Pollock was contrasting his approach with an artist like Benton, who was highly aware of the planned result long before the first brush touched canvas. However, to say that Pollock's approach was unconscious or irrational would be incorrect. Pollock was always in close interaction with the artwork as it was developing. But for him the work is always full of surprises, as the overall complexity of the painting emerges. The critical organizing function of the artistic self, the judging and planning part, may be unaware but the artist's keen intelligence and the attuned, affective engagement with the painting are very much involved.

These innovations allowed Pollock to circumvent many of the inhibitions with which he had struggled for years, and in addition they allowed certain strengths and talents which he brought to his art to be accentuated and their effect strengthened. In particular, Pollock was always fearful of periods (however brief) during the creative process in which he was not engaged with the artwork. In planning to begin a piece of work, or in moments of contemplation when he stepped back to "get acquainted" with the work, at these times his doubts could be crippling and his own assessment of the quality of the object could be withering. Paralysis frequently followed. However, with his gesture paintings he could re-engage the painting immediately "without memory or desire" (Bion, 1967, pp. 143–145). Then he could once again follow the spontaneous rhythm of the flying ribbons of paint and the bright, surprising splattering across the canvas.

The other advantage of this approach was that it allowed Pollock to engage the work with his whole body, rather than the cramped fumbling of his fingers and hands. Always recognized for his physicality, energy and almost animal-like presence, Pollock was able to interact with the canvass with his whole body – and this appeared to be an enlivening and relaxing experience for him. He could thereby respond to the work as it emerged beneath him, and he could react to each creative event immediately and with his entire being – mind and body were united as he worked. During these times of creative engrossment he could be happy, even elated. His artistic self was cohesive, vital and continuous and as a result his damaged self was restored – for a time.

A paternal aesthetic: Pollock's search for the Sublime

Pollock's most important aesthetic innovation was the overall, massive presence of many of his greatest works. He eliminated representation and all clear, formal organization in his paintings. This made him different from the abstract painters who had come before him, who organized their paintings around certain structures that highlighted and played on the relationships between certain dominant and ancillary forms. If Pollock's paintings had a structure it was spread out over the surface of the work, a unified field in which every inch seemed to contain the same tensions at the same time as the separate parts came together to create the complete, consistent effect of the whole. In this way his best paintings were both chaotic and lyrical at the same time. They conveyed energy, power and raw physical presence. The effect on the viewer was to create an aesthetic experience of intense, overwhelming beauty – of the Sublime.

Earlier we discussed the difference between the maternal and paternal dimensions of aesthetic experience. The maternal aesthetic is what we traditionally think of as beauty. The quality of formal balance, pleasing rhythm and harmony found in beautiful artworks resonates with our unconscious memory (or fantasy) of perfect attunement with mother. Beauty is about the ideal relationship and the vitality that comes with the experience of a perfect fit, of safety and joy. It evokes a sense of wholeness, rightness and the balance that comes with understanding and even love.

The paternal aesthetic reflects dynamic and multiple sets of representations that are organized around the child's experience of the father. It is what we have come to call the Sublime. The nature of the paternal aesthetic is a quality of formlessness, of vastness, of open space, rather than rounded or enclosed space. It is about movement and power. The paternal aesthetic rather than pleasing and reassuring provokes wonder, awe, even fear. As I noted in an earlier work:

> The Paternal Aesthetic found in sublime experience gratifies both the desire and the motivation to seek out the new and different and creates the opportunity for us to investigate and discover the world. Our sense of vigor and curiosity intensifies, and the inherent drive to individual and separate becomes united with the curiosity about the world around us.
>
> (Hagman, 2005, p. 132)

Hence for Pollock his immersion in the Sublime (the paternal aesthetic) offered opportunities for individuation and empowered his self-experience to express and actualize his ambitions. On the other hand he was stifled by beauty. For most of his early career he struggled to find balance, to achieve purity in his line, or to live up to the high standards of classical beauty promoted by mentors such as Benton. The qualities of the maternal aesthetic, associated as they were with his tormented attachment to his mother, were crushing to Pollock; the expectations, needs and judgments that accompanied his attempts to create "beautiful" works doomed him from the start. It was only when Pollock discovered how to move beyond beauty, to create an art of power and chaos, of formlessness and violence, that he was able to transcend the inner constrictions of the maternal and finally be free to create. Naifeh and Smith describe how this new aesthetic approach was the perfect antidote to the uncertainty, self-consciousness and impotence with which Pollock struggled all his life. In this new style Pollock found a successful identification with his lost father, distancing himself from the constriction and oppression of his mother's aesthetic. They write:

> The new technique changed all that. It took him away from the canvas – where Stella did her close work – and back to the upright position from which Roy Pollock did his manly work, from his mother's tight wrist movements, to his father's broad arm gestures. Standing over the canvas, flinging a stream of paint from the end of a stick, Jackson found the potency that had eluded him in real life.
> (Naifeh & Smith, 1989, p. 541)

Of course to simply express or represent these forces and elements would be overwhelming and would not have artistic merit, so the artist must capture the paternal aesthetic and give it form, structure and organization – even while fully expressing the wild and thrilling quality that is at the heart of the paternal aesthetic experience.

One of the problems with an art of chaos and formlessness is what you do afterwards. What is the next step in such a project? This is, as we will see, the looming obstacle in Pollock's work. Having freed himself from the checks and balances of traditional creativity, and having surmounted the restrictions of traditional standards of beauty, form and aesthetic value, what then? Having brought the modernist project to its logical and inevitable conclusion, there was really nothing left for Pollock to do. He would attempt to replicate his drip paintings time and again, and for a time he returned to representation, but he could never find anything beyond his modernist triumphs – he and modernist were finished.

Conclusion

In Pollock's action paintings modernist aesthetics came to its highest point. Unconstrained by the past, fully in tune with the subjective, his art immediately intelligible for what it was, this modern artist had broken free from western history, creating an art so dependent on his self that each painting was of necessity fully original and without precedent. This would lead to the ultimate crisis for Pollock (and for modern art as a whole). If the artist is going to maintain complete originality, then he or she must also find a way to be free of self-influence and self-imitation, especially if one is a success; the fear is that one will be accused of repeating oneself, at the urging of the public hungry for more of the same. And the reaction of Pollock's audience and the art world was understandably complex: fear, anger, devaluation and dissociation.

The personal sources of Pollock's aesthetic achievement were in the internal relationship between intense longings for his mother (and by extension family), anxiety about the psychological danger posed by those needs, and his hunger for merger with a paternal figure who was inevitably always distant, unreachable and disappointing. To join with his mother meant annihilation; to join with his absent father was impossible. So Pollock sought through his aesthetic ambitions to combine the mother's idealization of the arts and the labor of the artist with a workmanlike approach to the career of the artist. In the end his aesthetic accomplishment repudiated the classical maternal forms of traditional western art and instead assaulted the western art world with a purely paternal and violent aesthetic style in which structure, balance and standards of harmony and beauty were split apart, exploded and reorganized in a grand symphony of swirling lines, crashing splashes of color and rough, powerful compositions of formlessness and infinite spaces.

The years when Pollock was creating this highly personal new art form were the most stable and peaceful of his life. Although some biographers attribute this to the medications he was prescribed or the controlling influence of Lee Krasner, I believe that it was Pollock's immersion in the specific experience of the creative process, with its sense of enlivenment and self-confirmation, that sustained him during those years. For the first time in his artistic career he found the act of painting self-confirming. Creativity rather than resulting in doubt and self-loathing was now self-confirming, self-empowering, and he felt whole and cohesive as an artist and as a man.

Of course, as we have seen before, the selfobject experience and the resulting self-state, associated with productive creative work, is precarious and usually temporary, easily disrupted and almost inevitably accompanied by selfobject failure. Certainly Pollock had enough failure in his prior career. But the eventual failure which occurred in 1951, soon after the biggest success of his career, was associated not just with the pressures of celebrity and the inevitable jealousies and economic pressures, but in the failure of his creative selfobject tie.

At the height of his most productive period Pollock, buoyed by ambition, made the claim "I am nature" in response to Hans Hofmann's advice to paint from nature. What has rarely been noted was Hofmann's response: "Ah, but if you only work from inside you will repeat yourself." What Hofmann knew was that inevitably, sustained innovation in art required that the artist engage the other, the world apart from the self which would, to use Winnicott's idea, allow for "other than me substances to enter into the self" (Winnicott, 1971, p. 94). In fact, Pollock feared the world as much as he feared his own perpetual state of inner chaos. In the isolation of his studio he had found peace, even a fragile, healing grandiosity, in the rich dialectic with his own subjectivity. However, given the nature of his creative methods and the elimination of all outside influences, Pollock was continually forced to create out of the limits of his own inner life – repetition was inevitable. Pollock would often speak of his fear of repetition of style and self-imitation, the failure to be authentic. He feared being a phony.

And a phony would be not just an embarrassment but the deepest, most bitter shame imaginable. To be an artist whose just performed, who created art for show or profit, meant that the primary psychological support for his precarious and fragile self would be corrupted and it would turn not just into bad art, but a bitter revilement of his own self, which would collapse into a black hole of self-loathing, despair and terror.

The psychological benefits which came from Pollock's art were tied to his sense of creativity as confirming the specialness and grand nature of his talent, and thus of his self; the admiration which came with fame only confirmed and supported this sense of specialness and greatness. His ambitions as an artist were grounded in this need for creativity as a self-confirming process. This was tied to the recognition by others of his specialness through success in the marketplace and the broader art world.

The dream which came true for Pollock was that the powerfully subjective immersion in the reconciliation of the internal, painful lifelong split between his grandiose self and corrupted and reviled self brought them together and integrated them magnificently in a group of some of the greatest paintings of his age. These were given an entire article in *Life* magazine and represented the beginnings of worldwide notoriety and fame. The admiration of the external world, with a dramatic and unfortunately volatile experience of realized self-aggrandizement, and the satisfaction of archaic childhood longings for recognition and admiration, confirmed internal vitalization through creative success.

All of this set Pollock up for a dramatic and deadly fall into self-crisis, panic and death. After the article in *Life* magazine Pollock continued to struggle to produce new art. He felt the continual strain of innovation and quickly found that his store of ideas and inspirations were limited. He knew he couldn't simply keep repeating his poured paintings yet nothing half as compelling seemed possible. His creative needs increased, along with his uncertainty about himself and the tension of his precarious self-coherence as an artist. Some months later he was approached by a young filmmaker who asked to make a film of Pollock's controversial method of painting. With a canvas set up on a platform in the yard, the filming went on for hours each day, and Pollock was forced to repeat his actions over and over to recreate the images of a spontaneous event. Eventually, after the filming was complete, Pollock returned to his home and poured himself several large whiskeys. Months of sobriety came to an end and Pollock would continue to drink, struggle and eventually despair until his death in an automobile accident on a Long Island country road.

Pollock was the perfect artist to bring about both the culmination of modernism and its death. The level of his self-disorder was profound; the consequences for his family, his health and his mind were catastrophic. However, Pollock had the need to self-create out of his inner chaos, to bring order to his affective life and have the results admired. He was unable to manage the discipline and careful methods of traditional western painting (exemplified by Benton) and Greenberg's exhortation to abandon imagery and illusion to directly confront the canvas resonated perfectly with his need for an unmediated, unreflective creative process. His artwork was the creation of his body, of his body in motion, with pigment flowing from his fingertips, the painted canvas was the concrete presence of his emotions, his vitality and his grandiosity. In his best work he became Pollock, "the greatest living American Artist", transcending the fantasies of his mother and becoming the sublime and wild wunderkind of art.

Of course modernism died before Pollock did. The generation of artists who came of age with Pollock – Newman, de Kooning, Rothko, Stills, Kline, Motherwell – had all created their most important work. The cult of individual subjectivity and self-expression, which had dominated modern art for the past several generations, had come to an end. Imagery and representation had been destroyed thoroughly and traditional notions of beauty had been trampled and marginalized, replaced by the terrible and often violent aesthetic of the Sublime. However, abstract expressionism essentially exhausted itself; all that was left for the major artists was to repeat themselves, drink or commit suicide.

Yet even while modernism was dying, young artists were moving into New York City seeking success and fame. For them the older artists were far too masculine and much too self-important. For these new artists the grand arts of the past were a sort of joke, and the blotted, drunken bombast of the abstract expressionist rhetoric was repulsive. These artists valued the cool and ephemeral. They admired (or worked for) the new advertising industry and the expanding technology of the media. And there was one, a young artist from Pittsburgh, then a hot new illustrator of women's shoe ads, who would soon construct out of the odds and ends of both contemporary and historical western culture a postmodern art that would sweep around the world, changing everything.

Chapter 13

The birth of postmodernism: Andy Warhol's perverse aesthetics

> If you want to know all about Andy Warhol, just look at the surface: of my paintings and films and me, and there I am. There is nothing behind it.
> (Andy Warhol, quoted in Bockris, 2003, p. 195)

In final chapter I will discuss the transition from modern art and the psychology of modern artists to the postmodern arts and beyond, to the wildly diverse art world that exists today. As in earlier chapters I will look broadly at the forces that brought about these changes but most importantly, from a psychoanalytic perspective, the individual psychological dynamics of an important artistic figure that I believe played a major role in bringing about change.

In the 1960s a new art movement developed and enjoyed enormous public interest and excitement. Partially in reaction to the aesthetically Olympian world of the abstract expressionists (the dominant artistic school of the post-war western culture), pop art celebrated the mundane and "low brow" creative products of popular culture. However, beyond "popism" these new artists began to aggressively dismantle many of the fundamental values and principles of modern art. One of the artists at the forefront of this movement was Andy Warhol, who became a dominant cultural figure of the later decades of the twentieth century. In keeping with the focus of this book I believe it is important to look at the individual psychological dynamics of a major art leader such as Warhol and to link these to the larger cultural and social forces within which he worked. To this end this chapter will discuss the art and mind of Andy Warhol, and the role that his personality and artwork played in the development of the postmodern art world. In particular we will explore how Warhol's self, structured around the enactment of perverse relationships and vertically split by dissociation, determined the specific nature of his provocative approach to art, creativity and postmodern cultural values. To begin I will review the historical, cultural and economic context which contributed to Warhol's development as a person and as an artist.

The art world of Warhol's early years

Post-war America was a culture in massive transition. It was transforming from being one of the greatest industrial nations prior to the Great Depression and the Second World War to a society and economy based not only on industry but also services, technology and consumer spending. At no prior time in history had marketing, advertising and sales led to the accumulation of such power and wealth. In addition, the pre-war European art world, which had been organized around the residua of the once powerful Academy system, was dead and a new American art world characterized by new types of artists, new mediums, new marketplaces and a whole new schools of aesthetic value, artistic practice and art criticism emerged and flourished. Art would no longer be the product of a few specialized artists, but a vast industry out of which radically new forms of artistic expression would be manufactured and made available to the entire society. Whole new notions about the nature of art would be elaborated to the point where the traditional western art world would be superseded by a diverse and complex tapestry of forms of "art". Even art itself would be redefined as "anything that we call art", removing the aura of specialness and spreading out the definition of art to apply to almost anything. In post-war America art became an avenue to wealth for many, not only through the production of saleable artworks – artistic expression became a power behind advertising and product design, and many artists joined the business world, turning their aesthetic sensibility towards the marketing and sale of commercial products. A vastly expanded and improved educational system made art education available to the masses. New, fabulously wealthy sponsors and philanthropists promoted museums and foundations which supported the growth of new art, and a liberal national government, flush with revenues from the exploding economy, channeled money to artists who were suddenly freed from the accountability of rich patrons and fickle customers. The proliferation and development of technology created new mediums and new media outlets for artists. Traditional mediums and methods became cheaper and more broadly available and new mediums such as television, mobile cameras, light, electronic music, etc. became available, allowing for a range of innovations and expansions of artistic forms and methods. Television, magazines and inexpensive book production made information about art available to every level of society. Last but perhaps most importantly, an enormous, educated and increasingly affluent public came of age with little commitment or loyalty to the past and a hunger to experience (and purchase) the many new art forms that were increasingly being produced for their entertainment. This was an environment radically different from the Victorian and Edwardian worlds of tradition, rigid class structure and academic and artistic institutions within which (and in reaction to) early modernism developed. The aesthetic life of world culture would be profoundly and permanently transformed – modernism was doomed.

Andy Warhol's life and career are a perfect example of the dynamic origins of this new postmodern world. When Warhol's moved to New York and began his career in commercial art, abstract expressionism, the last great movement of modern art, was at its height and artistic heroes such as Jackson Pollock, Wilhelm de Kooning, Marc Rothko and Barnett Newman dominated the art world. But soon this movement would be on the wane: Pollock dead from a car accident and Rothko a suicide, and de Kooning a drunk and a has-been. However, it was not so much what the abstract expressionists did as what society did with them that set the stage for a new group of artists. First, in the 1940s and 1950s the attention and resources of the art world shifted decisively to America, specifically New York City. The surging media and affluent art world, backed by fabulously wealthy urban art sponsors, had promoted the reputations, personalities and products of these men on a previously unheard of scale. Artists had become "superstars" and the popular media (as well as a new expanding gallery world) couldn't get enough of these new, sexy artists with their wild art and wild lifestyles. With the abstract expressionists art became big business and a new form of entertainment, and artists moved into the realm of movie stars and rock stars. There were new opportunities to be found for young artists willing to do whatever was necessary to succeed, even if it meant (especially if it meant) the total destruction of western artistic traditions, values and beliefs.

Andrew Warhola (soon to be called Andy Warhol) was eager to create a reputation and make a lot of money in this new postmodern world. A successful commercial artist, Warhol began producing and exhibiting artworks that copied in sometimes large and other times repetitious images the cartoons, Campbell's soup cans, Coke bottles and Brillo boxes that surrounded contemporary men and women in their everyday lives. However, Warhol's creativity extended well beyond the gallery art world into movies, music, publishing and, most importantly, the promotion of perverse approaches to self-promotion (celebrity, superstardom), sexuality (exhibitionism and pornography) and aesthetics (machine-made art). Beginning in 1961 and building over the next several years Warhola, now Warhol, became the most famous and notorious "pop artist" and over the next 20 years he would impact virtually every aspect of contemporary art and culture. How did he do this and why? To answer these questions we need to understand Warhol's personality development and relationships, and the psychological strategies he developed to manage vulnerability and gratify deep narcissistic needs.

Andrew Warhola was born in August 1928 in Pittsburgh, Pennsylvania (biographical information about Andy Warhol is from Bourdon, 1989 and Brockris, 2003). At that time the city was a rough, polluted industrial city with great poverty and fabulous wealth intermingled in a volatile social mix. H. L. Mencken describes the extreme poverty of many of Pittsburgh's citizens, who he says "lived in unbroken and agonizing ugliness" in housing that he notes for its "sheer revolting monstrousness" (Brockris, 2003, p. 19). Class and ethnic tensions, and extreme economic hardship resulted in periodic and decisive repression of the disgruntled workers by the powerful families who ruled the city. Needless to say it was not a welcoming or supportive environment. Later, Andrew Warhola would describe his hometown as "the worst place I have ever been in my whole life" (Brockris, 2003, p. 21).

Ondrej Warhola (Andy's father) was a rough, hardworking and ambitious man. Frightening to his children, he was more absent physically than present in Andy's life, since he was often away at work and would leave the fathering of Andy to his older brothers or friends. Born to a Byzantine Catholic family in Eastern Europe, Ondrej Warhola had emigrated to the United States as a young man, returning to Miková in the Carpathian Mountains of Slovakia in 1909 to marry Julia Zavackys, Andy's mother. They were very different people: Ondrej abstemious, aggressive and tight-fisted; Julia emotional, exhibitionistic, and artistic, a lover of myth and storytelling. Andy would possess and make use of these seemingly contradictory traits of his parents.

Soon, under the threat of conscription, Ondrej had to return to America, leaving his pregnant wife in the ambivalent care of his family. Her life with the Warholas was dreary, full of hard work and loss. Within a few years she had lost a baby to illness and her mother to grief. Then came the First World War, bringing widespread racial violence, repetitive threats to her and her family's lives, more loss and death. Finally, in 1921, in the midst of the influenza epidemic that decimated an already traumatized European population, Julia left Miková for Pittsburgh.

Life in Pittsburgh was also hard. The Warholas were poor outsiders enduring prejudice and sometimes violence from the other immigrant families. However, Pittsburgh was also a city of opportunity and Ondrej was determined to succeed economically and create the financial groundwork for his family's success. The cost of this striving was that he was an often absent, hard and judgmental father. His children both respected and feared him. His youngest son, Andrew, simply feared him.

Julia dealt with the hardships of life in Pittsburgh by withdrawal into memories and stories of her idyllic life back in Miková. She refused for many years to learn English. Throughout the rest of her life she maintained the attitudes and appearance of her Carpathian origins. Her early losses resulted in extreme fears of illness and possible harm to her family. She clung to her children, especially Andy, who became her constant and sickly companion for many years. At the same time Julia could be friendly, creative and, most importantly, talkative, energetically and frequently spinning yarns of the old days of her youth when life, she felt, was perfect. Julia loved and doted on her children.

Andrew, the youngest Warhola, was a slight, light-skinned and blond-haired child. His physical vulnerability and artistic nature made him the perfect object of bullying for peers and of companionship for his mother, who longed for an audience. Andrew suffered from many childhood illnesses, but most significantly, starting at the age of nine, for several years he was virtually disabled by St. Vitus' dance, a disease associated with rheumatic fever. A central nervous system disease with no known treatment at the time, St. Vitus' dance resulted in lost coordination, spasms and disorientation. He was pulled from school and spent some months in the care of his mother, who created a special area in the home where he could be close to her. Thus these periodic times of illness were also refuges from the hard world, during which time Warhol would draw, read, watch movies and be entertained by his mother's storytelling. Many observers remember how as a young boy he was continually clinging to his mother, and when forced to leave her for school down the block, he frequently panicked, at first refusing to go, later suffering an attack of St. Vitus' dance when force was attempted to wrench him from her side. This situation would set the stage for a lifelong preoccupation with his body image, health and sexuality, resulting ultimately in his strange public persona and a perverse orientation towards the world.

He was also a shy and socially withdrawn boy. A childhood friend, Kiki Lanchester, remembered: "He was always serious and shy when we were with other people. Every picture of him he would have his head down and he would look up at you as though afraid or he didn't trust you" (Brockris, 2005, p. 35). Warhol would later note how as a child he felt people avoided and rejected him the more he longed for relationships, and that people only seemed to care, to want him, after he had given up and no longer felt a need for people. This was a lesson that dominated his adult life: indifference and solitude is good, love and sex are dangerous derangements that open you up to loss and abuse. As an adult he would say that love was a type of chemical imbalance and that he, the solitary dreamer and momma's boy, lacked the chemicals in his brain that supported responsibility and adult heterosexual desires.

Warhol's mother loved to draw and she was an expert crotchetier. Warhol was also an enthusiastic draughtsman and he loved to color with crayons. Early on his talent and potential was recognized and the conditions were set for artistic ambition as a means of self-enhancement, perhaps self-repair, at least defense. Ultimately Warhol created a persona as an artist and a form of artistic expression that both enhanced self-esteem through fame and protected the self through a perverse aesthetic, inverting the self-revealing values of modern art and replacing them with an aesthetic system based on reversal, disguise, irony and pretense.

As noted above, Andrew Warhola has a powerful attachment to his mother. She was his refuge and companion when he withdrew in sickness and fear from the world and over time their bond would deepen. When Andy was ten years old his father began to suffer from heart disease and over the next three years he was disabled. When Warhol was 13 years old his father died. The impact of his father's illness and death increased Julia's need for Andy and a permanent bond developed. Years later, when Warhol moved to New York, she followed him, and until several months before her death they lived together. This, of course, is one of the great oddities of Andrew Warhola's otherwise notorious life, the fact that he would cultivate a reputation for outrageousness, sexuality and drugs at his various "factories" and in the early morning go home to the townhouse where he lived with his mother, who shared his bedroom for several years (though he later housed her in a separate living space in the basement), cooked his meals and entertained the few friends whom he would invite home with stories of the old country.

Another important issue in Warhol's development and something he struggled with his entire adult life was his homosexuality. In his youth he was gay in a culture in which homosexuality was not just frowned on but also treated as sinful and hateful. Warhol's struggle with St. Vitus' dance and various skin conditions, and his small, pale appearance added to his sense of being deficient and unlovable. He was always treated roughly by boys and sought the friendship of girls. In later life he would remember frequent rejections, despite his longings for relationships and intimacy. Only when he had finally given up and attempted to deny his need for relationships did he feel that people began to pay attention and then long to know him. Despite the many relationships, which accompanied his fame, he struggled with his sexuality and his inability to actualize his sexual identity in an effective, satisfying way. He had few intimate relationships (let alone love) with men and his frequent infatuations led to frustration and at time despair.

Warhol's artistic talent and intelligence were recognized early on. Not only his family but his schoolmates and teachers were impressed with his abilities. The most important positive contribution which Ondrej Warhola made to his son's future was the setting aside of money for the boy's education. It was obvious to the father that Warhol was the son with the most potential. This confidence, whether it was ever expressed directly to Warhol, must have had an enduring impact on the boy. Warhol attended the Pittsburgh Institute of Art, an excellent school funded by the Morgan family. (Despite the dismal working-class life the Warholas lived throughout Andy's childhood, there was a vibrant and rich artistic culture in Pittsburgh and some of the best educational opportunities, especially in the several first-rate universities in the city.) In college Warhol realized that art would be his means of self-promotion and self-repair. Despite some rocky periods when he was almost dropped from the program, he did well in school, earned the respect of his professors and graduated. With his talent recognized and a small group of fellow artists in tow he left for NYC to pursue his career.

Andrew Warhola found success in New York. Over the next few years he would become associated with many top advertising firms and magazines. He became known for his stylish drawings and innovative designs, especially for women's shoes. By the time his mother moved to the city to live with him he was one of the most successful young commercial artists in New York. However, the fame and status of fine art attracted him and he wanted more than just commercial success – he wanted to be famous. He knew that the increasingly important gallery scene, which had come to worldwide notice with the success of the abstract expressionists, was the road to the fame and fortune he longed for. He looked around at the new artists: Rothenberg, Jasper Johns and Clas Oldenburg were beginning to exhibit works of an entire new form of art based on popular imagery and new, less expressive methods of production. He saw an opportunity to make his mark as a member of this new avant-garde and to accomplish this Andrew Warhola initiated a project that would dominate his career, his social life and ultimately world culture – the creation and promotion of Andy Warhol. More than a personality, this new celebrity would become a way of seeing things, of being, a way of relating to the world, an attitude.

> Before Warhol, in artistic circles there was Ideology – you took a stance against the crassness of American life. Andy Warhol turned that on its head, and created Attitude. And the attitude was "It's so awful, it's wonderful. It's so tacky; let's wallow in it. That still puts you *above* it, because it was so *knowing*. It placed you above the crassness of American life, but at the same time you could *enjoy* it."
>
> (Wolfe, 1975, p. 64)

The persona of Andy Warhol which was gradually elaborated by Andrew Warhola was not so much a character of fiction but a refinement and elaboration of psychological characteristics which had been quietly expressed by Warhola throughout his life. He had always maintained a split in his self between the *inadequate fearful boy* ravaged by illness and anxiety and the *special son* of a doting mother – talented, ambitious and admired. Up until this point in his life he had little occasion to develop the grandiose side of his self. However, sensing the opportunity for attention, even fame, that the contemporary art scene offered, the life of Andy Warhol began. However, to accomplish this project Andy Warhol would not just be a person, but an entire philosophy of art and life; he would contain and express the cultural revolution of which he would be both the product and originator. Most importantly, through a perverse aesthetic, fueled by a spirit of rebellion and fun, he would challenge some of the most important beliefs and values of western culture, especially those of modern art.

Over the previous decade, the artistic careers of Pollock and de Kooning promoted a view of the artist as aesthetic hero, creating works of art which embodied a feeling of pure subjectivity, of raw, unguarded self-expression. Both artists attempted to remove the formal barriers to an authentic, unrestrained connection between the unconscious and the medium. In this way they argued that paint, body and emotion are one single action, man as nature in pure expression. Traditional cultural standards of beauty were discarded as irrelevant, a hindrance to the artist's pursuit of authenticity. What was valued was the sublime, awesome power of man as a natural force, art as a product of pure action unconstrained by culture.

The aesthetic beliefs and artistic systems of the abstract expressionists were anathema to Warhol for both professional and personal reasons. His talent was for decorative imagery presented in a tentative manner. However, he realized that the gallery owners and "serious" artists he longed to emulate looked at his success in the commercial world with distain. Warhol saw that he could use his experience and invert his aesthetic focus by making the subject of his serious work the very world he had been part of. Further, he would convert the emptiness that commercial art was accused of into an aesthetic based on what he called "the essence of nothing". He would raise surface appearance and style into a high art even as the entire notion of high art would be subject to his ironic and perverse denigration.

Rather than repudiating popular cultural and aesthetic standards as the abstract expressionists had, Warhol was fascinated with popular culture as his primary subject and theme. His relation to "pop culture" was deeply ironic and even cynical. Fascinated by beauty, he nonetheless acknowledged the ambivalence which beauty evoked, and the many ways that beauty obscured and compensated for the ugly in everyday life.

> Warhol deflated the mystifications connected with high culture, but at the same time he devastated the adversary position of the avant-garde in relation to the middle class. Warhol let the middle class know that it was culturally contemptible while he assured it, don't worry; there is nothing about art that you don't understand. Thus, his art has no anguish, no doubt, no apology, no existentialism, and no expressionism, nothing except what it was.
> (Ron Sukenick, quoted in Brockris, 2003, p. 159)

And in Warhol's life art was ubiquitous. Personal style, interior decoration, painting, films, prose, all were important to him. He was an enormous promoter of art as available and relevant to daily life while at the same time he undermined the idealization that characterized the modern view of art. For Warhol art was simultaneously all important, and a sham. He would say his goal was to invent a way of creating art which anyone could do and where his identity as originator would be.

> The manner in which Andy handled the uproar over his work was indicative of his developing persona. His credo was, "don't think about making art, and just get it done. Let everyone else decide whether it's good or bad, whether they love it or hate it. While they're deciding, make even more art." Rather than defend himself he encouraged the attacks. It was true, he purposefully lied, and that anybody could do his works. In fact, he likes the idea. It was true, he said, that his subject was nothing. And it was true that his paintings would not last. By accepting all the criticism with open arms he deflated or ridiculed it.
> (Bockris, 2003, p. 157)

A perverse aesthetic

> Warhol generated intellectual energy, always, by disregarding and hence erasing boundaries that separated what one would have supposed to be logically distinct orders of things, and allowing them to explode into one another through conceptual collapse.
> (Danto, quoted in Brockris, 2003, p. 158)

In psychoanalysis a perversion had traditionally been understood as a deviant form of sexual behavior resulting from some form of conflict related to mature, successful genital intercourse. For example, worries about castration that might result from forbidden sexual wishes lead a person to combine sex activities with some type of reassurance against harm, such as a fetish, or non-genital sex (voyeurism, sadism, etc.). In most cases perversions can be overdetermined and it may be quite difficult to sort out the meanings bundled within quite obscure and unusual behaviors. Some relational psychoanalysts have expanded the definition of perversion to describe behaviors and attitudes that, though non-sexual in nature, still have qualities of deviance and opposition to social and moral norms as a defining feature. In particular some perverse behaviors seem to combine the intense involvement with others with a simultaneous hiding of the self and denial of human contact. Most importantly, the engagement in behaviors and relationships that allow the disguised expression of hatred and destructive feelings, intense attachment hiding the desire to control and destroy the other, seem to be particularly modern forms of perversions. Ruth Stein, in her paper Why Perversion?: "False Love" and the Perverse Pact, summarizes this understanding of perversions:

> Perversion is a dodging and outwitting of the human need for intimacy, love, for being recognized and excited; it is the scorning of the moral

imperative of coming face to face with another human being's depth and unfathomable nature, which becomes palpable when one is in touch with one's longings for the "inside" of the other sexually or otherwise. Perversion is the active replacement of intimacy by the sexualized, enticing "false love". Lack of real curiosity about the other and the absence of a sense of enigma and wonderment at the other's secret are masked by intense, omniscient, pseudo-naïve, but clandestine and tendentious interest in the other, an interest and an agenda that can be sexualized or non-sexualized.

(Stein, 2005, p. 782)

In the same paper Stein offers an extended clinical report of a patient whose dynamics are very similar to Andy Warhol's, thus providing us with a means to begin our discussion of Warhol's perverse aesthetic:

Alice dodged a genitality that she dreaded; she was phobic about "doing it", having sex, writing, exposing herself, expressing her subjecthood. Her dread arose from a deep sense of shame, although her direct experience was of not being up to these tasks, lacking the knowledge and resources it takes to grow up – she feared she "did not have it", that she was not a woman, that she was "castrated". Her inhibitions were neurotic; her fears of being a little girl were not directly amenable to analytic work. Rather she camouflaged her sense of paralysis with incessant transgressive acts, by flouting boundaries and scorning limitations.

(Stein, 2005, p. 10)

Another aspect of these perverse organizations is that they involve the person using dissociation to separate different self-state configurations (the dependent "momma's boy" and the "superstar artist", for example) that have been organized by the person as a result of developmental stresses and traumas in order to ensure and protect affective safety. In the best of cases the person flexibly and creatively shifts between these self-states in response to internal and/or external demands. People like Alice and Warhol construct ways of living (meaning behaviors and relationships, as well as the accompanying beliefs and values) that are directly counter to the approved cultural systems of their social group and families. These dissociated systems contain within them both needs and desires and their dissociated antithesis, the simultaneous refutation of need and desire. The end goal of these dissociations is the protection of a precarious and fragile self from the disruptive impingements of both the outside world (desires and intentions of others) as well as the disorganizing and ultimately fragmenting effect of one's own psychological and emotional states, the desires and affects associated with anxiety and need. By dissociating the vulnerable self from the grandiose sexualized and transgressive self, a person manages to keep apart both threats and liabilities (see Goldberg, 1995).

In many cases dissociation occurs in response to traumas and these defensively motivated psychological structures are elaborated unconsciously, as emergency measures to protect the self. However, dissociation can also be developed deliberately and adaptively as a creative response to the evolving needs of the person and the opportunities that arise in their environment. Such was the case with Warhol. The creation of the Andy Warhol persona was a purposeful and skillful response to social and career opportunities; Warhol cultivated it as a solution to old vulnerabilities and emotional ambitions. And it took a lot of work as he tried to convey the exact look, attitude and affective manner that would make him appear to others the most sophisticated, worldly and "with it" leader of the post-war generation of the New York art community. In addition it required him to dissociate his family (mother and Pittsburgh family) from his art world colleagues, playmates and co-conspirators, even if this meant banishing mom to the basement.

> If Andy had wanted to distance himself somewhat from his mother as he struggled to transform himself into a new kind of person, short of expelling her from the premises he could not have done it more effectively than by confining her to the basement. For the next 12 years she lived alone in the dark, dank subterranean room where she invented a world of her own that could have been in Depression Pittsburgh or in Miková.
>
> (Brockris, 2003, p. 147)

In addition, Warhol discovered that art could also function to support dissociation, especially the management of affect. For example, for many years he was preoccupied with his physical appearance, his health and the threat of death, and for a number of years in a series of dramatic, sometimes enormous silk screens, he depicted images of suicides, car accidents and electric chairs that shocked the art community. The fact that Warhol would have these concerns makes sense when one considers his childhood illnesses, his social anxieties and the losses in his family, hence the expression of these feelings, memories and fantasies through his art at first appears unremarkable. However, what is fascinating from a psychoanalytic perspective is how Warhol came to use his art to both express these anxieties and preoccupations while at the same time dissociating the meanings and affects that the images normally arouse. Warhol stated the following regarding his motivation for creating the "death series" of paintings:

> I guess it was the big plane crash pictures, the front page of a newspaper: 129 die. I was also painting the Marilyns. I realized that

everything I was doing must have been Death. It was Christmas or Labor Day – a holiday – and every time you turned on the radio they said something like "4 million are going to die." That started it. But when you see a gruesome picture over and over again, it doesn't really have an effect. But there was no profound reason for doing the death series, no victims of their time: there was no reason for doing it, just a surface reason.

(Warhol, quoted in Goldsmith, 2004, p. 60)

I think it is safe to say that most people can empathize with this type of an approach to traumatic memories and the intense affects they evoke. However, for Warhol art functioned in a more general way to support the dissociation of many non-traumatic emotional states, and the self states associated with them. His compulsive and ubiquitous engagement in creating, collecting and talking about art had a broad effect on his emotional world, splitting off affect and cultivating a feeling on unreality about his inner life. Another example is Warhol's fascination with tape recording and his constant taping of interviews with friends, acquaintances and strangers whom he encountered in his rounds of socializing and partying. In the following quote he describes how tape recording people talking altered his relationship to his inner life:

The acquisition of my tape recorder really finished whatever emotional life I might have had, but I was glad to see it go. Nothing was ever a problem again, because a problem just meant a good tape, and when a problem transforms itself into a good tape, its not a problem anymore ... I think that once you see emotions from a certain angle you can never think of them as real again. That's more or less what happened to me.

(Warhol, 1975, pp. 26–27)

In other words, Warhol was of two minds: the first associated with his continued dependency on his elderly mother and the rituals and religious practices associated with her; and the second oriented towards the grandiose and flamboyant playing out of the artist and impresario – Andy Warhol cultural provocateur and iconoclast. As long as he maintained these different selves as distinct and separate, he was able to both continue his childhood attachment to his mother while simultaneously promoting the flamboyant "superstar" known as Andy Warhol, who was what he appeared – an entertaining surface, without personal meaning or emotional depth. To do this he maintained two distinct and radically different households and families: the one a cluttered Upper East Side townhouse he shared with his mother, filled with antiques and personally meaningful items that he compulsively collected over the years; and the other "the Factory", a downtown gathering place and studio, where he would play and work with his avant-garde friends and socialites. These two worlds were characterized by separate aesthetic systems, the former focused on the past and traditional styles of furniture and decoration, the latter a hotbed of disruptive, provocative and perverse art, which poured from the factory into the galleries and media for a world audience hungry for the next wild thing the factory would produce in Warhol's endless and energetic search for what was New. It is this aesthetic, what I think of as Warhol's perverse aesthetic, which we will discuss in the following pages.

Approaching the Andy Warhol persona as a dissociation helps us to understand the extreme and perverse positions he took in regards to aesthetics, creativity and art. From this point of view we cannot take his pronouncements at face value, rather they are his attempt to articulate attitudes, standards and values characterizing the split-off self-structure associated with his grandiose self. Through the cultivation of negation and the promotion of style and attitude, Warhol aggressively cultivated a type of character, a self-creation which he felt would gain him the attention, praise and notoriety that would compensate for the lonely, damaged and vulnerable boy who still ate breakfast cereal with his mother every morning at the East Side townhouse. The development and maintenance of this persona required the continuous expression of ideas, attitudes and modes of feeling, which became associated with this new type of person. From one point of view, Andy Warhol was a fabrication and his pronouncements falsehoods, or at best exaggerations. However, this is also Warhol's point – that the notion of a unitary, authentic self is the real fabrication and that a modern society demands a new type of man free of the old restrictions, values and standards, which ultimately mean nothing. Belief in truth and selfhood, that's the real lie. It is only in the cultivation of an attitude "above it all" and apart from and critical of the ridiculous and pointless culture to which we cling so pathetically that we can be truly creative, alive and free.

In other words, by means of a perverse approach to aesthetics and art Warhol attempted to accomplish several things: 1) To disguise his vulnerabilities and true self behind a facade, a persona of aloof indifference and naïveté. He constructed a manner, attitude and way of relating to the world that became his artistic self, the new artist whose aloofness and cool attitude conveyed the highest form of aesthetic awareness. Over the years he would cultivate, refine and often transform this persona, "behind" which the "real" Andy Warhol would be an enigma, a mystery. By combining this cool blankness with an obsessive voyeurism (he would always look, take pictures, record and film many of the people he met), he made people believe that he was really interested in them and that they and he had a special encounter without any true contact. 2) By focusing on images from popular media he could avoid the anxiety and vulnerability of authentic creation and self-expression. Borrowing the striking images of others he once again could hide even as he engaged the other. Everyone shares a relationship to Brillo or Campbell's soup, so there is an intimacy that he plays with and amplifies, once again without revealing himself or recognizing the other. 3) By soliciting directives from others about what he should create, he dramatically distanced himself from identifying himself with the product, thus when he depicted violent and gruesome images of suicide, murder and accidents he could deny personal meaning and even insist that they are just curiosities. 4) By simplifying imagery and through copying crass popular images, Warhol also avoided the intensity of aesthetic experience. Many of his works seemed to make fun of or even denigrate standards of beauty. He would intentionally strive to create imperfect, even ugly images. He avoided perfection and always sought to highlight flaws, whether in art or in his depictions of others. 5) Even more, Warhol often split aesthetics into extremes of excessive, unreal beauty (the Monroe portraits) or ugliness (mutilated corpses, electric chairs, the face of a man getting a blow job). 6) Warhol's approach to art made creation easy, without serious meaning, and common; in this way he could provoke without risking real judgment. He could shock and enrage without any self-investment or identification of himself with his artworks. After all, he could say, it was easy, it means nothing.

Warhol's *perverse aesthetic* would extend the psychological character traits described by Ruth Stein into the realm of art, resulting in a transformation of the basic aesthetic system of western art. Let us contrast the modern and the perverse in order to illustrate Warhol's aesthetic project. As we will see, Warhol's was a *dissociated* belief system that articulated and promoted an attitude towards aesthetics, creativity and art that was defined by its differentiation, even opposition, to modern western art. I will examine a number of central principles of modern art and Warhol's perverse disruption of these values.

For the modernists aesthetic experience was an ideal subjective response to the formal elements of one's engagement with the world. In art, the cultivation and perfection of aesthetic experience, through the medium and tools of artistic production, was the ultimate goal. The intent was to produce out of a subjective interaction between the artist's inner life and the external world a new, original experience in which old forms of beauty are replaced by a fresh appreciation of form, color, shape, and rhythm. The resulting artwork was the means by which this ideal state of being was brought about. Warhol deliberately undermined this cherished assumption about aesthetic experience. In his repetitious and mechanical depiction of soup cans he removed all trace of the special or ideal. Common items from the cupboard were displayed as if they were masterpieces. Boxes and boxes of fake Brillo containers were stacked in galleries. Newspaper photos were enlarged and silk-screened, copy upon copy. The notion of a special aesthetic response to the formal elements of some ideal object was subverted and even ridiculed. Warhol elevated the common and vulgar in the place of the fine and artistic. Even in the creative process he seemed to allow no place for aesthetic experience as he grabbed at new ideas that others came up with and cranked out copy after copy of new work. He claimed to value the empty and meaningless, and promoted the notion that he purposely selected his imagery because it meant nothing to him.

Modern artists viewed the creative process as a private, profoundly subjective process in which the artist actualizes a deep personal vision of self and self-in-world through art. Warhol approached creativity as an exhibitionistic display that seemed to eliminate the private and replace it with a type of creative spectacle, involving other's who would often come up with new projects and also take part in producing the work. The development of ideas for new art depended on an almost arbitrary process of searching for the next new thing. Rather than engaging in a creative process whereby his personal subjective vision would be allowed to engage the world and a process of psychological investment and elaboration would allow new, unique ideas for art to emerge, he tended to ask other people: "What do you think I should do?" He would ask almost anyone. In fact, many excellent ideas came from this process and clearly Warhol was not a passive participant but an active part of the dialogue. He would ultimately select from the range of different ideas which his friends would offer the special one that would become the next project. This approach turned the classical notion of inspiration arising from some private, perhaps unconscious, source, a process unique to the individual artist and fundamentally private and mysterious, into an aspect of dialogue, in which the artist, through a give and take with colleagues and friends, elicited ideas which he or she then assessed to see if they were worth further elaboration. In this way modern assumptions about the creative process were subverted and transformed. At first this appeared to be a violation, a corruption of aesthetic values, but it was not; rather, Warhol was exploring the intersubjective creative process more deliberately and without ambivalence. Inspiration was not only a private process but could legitimately involve social dynamics and dialogue. To free himself from the heavy burden and vulnerabilities of meaning, Warhol promoted the opposite perspective: "I feel the less something has to say the more perfect it is" (quoted in Brockris, 2003, p. 179).

For modern artists the creation of art was essentially private, the artist retreating to his or her studio to wrestle with his or her own angels and demons. Warhol would almost invariably involve others in doing the work and at times he would completely remove himself so that the other, or in some cases the machine, the camera, was operating completely on their own. Warhol followed similar principles in the production of art. Rather than seeing himself as the solitary artist struggling with his own aesthetic demons to laboriously constructs a new personal art product, he always involved others in working on production, often giving them a major part of the labor. He would also at times give over the entire process to the other, not even participating in the production of some work.

Modern artists struggled and labored for perfect expression of inner vision. For them art was labor and the serious nature of art was invariably hard, often torturous work. Andy Warhol valued the effortless and the superficial. He wanted his work to look easy and even entertained the idea of making his art so uniform in style that anyone could create a work like Warhol. Warhol was famous for his remark that he wanted to be a machine: "The reason I'm painting this way is that I want to be a machine, and I feel that whatever I do and do machine-like is what I want to do" (quoted in Koch, 2002, p. 23). In fact, one of the qualities that he sought in his artwork was a feeling of coldness and lack of emotion, of style over affect. In many of his artworks Warhol attempted to make the art as clean and regular as possible, producing multiple copies of a single piece as if they had come off an assembly line. In this way he would try to eliminate any trace of subjectivity, any hint that might betray the personal sources of the work. *"There is nothing behind it,"* he would say.

Modern artists felt that the best art was special and that the artwork is singular and unique. Warhol was famous for his repetitions and copies. He emphasized how his art, as if produced by a machine, could be rolled out in a seemingly endless series. In his factories he produced products to meet demand. With his cameras and tape recorders he produced endless films and interviews that would be stored, most of them unviewed and unappreciated. As a collector and hoarder he was obsessed with finding and gathering, but the objects did not possess intrinsic value to him, it was the constant experience of finding, acquiring and producing that was of value. In this way nothing was truly important and the longing for the thing of beauty, the masterpiece, could be soothed by another repetition, the next purchase.

Modernists believed that art should be separate from the day-to-day commerce of social life and exist in a rarefied and transcendent realm. Warhol's creation of "the Factory" brought into being a new type of studio. Wildly social, with a constant flow of addicts, entertainers, socialites, political figures, and artists, the Factory was the opposite of the private, individual, creative spaces of modern artists. In the midst of this busy social scene Warhol would spread out canvases, make films or snap endless Polaroids. He promoted a perverse reversal of the normal western aesthetic environment within which artists cultivated the creative process.

Throughout the twentieth century artists turned away from the old aesthetic standards of the Academy, pursuing the creation of new forms of beauty. Warhol was preoccupied with beauty as a commodity, or an unremarkable aspect of everyday life. Through his technique of image reproduction he showed how beauty could be duplicated, sold, even discarded as if it were just another commodity. He saw beauty as a business, and he used beautiful people and things purely to make money. With Warhol the classical ideal of beauty was devalued and degraded even as he exploited it.

Modern artists believed in the immortality of great art; for them it was a special, transcendent object possessing within it a type of truth that would assure its continued relevance and value. Warhol promoted the notion of art, especially his art, as devoid of meaning, just surface appearance, a fad. He would often speak about how his work would eventually be forgotten, and he fantasized that he would not die physically but disappear, just pass into oblivion. To expect or long for one's art to endure, to be valued over time, would open oneself up to the anxiety of transience and mortality. If nothing matters, then nothing can be lost. If everything one creates is empty and superficial, then the artist doesn't have to worry about being known, or judged, or rejected.

Modernists believed that art was free of the corrupting influences of money and commerce, and that personal financial gain should never be a principal motive for its creation. Warhol flaunted his origins in the commercial art world and continued to blur the distinctions between high and low art. "Art for art's sake" was never something Warhol valued – to the contrary, fame, success and money made Warhol and Warhol's world go round. He wrote:

> Business art is the step that comes after art. I started as a commercial artist, and I want to finish as a business artist. After I did the thing called "art" or whatever it's called, I went into business art. I wanted to be an Art Businessman or a Business Artist. Being good in business is the most fascinating kind of art. During the hippie era people put down the idea of business – they'd say "Money is bad" and "Working is bad" but making money and working is art and good business is the best art.
>
> (Warhol, 1975, p. 92)

In this subversion of western aesthetic values Warhol created an aestheticized world in which his perverse orientation to self and other could be articulated, enacted and even admired. He sought through his art to engage the public in what Stein calls "the perverse pact", a disguised enactment of hatred and destructiveness that is actualized within a relational structure (Stein, 2005).

The notion of the *perverse pact* is a useful tool in understanding one of the most important and influential aspects of Warhol's artistic career – that is, his relationship to his audience and the importance of fame. Above all Warhol craved publicity and celebrity (if not notoriety). His search for new art forms, fresh images and ideas was driven not by aesthetic ambitions primarily but by the search for the next best thing that would "turn on" the public, media and critics and draw the maximum attention to Andy Warhol. However, Warhol's exhibitionism was combined with a powerful voyeuristic interest on his part. Everywhere he went he carried a camera or tape recorder. He seemed engrossed by others even as he was the object of their fascination. This resulted in the strange phenomenon of people feeling special in his presence, that anyone could be a star, and that Warhol found everyone fascinating. Of course he rarely looked beneath the surface of anyone and his random scanning of the room revealed his lack of recognition or caring for individuals and his love of style and appearance over subjectivity. His statement that "in the future everyone will be a star for 15 minutes" captured the issue – even if it were true, you would get a lot of attention, no one would really know you, nor would anyone truly care, as you'd be dropped soon after (intense narcissistic gratification followed by abandonment). This, of course, was Andy Warhol's dilemma in a nutshell. It expressed his fear of rejection and loss even as it assured him that he would be protected from being taken over by the other.

For Warhol this perversity was pronounced and his contradicting modern values would be better characterized as a subversive attack whereby the fundamental assumptions underpinning modern art were reversed and even degraded by the very nature of his aesthetic organization. In addition, Warhol was not just motivated by a desire to explore new aesthetic territories, he also seemed to get enormous pleasure and almost sexual gratification from the repulsion and shock that people experienced in reaction to his work. Pop art was not just about "the transfiguration of the commonplace" (Danto, 1981); Warhol reveled in perverse delight at the refutation of all that the modern world had come to value and idealize. He was saying "it is all shit and I am the best at revealing and displaying. I am famous for parading the contemporary emptiness of art before the whole world and laughing at the response." Warhol's perversion was more than a means to an end – the creation of new art forms – it was at the center of his aesthetic. It was at the heart of his aesthetic.

While modern artists promoted a mystique of authenticity and self-expression (most powerfully enacted by the abstract expressionists, who were at their height during the early days of Warhol's career), Warhol rejected authenticity and spent his life cultivating a created persona, an image of the artist that was antithetical to the modernist one. In a sense this way Warhol's first and most radical contribution, the notion that the artist is a social type, a performance, and that the new artist could construct a way of being an artist, create and sustain a performance which would become as important to his new aesthetic as the artworks themselves. In a sense this disguise provided Warhol with a new freedom; behind his mask he could be free of the restrictions of the self and the expectations that people had of him. This permitted Warhol to follow his interests and whims, to elaborate weird and often contradictory mediums and subject matter. He was no longer bound to his "authentic self", rather he could invent and play with the many permutations of the character known to the world as Andy Warhol.

Warhol's role in the creation of a new culture: Art after modernism

With the rise of the individual and the collapse of the traditional social structures used by generations to define artistic standards and manage the business of art making and selling, modern artists discovered the power of the intrapsychic in the creative process. No longer were artists obliged to honor mentors, constrain their style or suit the norm and the judges; rather, the artist was free to elaborate and refine his or her own subjectivity through the externalization of fantasy and the perfection of the resulting creations though a dialectic by means of which a dazzlingly new form of art crystallized.

Andy Warhol changed all this. He didn't return to the old traditions, or give himself over to some group creative project; rather, he stepped outside the subjective and cultural landscape and took a radically critical position. In a sense he "threw out the baby with the bathwater". According to the aesthetic philosophy of Andy Warhol, individual inspiration and creative effort was a nuisance, self-expression was a matter of technique, beauty was an unreliable and even hazardous illusion, and all art was contextual, ultimately meaningless and only as good as the size of its price tag. Of course these positions are also fabrications, and in the end one gets the feeling that Warhol never meant to irrevocably subvert traditional western values but rather wanted to have fun, to cause trouble and indulge his desire for notoriety and outrageousness. To value western traditions and the products of western culture (except as objects of a collector's fetish) would have run counter to Warhol (and Warhola's) central self-organization. He was a man organized around split selves, all of which needed to be maintained and differentiated by means of denial, negation and denigration. Through the subversion of these values and practices Warhol's influence was not just as a provocateur and "bad boy" of art. The result of the Andy Warhol phenomenon was that western art moved beyond the restrictions and dictates of modernism, freeing up other artists to question practices, and experiment with new mediums and even new ideas of what art can be. Andy Warhol was a contemporary incarnation of one of Shakespeare's fools – brilliant, ironic and infinitely playful – and he held up to modern society a funhouse mirror that freed the viewer from the painful, serious and ultimately despairing reflection of our true selves and gave all of us a lot to talk about. He subverted virtually all of the principle values and practices of modernism, and his perverse aesthetic became the cultural standard for artistic production, aesthetic judgment and the contemporary art world. After Warhol the art world (and the world) would never be the same.

Chapter 14

Postscript: The world after Warhol

> Warhol invented an entirely new kind of life for an artist to lead, involving music, style, sex, language, film, and drugs, as well as art. He changed the concept of art itself, so that his work induced a transformation in art's philosophy so deep that it was no longer possible to think of art in the same way that it had been thought of even a few years before him. He induced a deep discontinuity into the history of art by removing from the way art was conceived most of what everyone thought was its essence.
>
> (Danto, 2009, pp. 47–48)

In the last chapter we discussed Andy Warhol, his psychological development and its implications for his artistic career and aesthetic innovations. By emphasizing Warhol's perverse approach to art, culture and aesthetic values, and his aim to subvert and critique virtually everything that the modern western art world believed in and valued, I may have created an impression of Warhol as simply an iconoclast and a rebel – which of course he was. However, Warhol's ultimate influence has been enormously positive, and once we move beyond his antics, provocations and perversions, we can see how he liberated the contemporary art world in ways which continue up to the present day. Most importantly, Warhol altered the psychological function of art and challenged common assumptions about the creative process and the artist's relationship with his artwork and audience in ways which have stimulated innovation and productivity across the art world.

Warhol's immediate predecessors, Jackson Pollock and the other artists of the New York School, were the last representatives of the great modern movement in art. They saw themselves as working within a long tradition, the ultimate goal of which was the pure and unencumbered expression of subjectivity. They attempted to achieve this by means of a medium stripped to its essence, unconstrained by formal standards or expectations. They believed that they had brought western painting to its highest point, giving birth to an art form (abstract expressionism) with such potential that it would dominate the art world for a millennium. What a tremendous burden that must have been! What they didn't see was that the great western artistic tradition was coming to an end, and that even as the world applauded (and purchased) their masterpieces, other younger artists were plotting the total destruction of all they believed in and clung to.

By attacking and subverting western aesthetics, notions of creativity and the cultural role of the artist, Warhol and his gang brought vitality, freshness, freedom and renewed potential to art. No longer dominated by manly white men, battling with the past while wielding brushes like sabers, the new artist could just as easily be a woman or an African American. Artists such as Warhol, Rauschenberg and Jasper Johns were gay men, and from their outsider perspective they assaulted the heterosexual male power structure. These attacks challenged basic assumptions about who an artist is, and what the role of art is in society.

Over time the rebellion and critical onslaught evolved and was eventually transformed into a diverse, aesthetically enriched and infinitely creative art world. In a sense a permanent revolution has developed. However, artists are no longer rebelling against tradition; in fact, as the years pass there is an increasing historical distance between the present and the now distant world of modern art. Currently contemporary artists see themselves as part of an infinitely complex global community in which innovation and experimentation is the norm.

What are the implications of Warhol's popism and postmodernism for the psychological model of creativity, art and artists that we discussed in Chapters 2 and 3? Given the revolution that has occurred and the way in which traditional assumptions and standards about art have been relentlessly attacked, subverted, and seemingly replaced, what can we say with any definitiveness about art now? What is the relationship between the artist and his or her artwork now? Is there a creative process, or is it *any* means to *any* end? And what is the point of art, now, in our postmodern age? Does beauty matter? Does it even exist anymore? I would like to close this book with some thoughts of my own about these questions.

One of the problems with our traditional approach to art is that we often generalize about it based on the forms that it takes, or the functions that it may have at a given time or place. The postmodern critique taught us that western assumptions about the nature of art were culture-bound, limited and constricting. Now we see art as less specific, encompassing many forms, methods and mediums, some of these far from the aesthetically based artworks that we are used to. Given this, it may be better to view art not as a thing or an institution but an evolving and complex human process, a process in which artists seek to articulate in clear and convincing terms aspects of human experience and subjectivity – whatever that might entail. In fact, if we view the core of art as subjectivity as we have in this book, then it is inevitably diverse and unpredictable.

As we discussed in Chapter 2, human subjectivity is experienced in three dimensions (at least): the intrapsychic (internal, private psychological experience), the intersubjective (dialogue, shared communication) and the metasubjective (social, cultural). Each of these dimensions is determined by and dependent on the other. An artist creates out of private thoughts and feelings that emerge within dialogues that are defined and sustained by and within a culture. The fourth dimension would be *time*, given that human subjectivity is always changing, a process within processes, with no specific point in time that defines and delimits it.

Warhol and those who have come after him saw subjectivity as not limited to a particular medium or art form. Subjectivity saturates all human activity. It is all around us – even, and perhaps most importantly, in the common objects and experiences of everyday life. An artist is a person who makes the subjective aspects of an activity the object of his or her creative efforts. It is what the artist does with that expression, and what he makes of it, that is important. Warhol asserted that the artist's subjectivity was his or her entire life world – an infinite set of possibilities for self-experience was now available and acceptable. Radically, he took personal claim to the whole of popular culture, making the literal reconstruction of a Brillo box into a personal statement, forever associated with "Andy Warhol".

Building on the innovations of Duchamp, Warhol saw art not as things, or products, so much as ideas, psychological phenomena contained within and caused by the encounter with artwork, but not synonymous with it. Since then many contemporary artists, especially cognitive artists, eschew sensuous experience and focus on thoughts, ideas and language. However, they are just as subjective as sensuous art, emphasizing the perfection of concepts and language usage. In cognitive art it is the manipulation of the mind not the senses that is the focus. But just as with other forms of art the cognitive artist also seeks to "get it right", to capture the idea precisely, and to perfect the mental dimension of human subjectivity.

Contemporary artists have also focused on the cultural dimension of subjectivity, most importantly through the deconstruction of traditional art forms and artistic values. The goal is to find the perfect critique, the most affecting new view on old forms, to express new ideas through an ironic restructuring of traditional standards and values. In this way artists seek to find fresh art forms by reorganizing the old. For these new artists there is no clear distinction between inner and outer, between self and culture, we are all ineluctably embedded and co-determined. The old notion that creativity arises from some isolated unconscious mind, the well of inspiration and innovation, has been debunked. Artists now engage in culture, politics and economics, they view the self as contingent and protean, an actor in, to quote Prospero in Shakespeare's *The Tempest*, "an insubstantial pageant" – participants in the "festival", as Gadamer (1986, p. 39) refers to the art world.

Given this, how can we still claim that the artist seeks to *perfect* his subjectivity? Contemporary artists do not just try to make art beautiful (of course that may be their intention – anything may be intended); rather, they try to get it right. Getting it right is variable and idiosyncratic. The artist judges his work according to standards and values which may be highly personal, but which are also grounded in the pursuit of his art within a social system (society as a whole, and the art institutions where he studied and worked) and in the midst of relationships (family, friends, other artists, critics, etc.) which also affect how he experiences his creation and guide the process of his refinement of the work. In the end the artist seeks to bring the artwork to a point where he feels that it possesses some *ideal* quality. By this I mean that he feels it is as perfect an expressions of his subjectivity as he is capable of creating at that point in time.

However, viewing subjectivity as a process also means that the artist is not simply representing some pre-existing stable subjectivity by means of an artistic medium. In fact, I believe that during the creative process the artist is changed to a greater or lesser degree and perhaps in unexpected, sometimes disturbing ways by the artwork. In other words the artist's subjectivity evolves through the creative interchange with the very thing he is creating, in the context within which he creates it and displays it. Thus the successful outcome of any artist's creative effort may be the discovery of aspects of the artist's subjectivity that were unknown, perhaps non-existent, prior to entering into the artistic project. Given that artists are no longer limited by standards of composition, or other formal traditions, the potential for expression is endless; they can now experiment with mediums and methods which allow for expressions of subjectivity unheard of in prior times.

Perhaps the creative process has not changed much. At some point in time, perhaps even *after* initiating a particular artwork, an artist is inspired or imagines an image, an idea or a thing, and tries to make it happen, building something or putting something together. Along the way they judge if it feels right or wrong (whatever that may mean – it is often just a feeling). They adjust it and step back, and think and/or feel. The process is frequently fraught with doubt, confusion and anxiety. Artists still take risks, big risks. They struggle to get it right, and they feel good when they succeed. The result always brings satisfaction, even joy, the emotional response making it all worth it. In this sense artists still idealize art, they still believe that art is one of the best things to do, and they feel excited and more alive when it turns out well. To be a successful artist you have to believe in the process, you have to invest your Self in it, you have to care deeply (passionately) about the results.

Of course, in the end the artist will not be the sole judge of his work (nor will his experience of the work remain static over time). In almost all cases others will view the work and they will respond with their own mixture of subjectivity, experience and point of view. The artwork will be known by other eyes, and new meanings, unrecognized by the artist, may be perceived and valued, and altogether strange and unexpected perfections identified. In the end the subjective meaning of the artwork may be entirely changed by the audience, and the communal value of the work may be totally out of sync with the artist's "original intent" (if that can be known).

Contemporary art has been freed of its traditional formal constraints. As Duchamp and Warhol have shown us, aesthetics is not necessary to art. Aesthetic experience is a dimension of subjectivity, but not a necessary condition *for* subjectivity. Some forms of art lack an emphasis on aesthetic experience, and some art forms may appear to have no aesthetic quality whatsoever. Beauty, which was once considered the essential element in art and aesthetic experience, is important to understanding art as cultural phenomena, but it is not necessary to any general definition of art. The reason that beauty has been so central to art is the way in which aesthetics amplifies meaning; in particular it gives a refined form to what is being communicated, imbuing it with an affective quality that heightens and enhances its meaning. Warhol showed us how beauty could be exploited to make a point, but on the other hand even an artist of Warhol's perversity cannot eliminate the power of beauty – it still matters to us, but no longer just in traditional forms. Beauty has changed with the times just as Baudelaire claimed it must over a century ago.

In other words, artists do not set out to create "beauty", nor is the beauty of art an adequate measure of an artwork's value. Then why do we value artworks for their beauty? When we say something is beautiful we often mean it feels right: an idea exquisitely articulated, perfectly executed and special – all beautiful things stand out (are special) and resonate with our biologically and developmentally based readiness for idealization. When something is done really well we often experience it as beautiful. When the articulation of an idea, a perception, a feeling, or other subjective experience is conveyed in a particularly clear, precise or interesting way we feel beauty in it – and the feeling of beauty is always special. In response we feel energized, happier and more whole as a person. Appreciating art involves a type of selfobject experience. Even when art is disturbing and disruptive, part of us responds with excitement, even joy. The source of art's power still lies in the opportunity for idealization (e.g. a selfobject experience). The artist desires to express him or herself, but only when that expression stirs emotions which are simultaneously authentic (fear, sadness, joy) but also self-enhancing (self-cohesion, vitality, efficacy).

Finally, it was under Warhol's manic leadership that the art world became fun. Any notion of classical standards and "fine" art had to give way before hundreds of coke bottles, cow heads, blowjobs, and silver balloons. As the weight of tradition and seriousness of art lifted there was an explosion of creativity as new forms of art and new types of artists emerged. No longer burdened by the long, often drunken slog towards greatness, these new artists are less serious and more spontaneous. Since Warhol revealed how anything could be art and anybody could be an artist, the new artists have taken him at his word, and followed his example. The result is the excitement, confusion, conflict and creativity of our contemporary art world.

References

Anderson, W. J. (2006). Frank Lloyd Wright: A psychobiographical exploration. In Winer, J., Anderson, J. W., & Danze, E. (Eds.), *Psychoanalysis and Architecture*. Catskill, NY: Mental Health Resources.

Beebe, B. & Lachman, F. (2002). *Infant Research and Adult Treatment*. Hillsdale, NJ: The Analytic Press.

Bion, W. (1967). *Second Thoughts: Selected Papers on Psychoanalysis*. London: Karnac Books.

Blair, L. (1998). *Joseph Cornell's Vision of Spiritual Order*. London: Reaktion Books.

Bloomer, K. & Moore, C. W. (1977). *Body, Memory, and Architecture*. New Haven: Yale University Press.

Bourdon, D. (1989). *Warhol*. New York: Abrams.

Brockris, V. (2003). *Warhol: The Biography*. Cambridge, MA: Da Capo Press.

Bromberg, P. (1996). Standing in the spaces: The multiplicity of self and the psychoanalytic situation. *Contemporary Psychoanalysis*, *32*: 509–536.

Carlson, A. (1999). *Aesthetics and the Environment: The Appreciation of Nature, Art and Architecture*. London: Routledge.

Cornell, J. (1993). *Joseph Cornell's Theater of the Mind: Selected Diaries, Letters and Files*. Caws, M. A. (Ed.). New York and London: Thames and Hudson.

Danto, A. (1981). *Transformation of the Commonplace*. Cambridge: Harvard University Press.

Danto, A. (2009). *Andy Warhol*. New Haven: Yale University Press.

Deri, S. (1984). *Symbolization and Creativity*. Madison, CT: International Universities Press.

Dissanayake, E. (1992). *Homoaestheticus: Where Art Comes From and Why*. New York: The Free Press.

Dissanayake, E. (2000). *Art and Intimacy*. Seattle and London: University of Washington Press.

Eagleton, T. (1990). *The Ideology of the Aesthetic*. London: Blackwell.

Ehrenzweig, A. (1967). *The Hidden Order in Art*. London: Paladin.

Field, J. (1957). *On Not Being Able to Paint*. Los Angeles: J. T. Tarcher, Inc.

Flam, J. (1986). *Matisse, the Man and His Art: 1860–1918*. Ithaca, NY: Cornell University Press.

Flam, J. (1995). *Matisse on Art*. Berkeley and Los Angeles: University of California Press.
Frascina, F. & Harrison, C. (1987). *Modern Art and Modernism: A Critical Anthology*. New York: Harper & Row.
Freud, S. (1908). Creative artists and daydreaming. *Standard Edition*, 9: 142–153. London: Hogarth Press, 1959.
Freud, S. (1910). Leonardo da Vinci and a memory of childhood. *Standard Edition*, 11: 59–137. London: Hogarth Press, 1959.
Freud S. (1925a). Note upon a "mystic writing-pad.' *Standard Edition*, 20: 87–174. London: Hogarth Press, 1959.
Freud, S. (1925b). An Autobiographical Study. *Standard Edition*, 20: 7–74. London: Hogarth Press, 1959.
Gadamer, H. G. (1986). *The Relevance of the Beautiful and Other Essays*. Cambridge: Cambridge University Press.
Gill, B. (1988). *Many Masks: A Life of Frank Lloyd Wright*. New York: Ballantine.
Goldberg, A. (1995). *The Problem of Perversion: The View from Self Psychology*. New Haven: Yale University Press.
Goldsmith, K. (2004). *I'll be Your Mirror: The Selected Andy Warhol Interviews*. New York: De Capo Press.
Gordon, R. (1998). *Degas*. New York: Abrams.
Greenacre, P. (1953). Penis awe and its relation to penis envy. In *Emotional Growth: Psychoanalytic Studies of the Gifted and a Great Variety of Other Individuals*. Madison, CT: International Universities Press, 1971, pp. 31–49.
Greenacre, P. (1956). Experiences of awe in childhood. In *Emotional Growth: Psychoanalytic Studies of the Gifted and a Great Variety of Other Individuals*. Madison, CT: International Universities Press, 1971, pp. 67–92.
Groom, G. (2001). *Beyond the Easel: Decorative Painting by Bonnard, Vuillard, Denis, and Roussel*. New Haven: Yale University Press.
Hagman, G. (1996). Flight from the subjectivity of the other: Pathological adaptation to childhood parent loss. In Goldberg, A. (Ed.), *Progress in Self Psychology*. Hillsdale, NJ: The Analytic Press.
Hagman, G. (2002). The creative process. In Goldberg, A. (Ed.), *Progress in Self Psychology*, Vol. 16, pp. 277–297. Hillsdale, NJ: The Analytic Press.
Hagman, G. (2005). *Aesthetic Experience: Beauty, Creativity and the Search for the Ideal*. Amsterdam: Rodopi Press.
Higgins, L. (2002). *The Modernist Cult of Ugliness*. New York: Palgrave Macmillan.
Hyman, T. (1998). *Bonnard*. London: Thames & Hudson.
Karmel, P. (1999). *Jackson Pollock: Interviews, Articles and Reviews*. New York: Museum of Modern Art.
Kirwan, J. (1999). *Beauty*. Manchester: Manchester University Press.
Kligerman, C. (1980). Art and the self of the artist. In Goldberg, A. (Ed.), *Advances in Self Psychology*. Madison, CT: International Universities Press.
Koch, S. (2002). *Stargazer: The Life, World, and Films of Andy Warhol*. New York and London: Marian Boyars.
Kohut, H. (1971). *The Analysis of the Self*. Madison, CT: International Universities Press.
Kohut, H. (1985). *Self Psychology and the Humanities*. New York: Norton.

Kohut, H. (1966). Forms and transformations of narcissism. In Strozier, C. (Ed.), *Self Psychology and the Humanities*. Norton: New York, 1985, pp. 97–123.
Kris, E. (1952). *Psychoanalytic Explorations in Art*. Madison, CT: International Universities Press.
Kuspit, D. (1993). *The Cult of the Avant-Garde Artist*. Cambridge: Cambridge University Press.
Lavin, S. (2004). *Form Follows Libido: Architecture and Richard Neutra in a Psychoanalytic Culture*. Cambridge, MA: MIT Press.
Lee, H. B. (1947). On the esthetic states of mind. *Psychiatry*, X: 281–306.
Lee, H. B. (1948). Spirituality and beauty in artistic experience. *The Psychoanalytic Quarterly*, 17: 507–523.
Lee, B. (1950). The values of order and vitality in art. In Roheim, G. (Ed.), *Psychoanalysis and the Social Sciences, Vol. 2*. New York: International Universities Press, pp. 231–274.
Loyrette, H. (1993). *Degas: The Man and His Art*. New York: Abrams.
McShine, K. (1995). *Joseph Cornell*. New York: Museum of Modern Art.
Maritain, J. (1953). *Creative Intuition in Art and Poetry*. Princeton, NJ: Princeton University Press.
Mcmullen, R. (1984). *Degas: His Life, Times, and Work*. New York: Houghton Mifflin Co.
Meyers, J. (2005). *Impressionist Quartet: The Intimate Genius of Manet and Morisot, Degas and Cassatt*. New York: Harcourt.
Milner, M. (1957). The role of illusion in symbol formation. In Klein, M., Heimann, P. & Money-Kyrle, R. E. (Eds.), *New Directions in Psychoanalysis*. New York: Basic Books, pp. 82–108.
Milner, M. (1987). *The Suppressed Madness of Sane Men*. London: Tavistock.
Mitchell, S. (1993). *Hope and Dread in Psychoanalysis*. New York: Basic Books.
Naifeh, S. & Smith, G. W. (1989). *Jackson Pollock: An American Saga*. New York: Potter.
Oremland, J. (1997). *The Origins and Dynamics of Creativity*. Madison, CT: International Universities Press.
Pater, W. (1886). *The Renaissance: Studies in Art and Poetry*. Oxford: Oxford University Press.
Pfeiffer, B. (1992). *Frank Lloyd Wright Collected Writing Volume 1: 1894–1930*. New York: Rizzoli.
Press, C. (2002). *The Dancing Self: Creativity, Modern Dance, Self Psychology, and Transformative Education*. Cresskill, NJ: Hampton Press.
Protter, E. (1997). *Painters on Painting*. Minneola, NY: Dover Publications.
Read, H. (1963). *The Form of Things Unknown: Towards an Aesthetic Philosophy*. Pittsburgh: Horizon Press.
Roland, A. (2002). *Dreams and Drama: Psychoanalytic Criticism, Creativity and the Artist*. Middletown, CT: Wesleyan University Press.
Rose, G. (1980). *The Power of Form*. New York: International Universities Press.
Rotenberg, C. (1988). Selfobject theory and the artistic process. In Goldberg, A. (Ed.), *Learning from Kohut: Progress in Self Psychology, Vol. 4*. Hillsdale, NJ: The Analytic Press, pp. 193–213.
Rotenberg, C. (1992). Optimal Operative Perversity: A Contribution to the Theory

of Creativity. In *New Therapeutic Visions: Progress in Self Psychology, Vol. 8*. Hillsdale, NJ: The Analytic Press, pp. 167–188.

Rutter, M. & Taylor, E. A. (2002). *Child and Adolescent Psychiatry*. Hoboken, NJ: Wiley-Blackwell.

Santayana, G. (1896). *The Sense of Beauty*. New York: Dover.

Secrest, M. (1998). *Frank Lloyd Wright: A Biography*. Chicago: University of Chicago Press.

Segal, H. (1991). *Dream, Phantasy and Art*. London: Routledge.

Siegel, A. (1995). *The Private Worlds of Marcel Duchamp*. London: Penguin.

Singleton, J. L. & Tittle, M. D. (2000). Deaf parents and their hearing children. *Journal of Deaf Studies and Deaf Education*, 5: 3. Oxford: Oxford University Press.

Solomon, D. (1997). *Utopia Parkway*. New York: Farrar, Straus, & Giroux.

Spurling, H. (1998). *The Unknown Matisse*. New York: Knopf.

Spurling, H. (2005a). *Matisse the Master: The Conquest of Color, 1909–1954*. New York: Knopf.

Spurling, H. (2005b). Matisse's Pajamas. *New York Review of Books, Volume 52*: 13, pp. 33–36.

Stein, R. (2005). Why perversion?: 'False love' and the perverse pact. *International Journal of Psychoanalysis*, 86: 775–799.

Stern, D. (1984). *The Interpersonal World of the Infant*. New York: Basic Books.

Stokes, A. (1957). Form in art. In M. Klein, P. Heimann, & R. E. Money-Kyrle, (Eds.), *New Directions in Psychoanalysis*. New York: Basic Books, pp. 406–420.

Tomkins, C. (1996). *Marcel Duchamp: A Biography*. New York: Owl Books.

Turner, E. H. (2002). *Pierre Bonnard: Early and Late*. Washington, DC: Philip Wilson Publishers.

Warhol, A. (1975). *The Philosophy of Andy Warhol (From A to B and Back Again)*. New York: Harcourt Brace.

Whitfield, S. & Elderfield, J. (1998). *Bonnard*. New York: Museum of Modern Art.

Wilde, O. (2007). *The Collected Works of Oscar Wilde*. Hertfordshire: Wordsworth Edition, Ltd.

Winer, J., Anderson, J. & Danze, E. (2006). *Psychoanalysis and Architecture*. Catskill, NY: Mental Health Resources.

Winnicott, D. W. (1971). *Playing and Reality*. New York: Basic Books.

Wolfe, T. (1975). *The Painted Word*. Farrar, New York: Straus & Giroux.

Wright, F. L. (1943). *Frank Lloyd Wright: An Autobiography*. New York: Barnes and Noble Books.

Wright, F. L. (1955). *An American Architecture*. New York: Horizon Press.

Wright, F. L. (1986). *The House Beautiful*. Rohnert, CA: Pomegranate Art Books.

Index

admiration 22, 51; Cornell's response to 103–4; maternal 111; Wright's quest for 110, 111, 116–17
aesthetic empathy 115–16
aesthetic experience: aesthetic resonance *see* aesthetic resonance; aesthetic tension 122–3; and the aesthetic unconscious 64–5, 66, 71; and anxiety 14–15; archaic 16; art appreciation 13, 15, 18, 19, 36, 165; of the artist 14–15; artist's subjectivity as centre of 2, 34; avoiding intensity of 155; of beauty, ugliness and the sublime 11–14; culture as aesthetic idiom of 25–6; embodying relationship of order and complexity 125–6; and the fading of the primary conception 48–9, 50, 52, 54; festival of 15–17; fundamental to human experience 3–4; healing function of 113–17 *see also* art: restorative function of; intersubjective source of 7–10; intersubjectivity of 27; modernism and 37; and the mother–infant dyad 3–4, 43–4; psychoanalytic views of *see* psychoanalytic aesthetics; psychoanalytic model of aesthetic experience, new; relationship to art 11–12, 16; repose 119–23; resolution through art of maternal and paternal aesthetics 44, 119–23; self-expression in 27, 69; self-organization and 13; subjectivity of twentieth century aesthetics 114; for "the breather" 84; transcendence of tragic man through 14; Warhol's undermining of modernist assumptions about 155–60
aesthetic forms/approaches: aesthetic idealization of masculine authority 56; aesthetic of "delay" 82–4; and the affective dimensions of light 54–6; beauty as maternal aesthetic 6, 137; breathing and 84; color *see* color; form as the objectification of subjectivity 79; of intimism 48; line *see* line; need to disrupt traditional forms and values 67; paternal aesthetic and the search for the Sublime 136–8; Pollock's action-based method of self-expression 134–6; psychological states interacting with 32, 34 *see also under specific artists*; the quick sketch preceding subjective reconstitution of experience 49–50, 52; reconciling maternal and paternal aesthetic form 44, 119–23; and the resolution of creative anxiety 59, 65–71; synthesis of 69–70; Warhol's perverse aesthetic 146, 148–9, 150–60
aesthetic organization 4, 67–8; ugliness and the violation of 6, 12, 64, 67–8, 71, 159
aesthetic quality 1, 165; aesthetic standards 16
aesthetic resonance 23; and selfobject experience 28–30, 31
aesthetic unconscious 64–5, 66, 71
aggression 65, 66; primitive aggressive fantasies 94–5
alienation 73, 82, 86; of the artistic self 112

Index

American modern art 87–90, 143–4; *see also individual artists*
Anderson, J. W. 108–9
anxiety: aesthetic experience and 14–15; Cornell 94–5, 104; creative 58–71; and the creative process 119; disintegration 83; Pollock 131–2, 138–9; selfobject failure and 66; and the sense of beauty 105; Wright 110, 119–20
architecture 107–8; and the body 123–5; and the healing function of aesthetic experience 113–17; "organic" 109; Wright and the selfobject function of 107–27
art: as affirmation of mankind's basic nature 4; appreciation 13, 15, 18, 19, 36, 165; and the artist's mind *see* psychoanalytic perspectives on art and artists; and the beautiful 11–12 *see also* beauty; as a business 157–8; cultural activities and the archaic sources of 16; cultural preservation through 4; defining art as a psychological activity 18–19, 31–2; devoid of meaning 158; dissociation and 152–5; festival 15–17; as human subjectivity externalized and perfected 24, 27–8, 78, 79–80; intersubjectivity of 16–17; modern *see* modern art; after modernism 160, 161–6; as opening to the transcendent 2, 114; as opportunity for dialogue 14, 16–17, 21; as perfecter and provider of meaning 4; Picasso on 37; postmodern critique of 162–6 *see also* postmodernism; pre-nineteenth century communal themes of 33–4; psychoanalytical understandings of *see* psychoanalytic perspectives on art and artists; psychopathology and the creative arts 30–1, 131–2, 137–41; relationship to aesthetic experience 11–12, 16; reparation of 14; restorative function of 19, 37–8; source of power and ubiquity of 3–4; as a subjective object 24, 28; viewed as sublimation 7, 18–19; works as products and commodities 88, 157–8
artistic dyads 26

artistic self 44, 60–1, 111–12; Duchamp 72, 77–9; function in self-experience 63; Matisse 59–63, 68–9; Wright and the psychological functions of 111–13, 116
artists: and admiration *see* admiration; aesthetic experience of 14–15; art and the artist's mind *see* psychoanalytic perspectives on art and artists; artistic engagement with the other 139; artistic self *see* artistic self; groupings of 26; intrapsychic approach to 7; modern artists 33–6 *see also individual artists*; motivation for art creation 22–3, 51, 65–6 *see also* aesthetic resonance; selfobjects and *see* selfobjects; societal and cultural roles 4–5, 33–5; subjectivity as centre of creative process 2, 34; surprise and shock at own creations 67; the three dimensions of the artist's subjectivity 25–7, 163
assemblage 91–2
astonishment 13
authenticity 69, 139–40, 149; Warhol's rejection of 154, 159–60
awe 12–13, 51, 137

Bauhaus School 107
beauty: Benton's idealizations of classical standards of 131; Bonnard and the seduction of 47–57; as a commodity 157–8; Cornell's quest for 104–6 *see also* Cornell, Joseph; enduring power in changing forms 165; fantasies of 119; idealizations of 3–4, 11, 131; of indifference (Duchamp) 77, 80–1 *see also* Duchamp, Marcel; and love 3–4, 54, 117–18, 137; as maternal aesthetic 6, 137; perfection and 11, 51; and the restoration of the self 38; sensation of 50, 52; the sense of beauty as a selfobject experience 50–2, 105, 117–19; from shared love and idealization 3–4; subjective reconstitution of experience of 49–50; sustained wonder at the beauty of the moment 54–5; ugliness, the sublime and 11–14; Wright's love of 117–19

Beebe, B. and Lachman, F. 75
Bellelli Family (Degas) 40–1
Bellelli, Gennaro 40
Bellelli, Laura 40
Benton, Thomas Hart 87, 130–1, 134, 136
Bion, W. 96, 102
Blair, L. 94, 99
Bloomer, K. and Moore, C. W. 115, 123–4
Bonnard, Marthe (neé Boursin) 50, 53–4
Bonnard, Pierre 47–57; creative sensibility and the "primary conception" 48–9, 50, 52, 54; Marthe and 50, 53–4; and the selfobject experience 52–6; use of light and color 54–6
boundaries: architecture and the body 123–5; of the circle 120; ego boundaries 8; fluid 26, 97; of the frame 96; Warhol's erasing of 150; *see also* containment/container, psychic
Boursin, Marthe 50, 53–4
breathing 84
Brockris, V. 149, 150, 152
Bromberg, P. 27

Calder, Alexander 91
Cézanne, Paul 69–70
chaos 12, 32, 67–8, 101, 140; dissociation and 27; *see also* disorder
childlike perception 48
circles/curves: boundaries and 120; the circle within the square as symbol of maternal and paternal aesthetic 122; representing the maternal aesthetic 71, 120
classical psychoanalytic aesthetics 7, 12
color: Bonnard 54–6; Degas 42–3, 45–6; emotional expression through 70–1; Matisse 64, 67, 70–1; and meaning 64
complexity 32, 125–6
Cone sisters 69
containment/container, psychic 96–7, 101–4
Cornell, Joseph 88–90, 91–106; biographical background 92–5; creative process 97–8, 100–3; death of his father 94–5; psychological meanings of his boxes 97–100, 101–4; quest for beauty 104–6; self experience 103–4; use of potential space 95–7
creative imagination 8
creative process 8–11, 22–5, 27–8; through aesthetic resonance *see* aesthetic resonance; Bonnard 48–50, 52, 54–5; Cornell 97–8, 100–3; Degas 43–4; of disruption and repair 67–8; Matisse 65–9; Pollock 134–6; regression and 67; self-experience and 43, 63, 66, 103–4; and the selfobject experience 79–80 *see also* selfobjects; serving selfobject functions 118–19; Warhol 156–7; after Warhol 164
creativity: and aggression 65, 66; artist's subjectivity as centre of creative process 2, 34; artists' surprise and shock at own creations 67; chaos, complexity and 32; the co-creative bond 115–16; creating something 'new' 20–1; creative anxiety 58–71; Duchamp's coping with 79–80; Kligerman and the currents to the creative drive 51; love and 14; and the mother–infant dyad 20, 43–4; motivators of 22–3, 51, 65–6 *see also* aesthetic resonance; and pre-nineteenth century communal themes 33–4; process of *see* creative process; psychoanalytic views of the creation of art 19–23 *see also* psychoanalytic perspectives on art and artists; psychopathology and the creative arts 30–1, 131–2, 137–41; regression and 7–9, 67 *see also* regression; self-fulfillment through 2; of specific artists *see specific artists*; viewed as sublimation 7
culture: as an aesthetic idiom 25–6; artist's role in context of cultural change 4–5, 34–5; cultural activities and the archaic sources of art 16; cultural dimension of subjectivity 163–4; Duchamp's influence on 73; pop culture 142, 149, 163 *see also*

pop art/popism; and pre-nineteenth century communal themes of art 33–4; in transition, in post-war America 143–4
curves *see* circles/curves

Danto, A. 150
de Kooning, Willem 128, 141, 144, 149
deconstruction 2, 12, 65, 66, 87, 163
Degas, Auguste 39–43
Degas, Celestine 39
Degas, Edgar 37, 38–46; ambivalent relationship with father 39–42; *The Bellelli Family* 40–1; letter to Evariste de Valerenes 42, 44; as a long-suffering artist 42–4; transition to modernism 44–6
Delacroix, Eugène 45, 64
delay, aesthetic of 82–4
Denis, Maurice 48
Derain, André 69
Deri, S. 21
detachment 79, 80, 81, 129
diagonals 120, 123
disintegration 8, 12, 38, 122; anxiety 83; Duchamp 83, 84
disorder 53, 67–8; narcissistic 52; self-disorder 42, 43, 49, 113, 140; *see also* chaos
Dissanayake, E. 3, 10, 16
dissociation 19, 27, 111, 151–5
dissonance 12, 28, 29
Dove, Arthur 87
dreams 23–4, 93, 94
Duchamp, Lucie 73–6
Duchamp, Marcel 72–86, 87, 91, 163, 165; aesthetic of "delay" 82–4; aesthetic sequelae of developmental failures 76–7, 79, 80, 82–4; artistic self 77–9; and the beauty of indifference 77, 80–1; biographical background 73–6; coping with creativity 79–80; and the empty object 81–2; expression of aesthetics through breathing 84; *Given* (*Étant donnés*) 84–6; impact of a failed maternal environment 73–6; *The Large Glass* 82–4; *Nude Descending a Staircase* 73; and the readymade 81–2

Eagleton, T. 44
ego-psychological approaches to aesthetics 7–9
Ehrenzweig, A. 98, 102
empathy 115–16
externalization 13; aesthetics and 27; art as human subjectivity externalized and perfected 24, 27–8, 78, 79–80; of the ego ideal 8

fantasies: of beauty 119; creativity and 20; of the grandiose self 111, 116; merging of real objects with unconscious fantasy 95–6, 101; of the mother 45; primitive aggressive 94–5; regression and unconscious fantasy 67; of renewal and transformation 69; self-disorder and 43; unconscious fantasy made manifest 17
fathers: developmental source of refuge and prospect 125; the "disconfirming" father 110–11; the early loss of a father 94–5; paternal aesthetic 44, 71, 119–23, 136–8; paternal mirroring 41; repressive presence of the father/tradition 39–42, 69; throwing down the gauntlet to the father 61–2
feminine subjectivity 56
festival, of art and aesthetic experience 15–17
Field, J. (M. Milner) 20
Flam, J. 69, 70
freedom of expression 1–2
Freud, S. 7, 18–19

Gadamer, H. G. 1, 15, 163
Gill, B. 110
grandiose self 29, 51, 97, 111, 116, 140, 154
Greenacre, P. 12
Greenberg, Clement 133, 141

healing function of aesthetic experience 113–17; *see also* art: restorative function of
Henderson, Joseph 132, 133
Henri, R. 11
Higgins, L. 56
Hofmann, Hans 139

holding (refuge) 124–5
homosexuality 147, 162

iconoclasm 16, 59, 73, 87; Warhol as iconoclast 153, 161
idealization: aesthetic idealization of masculine authority 56; aesthetic resonance, selfobject experience and 28–9; archaic 51; beauty and 3–4, 11, 50–2, 131; fantasies of 116; the ideal other 43, 54, 100; the ideal self 29, 118; maternal failure and the suppression of 77; reality and the processes of 13; selfobject experience, beauty and 50–2
identity: the artistic self *see* artistic self; fear of a fixed identity 78; and the parent's gaze 79, 111; restrictions on the sense of self 39–40; self-experience *see* self-experience
indifference 38, 63, 73, 146, 154; beauty of 80–1; Degas 40; Duchamp 72, 74–6, 77, 78–9, 80, 81, 82, 83–4; the indifferent mother 73–6, 79, 80, 81, 130; Matisse 63
individualism 34
infant–mother dyad *see* mother–child relationship
inspiration 24, 64, 67, 79, 156, 160; of "primary conception" (Bonnard) 48–9, 50, 52, 54; subjectivity as source of 34
internalization 54, 75, 76
intersubjectivity: of aesthetics 27; of art 16–17; of the artist 25; artistic dyads/groups and 26; intersubjective source of aesthetic experience 7–10; Rotenberg 22
intimate mutuality 10
intimism 48
intrapsychic approach to art and the artist 7, 26
intrasubjectivity/the intrapsychic 3, 7, 25, 26, 160
isolation 13, 86; Bonnard 53, 54, 55; Cornell 95, 100; Pollock 128, 139; Wright 111, 122

Johns, Jasper 148, 162
joy 15, 51, 55, 82; Wright 89, 126–7

Kligerman, C. 9, 11, 51, 52
Kohut, H. 26, 30, 50–1, 54, 66, 79, 102, 130
Krasner, Lee 132, 139
Kris, E. 7, 98
Kuspit, D. 37–8, 65, 83, 114

Lanchester, Kiki 146
light, affective dimensions of 54–6
line: Degas 45–6; diagonals 120, 123; Matisse 64, 67, 71; straight line representing paternal aesthetic 71, 122; Wright 123
Lloyd Jones, Anna 108, 112, 116
love: beauty and 3–4, 54, 117–18, 137; creativity and 14; "false love" 150–1; Warhol's view of 146

Maillol, Aristide 69
Mann, David 103
Maritain, J. 11
maternal aesthetic 6, 44, 71, 119–23, 137
Matisse, Amelia 69
Matisse, Anna 60, 62, 68–9
Matisse, Henri 58–71; and the artistic self 59–63, 68–9; biographical background 59–62; on Bonnard 47; and color 64, 67, 70–1; creating an art of subjectivity 63–5, 66–7; creative anxiety 58–71; creative process 65–9; experience of self 63, 66; and line 64, 67, 71; synthesis and originality 69–70
Matisse, Hippolyte 60, 61–2
meaning: art as provider of 4; art devoid of 158; color and 64; psychological meanings of Cornell's boxes 97–100, 101–4
Mencken, H. L. 145
metasubjectivity 16, 25, 26
Milner, M. 20, 21, 95–6
mirroring: by the artwork 22, 32, 118; child development and 75; of grandiosity 9, 51, 97, 116; of the ideal self 29; in the parent's gaze 79; paternal 41; and the selfobject experience 29, 105–6, 116; shame from failure in 122; Warhol's funhouse mirroring 160
modern art 33–6; aesthetic quality of 1; in America 87–90, 143–4 *see also*

individual artists; and the artist's subjectivity 34 *see also* subjectivity; deconstruction and 2, 12, 65, 66, 87, 163; defined as a category 1; psychological functions of *see* psychological functions of modern art; self-critical nature of 1–2; transition to postmodernism and beyond 142–60; Warhol's differentiation from 155–60; *see also* modernism

modern artists 33–6; need to disrupt traditional aesthetic forms and values 67; and the perverse aesthetic of Warhol 155–60; subjectivity of 34 *see also* subjectivity; *see also individual artists*

modernism 1, 34–5, 87–90, 107–27; aesthetic experience and Warhol's undermining of modernist assumptions 155–60; Cornell 91, 97–106; dynamics behind Degas' transition to 39–46; and the "liberation" of aesthetic life 37; Pollock and the culmination and death of 133–41, 161–2; Wright 109–10, 113–27

Moreau, Gustave 45

Morris, William 119

mother–child relationship: and aesthetic sequelae of maternal failure 76–7, 79, 80, 82–4; ambivalence in 72; and approval-seeking 62; and the artistic self 62, 72; attachment to the mother 3–4, 39, 137, 146, 147, 153; beauty and 12 *see also* maternal aesthetic; creativity and 20, 43–4; Degas and 40–1, 43–4; developmental source of refuge and prospect 125; and the drive for psychological healing 116; Duchamp and his failed maternal environment 72, 73–6, 79, 80; the indifferent mother 73–6, 79, 80, 81, 130, 154; maternal admiration 111; and the maternal aesthetic 119–23 *see also* maternal aesthetic; maternal detachment and neglect 129–30; maternal narcissism 131; rematriation 8, 9; role in early development 75–6; sense of failing the mother 129; a son's fantasies of the mother 45; as source of aesthetic experience and art 3–4, 8–9, 10, 40–1, 43–4 *see also* maternal aesthetic

multiple selves 77, 111–12

Nabis artists 47–8; *see also* Bonnard, Pierre

Naifeh, S. and Smith, G. W. 132, 133, 137–8

narcissism: maternal 131; narcissistic disorder 52; narcissistic gratitude followed by abandonment 159; narcissistic injury 66; narcissistic vulnerability 53; and Wright's practice of architecture 112–13

Neutra, Richard 114–15

Newman, Barnett 141, 144

objects: art as a subjective object 24, 28; creation of a 'new' object 20–1; the empty object: readymades 81–2; as objectifying medium 24; selfobjects *see* selfobjects; Winnicott's two ways of dealing with 20–1

Oldenburg, Clas 148

order 125–6; *see also* disorder

Oremland, J. 7

originality 69–70, 114, 138, 155

otherness 13; artistic engagement with the other 139; brought into the self 20; the ideal other 43, 54, 100

Pagans, Lorenzo 41

parental gaze 79, 111, 120

Pater, W. 56

paternal aesthetic 44, 71, 119–23, 136–8

perception, childlike 48

perfection: art and 4, 11–12, 27–8, 164; beauty and 11, 51; fall from paradise and 51; fantasies of 116; and the recovery of lost time 99; restoration of the self through the process of 38; selfobjects and the regaining of 51

perversion 150–1; the perverse pact 158; Warhol's perverse aesthetic 146, 148–9, 150–60

phallus 12

Picabia, Francis 87

Picasso, Pablo 37, 69–70, 91

pointillism 70

Pollock, Jackson 88–90, 128–41, 144, 149, 161; aesthetic innovations 133–8; and the artist's relationship to his artwork 135–6; biographical background 129–33; creative process 134–6; and the culmination and death of modernism 138–41, 161–2; internal maternal/paternal relationships 138–9; paternal aesthetic: search for the Sublime 136–8
Pollock, Roy 129
Pollock, Sande 131
Pollock, Stella 129–30
pop art/popism 142, 148, 149, 159, 162–6; Warhol's perverse aesthetic 146, 148–9, 150–60
postmodernism: birth of 142–60; the world after Warhol 161–6
potential space 20, 21, 27–8, 95–7
primary conception (Bonnard) 48–9, 50, 52, 54
prospect (release) 124–5
psychoanalytic aesthetics: art and the artist's mind *see* psychoanalytic perspectives on art and artists; classical 7, 12; ego-psychological approaches 7–9; and the mother–infant dyad 3–4, 8–9, 10, 40–1, 43–4; new *see* psychoanalytic model of aesthetic experience, new; regression and 7–9; rematriation and 8, 9; self-psychological approaches 9–10; ugliness and 12
psychoanalytic model of aesthetic experience, new 6–17; aesthetic experience of the artist 14–15; beauty, ugliness and the sublime 11–14; festival 15–17; intersubjective source 7–10
psychoanalytic perspectives on art and artists: and aesthetic experience 7–10 *see also* psychoanalytic aesthetics; psychoanalytic model of aesthetic experience, new; aesthetic resonance and selfobject experience 28–30; art as subjectivity externalized and perfected 24, 27–8, 78, 79–80; artistic self *see* artistic self; the creative process *see* creative process; defining art 18–19, 31–2; development of 7–10, 18–23; functions of modern art *see* psychological functions of modern art; a new perspective 23–5; perversion and aesthetics 150–60; psychopathology and the creative arts 30–1, 131–2, 137–41; selfobjects *see* selfobjects; subjectivity *see* subjectivity; sublimation theories 7, 18–19; the three dimensions of the artist's subjectivity 25–7, 163; *see also under specific artists*
psychological functions of modern art: the "breakthrough" and restoration of the self 37–8; and the dynamics behind Degas' transition to modernism 39–46; embodiment of relationship between order and complexity 125–6; healing function of aesthetic experience and 113–17; restorative function 19, 37–8; support of dissociation (Warhol's perverse aesthetic) 152–5; Wright and the selfobject function of art and architecture 107–27
psychologizing of art 88
psychopathology, and the creative arts 30–1; Pollock 131–2, 137–41

Rauschenberg, Robert 162
readymades 81–2
refuge 124–5
regression 7–9, 67, 86; Cornell's alternative to 98, 103, 105–6
release (prospect) 124–5
rematriation 8, 9
Renoir, Pierre 49
representation 44, 64, 65, 97, 141; Pollock and 136, 138
Roland, A. 60–1, 77–8, 111–12
Rose, G. 7, 8, 22–3
Rotenberg, C. 22, 41, 67–8
Rothenberg, Susan 148
Rothko, Mark 128, 144
Russell, John Peter 69
Ryder, Albert Pinkham 134

Santayana, G. 11, 117
Schwiters, Kurt 91
Secrest, M. 112–13
seeing, as an activity 86
Segal, H. 19
Seigel, J. 80

self: artistic *see* artistic self; "breakthrough" of the 37–8; as contingent and protean 163; Cornell's "self in a box" 103–4; grandiose self 29, 51, 97, 111, 116, 140, 154; the ideal self 29, 118; multiple selves 77, 111–12; parent's gaze as early source of 79; Wright and the vulnerable self 108–11
self-criticism 1–2; Degas 42
self-development: effects of a parent's death in childhood 94–5; potential space and 20, 95–7
self-disorder 42, 43, 49, 113, 140
self-experience: and the creative process 43, 63, 66, 103–4; disruption through the death of a parent 94–5; function of the artistic self in 63; selfobject experience *see* selfobjects; Wright's architecture and the earliest modalities of 124
self-expression 7; in aesthetic experience 27, 69; emotional expression through color 70–1; Pollock's action-based method of 134–6; *see also* creativity
self-fragmentation 113
self-fulfillment 2
self-identity *see* identity
self-organizations 13, 27, 89, 119, 160; artistic self *see* artistic self; Pollock's inability to self-regulate 130; splitting in 111, 116, 148
self-psychological approaches: to aesthetics 9–10 *see also* ego-psychological approaches to aesthetics; to art 22
selfobjects: aesthetic resonance and selfobject experience 28–30, 31; archaic 51; art appreciation as a selfobject experience 165; artist's confrontation with selfobject failure 9, 29, 51, 52, 54, 63, 66, 76–7, 80–1, 122, 139; Bonnard and the selfobject experience 52–6; coping with creativity and the selfobject experience 79–80; creative anxiety and the selfobject milieu 63, 66, 69; creative process serving selfobject functions 118–19; idealization and 29, 50–2; impact of a failed maternal environment 73–6, 79; meeting compensatory selfobject needs 116; mirroring and the selfobject experience 29, 105–6, 116; and the regaining of perfection 51; Rotenberg 22; the sense of beauty as a selfobject experience 50–2, 105, 117–19; the shared selfobject experience 54; Wright and the selfobject function of art and architecture 107–27
shame 58, 61–2, 122, 140, 151
Shchukin, Sergei 69
Sheeler, Frank 87
space: architectural space and the body 123–5; potential 20, 21, 27–8, 95–7
splitting 111, 116, 148; of aesthetics 154, 155; and dissociation 151–5 *see also* dissociation
Spurling, H. 58–9, 60, 61, 63, 68
Stein family 69
Stein, R. 150–1, 158
Stella, Joseph 87
Stern, D. 8–9
Stokes, A. 14
subjectivity: aesthetic form as the objectification of 79; art as a subjective object 24, 28; art as the externalization/embodiment of 19, 24, 27–8, 66–7, 78, 79–80; of artist as centre of creative process 2, 34; beauty and the investment of reality with 11; Cornell's creating of his own subjectivity 102–3; cultural dimension of 163–4; dialectic between internal and external aspects of 22, 24–5; embodied through color and line 64; expressed through symbol and narrative 63–4; feminine 56; indifference and the removal of 81; Matisse, creating an art of 63–5, 66–7 *see also* Matisse, Henri; of the modern artist 34; mutual transformation of objective reality and 20–1; as a process 163–4; subjective reconstitution of experience of beauty 49–50; the three dimensions of the artist's 25–7, 163; of twentieth century aesthetics 114; after Warhol 162–5
sublimations 7, 18–19

the Sublime 12–13; paternal aesthetic of 136–8; and the transcendent 13 *see also* transcendence/the transcendent
Sukenick, Ron 149
Sullivan, Louis 108, 109
surrealism 88, 93
symbolism 7, 63–4, 92; assemblage and 92; Wright 122
systems theory 32

time, recovery of 99
Tomkins, C. 74, 76, 81
tragedy/the tragic 13–14
transcendence/the transcendent: aesthetic experience and 13–14, 23; creativity and art as openings to 2, 114; Degas and the transcendence of the moment 55; idealization and 17; and the restoration of the self 38, 44; the Sublime and the transcendent 13 *see also* the Sublime; transcendence of tragic man through aesthetic experience 14

ugliness 12, 117, 155; as negative empathy 115
the unconscious 103; aesthetic unconscious 64–5, 66, 71; unconscious fantasy 17, 67, 95–6, 101
unconscious scanning 98, 102
United States, modern art 87–90; *see also individual artists*

Valéry, Paul 42
Van Gogh, Vincent 43
Vischer, Robert 115
Vlaminck, Maurice de 69
Vollard, Ambroise 42
vulnerability: and the artist's aesthetic experience 14; and defence mechanisms 43, 95; dissociation and 151–2; narcissistic 53; and the protection of Cornell's boxes 100; to self-crises 112–13; the Sublime as safe experience of 13; transcended through aesthetic experience 14; Wright and the vulnerable self 108–11

Warhol, Andy 142–60, 161, 162, 163, 165–6; and the art world of his early years 143–50; attachment to his mother 146, 147, 153; biographical background 144–8; business art 157–8; creative process 156–7; dissociation 151–5; perverse aesthetic 146, 148–9, 150–60; rejection of authenticity 154, 159–60; role in creation of a new culture 160; St Vitus' dance 146; struggle with his homosexuality 147
Warhola, Julia 145–6
Warhola, Ondrej 145
Wilde, O. 31
Windham, Donald 100
Winnicott, D. W. 20–1, 95–6
Wolfe, T. 148
Wright, Frank Lloyd 88–90, 107–27; architecture and the body 123–5; artistic self 111–13, 116; biographical background 108–11; childhood memories with Uncle John 120–2; genius and the vulnerable self 108–11; and the healing function of aesthetic experience 113–17; joy and influence 126–7; love of beauty 117–19; order and complexity 125–6; reconciling maternal and paternal aesthetic form 119–23; and "repose" 119–23; and the selfobject function 107–27
Wright, William Carey 108, 110–11

Zavackys, Julia, later Julia Warhola 145; *see also* Warhola, Julia